Reading the Bible Badly

Reading the Bible Badly

How American Christians Misunderstand and Misuse Their Scriptures

Karl Allen Kuhn

CASCADE *Books* · Eugene, Oregon

READING THE BIBLE BADLY
How American Christians Misunderstand and Misuse Their Scriptures

Cascade Books
An Imprint of Wipf and Stock Publishers
199 W. 8th Ave., Suite 3
Eugene, OR 97401

www.wipfandstock.com

PAPERBACK ISBN: 978-1-7252-6698-8
HARDCOVER ISBN: 978-1-7252-6699-5
EBOOK ISBN: 978-1-7252-6700-8

Cataloguing-in-Publication data:

Names: Kuhn, Karl Allen, author.

Title: Reading the Bible badly : how American Christians misunderstand and misuse their Scriptures / by Karl Allen Kuhn.

Description: Eugene, OR: Cascade Books, 2020 | Includes bibliographical references.

Identifiers: ISBN 978-1-7252-6698-8 (paperback) | ISBN 978-1-7252-6699-5 (hardcover) | ISBN 978-1-7252-6700-8 (ebook)

Subjects: LCSH: Bible—Hermeneutics. | Bible—Evidences, authority, etc.

Classification: BS480 .K75 2020 (print) | BS480 (ebook)

Manufactured in the U.S.A.   08/31/20

For Pastor Kim

Contents

Acknowledgments

PERHAPS IT IS FITTING that a book for the church should have its start in the church. *Reading the Bible Badly* began as a Monday night adult-education study of the same name at Grace Congregational United Church of Christ in Two Rivers, Wisconsin, in the winter of 2018. During our first session together, I noted how disturbing it was that so many of them were willing to come back to church on a cold winter night to learn how to read the Bible badly! But kidding aside, I am grateful for the many studies I have shared with this congregation over the years as together we have struggled to discern what it means to read the Bible, our faith, and the times in which we live well. I am also deeply appreciative for their continuing support of my ministry in the academy and the church, and the Grace Chair of Religious Studies which I am honored to hold at Lakeland University.

The twenty years and counting I have served at Lakeland have been a tremendous blessing. This liberal arts college related to the United Church of Christ, nestled among the farm fields of rural Wisconsin, has shaped my ministry of teaching and scholarship in profound ways. I have learned much from my colleagues and students. A sabbatical leave the fall of 2019 enabled me to complete most of the manuscript for this book. Then, in spring 2020 I shared a draft of the text with students in my "Interpreting Sacred Traditions" course, whose comments and encouragement gave me the sense that the work was on the right track and led to several improvements. Their names are Nicholas Broder, Kyle Ericsson, Nicole Herda, Mark Schmitt, Erin Tomlinson, and William Young. I also very much appreciate Lakeland librarian Jamie Keller, for the scores of inter-library loan requests he processed to support my research.

Others have also made valuable contributions to this book. My wife, Kathryn, a gifted UCC pastor and preacher, read through several chapters and encouraged my attempts to reach a general audience while cautioning me not to get too "gimmicky." My sister, Louise Hubert, also commented on several chapters of the work. Her perspective was quite valuable as I sought to discern how the book might be useful to those on the more conservative side of our tradition. I am incredibly grateful for the tireless work of Kim Thimmig, who proofed and commented on the entire manuscript. Her efforts have improved the work in substantial ways.

Finally, I thank Wipf and Stock for this opportunity to publish under their Cascade imprint, and for the able work of their staff, including editor Rodney Clapp, whose expertise further improved the book and guided it to completion.

INTRODUCTION

Reading Glasses

"I don't interpret the Bible. I just read it!"

THE SPEAKER PUNCTUATED HIS pronouncement with a dramatic fist pound on the heavy oak table.

Gathered around were members of a Sunday morning Bible study I had been asked to lead for several weeks. Nods from a couple of others indicated that the gentleman speaking these words was not alone in his frustration. Perhaps I was being too pushy.

These folk, after all, had been meeting long before I joined the congregation. Over the years, the group had established its own method for reading Scripture. In fact, their way of making sense of Scripture just seemed so natural to them it was not even a "method" at all. They just read it.

My years of teaching biblical studies have led me to discern that there are many Christians for whom understanding Scripture is pretty much a matter of just reading it. What appear to me as rather complex arrays of assumptions about the character of Scripture and sophisticated interpretive dances with biblical texts become learned patterns of reading behavior that are absorbed—unconsciously it seems—by groups and individuals. They have trouble imagining reading Scripture any other way, because their way of reading Scripture is not a "way" at all. It is simply reading. Like breathing.

I have noted another common tendency in how Christian readers engage the Bible. They look to faithful experts to tell them what the Bible has to say. Such folks recognize their own limitations in unveiling the truth of Scripture and in varying degrees rely on pastors, evangelists, scholars, and online bloggers to do the reading for them. Some will shop around and gravitate to those experts who read Scripture in a way that resonates with them. Others remain devoted to a particular pastor or teacher.

1

But, in most cases, the "methods" of these experts are of little interest to those who listen to them and learn from them and even read the Bible like them. Followers may believe that the way *their* expert reads Scripture is the right way, as opposed to others. But the rightness of any way of reading Scripture is for most folks more about the results than the process. The results are the foreground. The method is the background. As background, it is easy to forget that it is even there.

But as with nearly all things, what you get out of Scripture has a heck of a lot do to with what you put into it.

The Necessity of Interpretation

"I don't interpret the Bible, I just read it."

I noted that not everyone in that Bible Study group was nodding in agreement with the fist-pounding but otherwise dignified gentleman sitting across the table from me. This gave me a ray of hope that some in the group might find what I had to say helpful. I had been attempting to explain the importance of reading biblical texts in relation to their historical and cultural contexts (which we will discuss in the next chapter). Looking back to that Bible study session, perhaps it would have helped if I had begun by talking about the necessity, the unavoidability, of interpretation.

Perhaps that would be a good place for us to start.

Making Meaning

Any act of discerning meaning is an act of interpretation. Please do me a favor and reread that statement. It is really important.

Any act of discerning meaning is an act of interpretation (okay, sorry, just to be sure).

Few such blanket statements are to be trusted as true in every circumstance. But I think this statement probably qualifies as one of those few. Beyond primal, instinctive impulses (such as "*ouch!*" or "*run!*"), we simply cannot make sense of *anything* without interpreting it. No matter the object of our consideration, for us to make the transition from the sensory stimulation caused in us by that object to an understanding of that object in relation to ourselves and our world we must engage that object through a complex, calculating, mental process. We must *interpret* its significance in relation to what we already know to be true about the world and ourselves. This is worth repeating: any act of discerning meaning is an act of interpretation.

The fact that most of the time we may not be consciously aware that we are actively interpreting all sorts of sensory and mental stimuli as we go about our daily lives does not mean we are not doing it. It often is, as I stated above, like breathing. That which is most essential to our cognitive functioning, like a beating heart is to our physical functioning, is something we often take for granted. It is so "under the radar" that we are often unaware it is occurring. But, in reality, everything we know is the product of a complex web of associations we weave in our minds guided by a host of factors such as our mental and emotional state at that moment, life experiences, culture, environment, relationships, views on life and the world.

Most of us do not become aware of how critical these hidden "meaning-making processes" are until they are challenged by extraordinary events, or compromised by a physical impairment impacting our cognitive faculties. When encountering a traumatic, life-altering situation, many find it difficult to make immediate sense of what has just occurred, and what it means for them moving forward. Very simply, they need time to "process" the experience. Sometimes, their views of themselves, the world, and even their faith shift as a result of the experience. Many in the early stages of dementia come to the heartbreaking realization that their ability to make sense of their environment and the lives they once knew—their ability to interpret their world—is deteriorating. Trauma and illness have a way of leading us to recognize numerous things we take for granted. Our ability to interpret, our *need* to interpret, can be one of them.

Making Meaning Differently

There are, of course, countless indications that the world in which we live and the situations, persons, and objects we encounter within it need to be interpreted in order to be comprehended. Among the most obvious is that we human beings often disagree with one another about how to understand the situations, persons, and objects we encounter. Some of these disagreements are trivial. Others have far-reaching, sometimes tragic consequences for individuals, couples, families, communities, countries, and even the world. Not only is interpretation an inescapable reality for all thinking minds on this planet, it is also an extraordinarily important, and contentious, reality. We make meaning differently.

The Necessity of Biblical Interpretation

Just as any object we encounter needs to be interpreted in order for us to make sense of it, so too does Scripture. With all due respect to that gentleman sitting across the table from me those many years ago, and to all who think as he did, there simply is no such thing as "just reading it."

I have this on good authority. Scripture itself makes clear that the actions and will of God need to be discerned, or figured out. Scripture itself tells us interpretation is essential to the vocation of God's people.

God, Help Me Understand

The Bible affirms this reality in countless ways. One of the more obvious is when voices in Scripture ask for God's guidance in determining what God wants them to do. Consider, for instance, these words from Psalm 25, a psalm in which the psalmist pleads for deliverance from pernicious, nasty foes. We might expect the psalmist in this situation simply to ask God to "blast those evil buggers!" But remarkably, the psalmist not only calls on God for deliverance from the deadly adversaries, but also from his or her own propensity to stray from God's will.[1]

> [4] Make me to know your ways, O LORD;
>   teach me your paths.
> [5] Lead me in your truth, and teach me,
>   for you are the God of my salvation;
> for you I wait all day long.
> [6] Be mindful of your mercy, O LORD, and of your steadfast love,
>   for they have been from of old.
> [7] Do not remember the sins of my youth or my transgressions;
>   according to your steadfast love remember me,
>   for your goodness' sake, O LORD!
> [8] Good and upright is the LORD;
>   therefore he instructs sinners in the way.
> [9] He leads the humble in what is right,
>   and teaches the humble his way.
> [10] All the paths of the LORD are steadfast love and faithfulness,
>   for those who keep his covenant and his decrees.

The psalmist, in other words, needs help figuring out what it means to walk in God's ways and paths in the midst of these trying circumstances. Notice the references to "teach," "know," "instruct," "lead," "right," "truth,"

---

1. Unless otherwise indicated, all Scripture texts are taken from the NRSV.

"way," "path"—many of which are repeated. Notice the psalmist's desire to leave behind "the sins of my youth." This is an individual crying out for instruction and transformation! The psalmist already knows God as Savior (v. 5), God's steadfast love and mercy (vv. 6, 7), and God's "covenant and decrees" (v. 10). But even so, the way forward is not altogether clear. The psalmist needs help interpreting God's instruction in order to live it out faithfully in his or her troubled present.

Note the similar chords struck by Paul at a key transitional moment in his letter to the Romans. Here, Paul urges members of the Roman church, in response to God's great act of mercy in Jesus, to orient their actions, hearts, and minds anew—to be transformed or "metamorphisized"—so that they may be able to rightly discern the will of God.[2]

> I appeal to you therefore, brothers and sisters, by the mercies of God, to present your bodies as a living sacrifice, holy and acceptable to God, which is your spiritual worship. Do not be conformed to this world, but be transformed by the renewing of your minds, so that you may discern what is the will of God— what is good and acceptable and perfect (Rom 12:1–2).

Incomplete and Misguided Understandings of God's Ways

Turning to the Gospels, we find the disciples repeatedly asking Jesus to clarify his teaching, and with a regularity that sometimes exasperates him: "Do you not understand this parable? How then will you understand any of the parables?!" (Mark 4:13). But, of course, Jesus always goes on to explain.

We also encounter numerous examples of biblical interpretation gone awry. At the center of Jesus' many disagreements with his fellow Israelites were their very different modes of interpreting their sacred tradition—the law (Torah) and the prophets—what Christians know as the Old Testament. Near the start of his "Sermon on the Mount" (Matt 5:1–7:29), Jesus announces,

> [17]"Do not think that I have come to abolish the law or the prophets; I have come not to abolish but to fulfil. [18]For truly I tell you, until heaven and earth pass away, not one letter, not one stroke of a letter, will pass from the law until all is accomplished. [19]Therefore, whoever breaks one of the least of these commandments, and teaches others to do the same, will be

2. The Greek verb Paul uses here which the NRSV translates as "be transformed" is *metamorphēo*.

called least in the kingdom of heaven; but whoever does them and teaches them will be called great in the kingdom of heaven. [20]For I tell you, unless your righteousness exceeds that of the scribes and Pharisees, you will never enter the kingdom of heaven." (Matt 5:17–20)

In the verses to follow, specific differences in the interpretative stances of Jesus and his opponents become clear. Jesus prefaces a series of teachings with the rather audacious refrain, "You have heard it was said to those of ancient times . . . But I say to you . . ." (see Matt 5:21–48). He then goes on to offer what his detractors would have surely thought were quite radical (and wrong) takes on God's Torah. As if anticipating their objections, Jesus then offers concrete examples of how the Pharisees and scribes, among others, fail to correctly interpret and embody the will of God (see 6:1–7:12). Jesus criticizes the religious leaders and those who follow them for their pursuit of honor and wealth, collusion with the elite, condemnation of others, and lack of love. Then the final words of Jesus' sermon underscore the ramifications of failing to interpret God's will with humble, justice-guided, other-centered hearts (7:13–20), and failing to truly live out the truth revealed by Jesus:

Everyone who hears these words of mine and acts on them will be like a wise man who built his house on rock . . . and everyone who hears these words of mine and does not act on them will be like a foolish man who built his house on sand (see 7:24–29).

As Matthew emphasizes throughout his Gospel, it is *Jesus'* interpretation of the Torah and prophets that is to empower the lives of the righteous. More than just reading Scripture is required. One must read it guided by the one who fulfills the very purpose of Scripture and, unlike the scribes and Pharisees, truly opens the way into God's realm.

Jesus' Followers Interpreting Their Traditions

Examples of various characters interpreting their sacred traditions abound throughout both testaments, but are especially prevalent throughout the New Testament as the early believers sought to make sense of their experience of Jesus. Many of these examples indicate that the relationship between Jesus' life, death, and resurrection and the Israelite Scriptures was *not*—as many Christians today often assume—self-evident. It needed to be explained. In Luke 24, the resurrected Jesus repeatedly corrects the disciples' misapprehension of the events that have just taken place by turning to Scripture. For example,

Then he said to them, "Oh, how foolish you are, and how slow of heart to believe all that the prophets have declared! Was it not necessary that the Messiah should suffer these things and then enter into his glory?" Then beginning with Moses and all the prophets, he interpreted to them the things about himself in all the scriptures. (See also Luke 24:44–47.)

In Acts of the Apostles, we find the early believers taking up Jesus' ministry of interpretation and proclamation. The speeches of Peter in the opening chapters, and those of Paul and others to follow, aim to help both Jews and Gentiles make sense of a crucified and risen messiah, a reality that radically conflicted with Israelite expectations of how God would redeem Israel and the world.[3] Consider this moving scene from Acts 8.

[26]Then an angel of the Lord said to Philip, "Get up and go to-wards the south to the road that goes down from Jerusalem to Gaza." (This is a wilderness road.) [27]So he got up and went. Now there was an Ethiopian eunuch, a court official of the Candace, queen of the Ethiopians, in charge of her entire treasury. He had come to Jerusalem to worship [28]and was returning home; seated in his chariot, he was reading the prophet Isaiah.[29]Then the Spirit said to Philip, "Go over to this chariot and join it." [30]So Philip ran up to it and heard him reading the prophet Isaiah. He asked, "Do you understand what you are reading?" [31]He replied, "How can I, unless someone guides me?" And he invited Philip to get in and sit beside him. [32]Now the passage of the scripture that he was reading was this:

"Like a sheep he was led to the slaughter,
    and like a lamb silent before its shearer,
    so he does not open his mouth.
[33] In his humiliation justice was denied him.
    Who can describe his generation?

For his life is taken away from the earth."

[34]The eunuch asked Philip, "About whom, may I ask you, does the prophet say this, about himself or about someone else?" [35]Then

---

3. The notion of a crucified and resurrected messiah does not appear to have existed in Israelite thought prior to the time of Jesus. The Israelite Scriptures and other Israelite traditions refer to righteous ones who suffer due to their faith in God or on behalf of Israel, such as in the Psalms, the Maccabean traditions, or the Servant Songs of Isaiah (e.g., Isa 52:13–53:12). But there are no surviving Israelite texts prior to Jesus that specifically foretell the crucifixion and resurrection of God's anointed. For this reason Paul refers to Christ crucified as "a stumbling block to Jews and foolishness to Gentiles" (1 Cor 1:23).

Philip began to speak, and starting with this scripture, he proclaimed to him the good news about Jesus. (Acts 8:26–35)

The eunuch read an eloquent, profound, and penetrating piece of
Scripture. But his act of reading—just reading—wasn't nearly enough.
"How can I understand this unless someone guides me?" he laments. Then
Philip begins to speak.

The Challenge of Biblical Interpretation

Any act of discerning meaning is an act of interpretation (again, my
apologies).

I hope that the preceding discussion has also made it quite evident that
the act of discerning meaning from Scripture also necessitates interpretation. We never "just read it." In fact, interpretation is an essential part of our
vocation as followers of Jesus.

But the biblical examples of biblical interpretation that we glanced at
above also make it clear that there are helpful and unhelpful ways of interpreting Scripture. Furthermore, the history of Christianity has also made it
clear that Christians themselves have often disagreed over what are helpful
and unhelpful, faithful and unfaithful, ways of reading Scripture.

And sadly, throughout our history, there have been ways of reading
Scripture that have resulted in horrific acts of injustice against others. In
our own American story, scores of Christians have used Scripture to justify the practice of slavery. We have also used it to promote the doctrine of
Manifest Destiny—the notion that white colonists were destined by God to
"settle" the west and lead indigenous Americans to civility and faith, even
at the cost of their lands, liberty, lives, and children. Even today, many use
Scripture to justify discrimination against members of LGBTQIA+ communities, women, Jews and Muslims, and ignore Scripture's ever persistent
call to choose love over fear.

But Christians have also been inspired and empowered by Scripture to
rail against slavery and the physical and cultural genocide of native Americans, and to name homophobia, patriarchy, Islamophobia, and racism as the
injustices they are.

How are we to account for these incredibly disparate ways of reading
Scripture by Christians, beyond saying that some are clearly the result of
human selfishness, anxiety, and short-sightedness? How are we to account
for the multitude of disparities in how Christians today read Scripture?

Factors that Complicate Our Interpretation of Scripture

Interpretation is a human endeavor. Like all human endeavors it can be blessed by human ingenuity, creativity, brilliance, and openness to the guidance of God, or it can be marred by human fallibility, small-mindedness, and ignorance. Perhaps more common still, it can be influenced by some combination of several of those tendencies, both good and bad.

Our own personal histories and cultural settings also impact the meaning we discern from a biblical passage. New Testament scholar Mark Allan Powell has investigated, catalogued, and reported on differences in the ways readers understand scriptural passages. Particularly illuminating is a study Powell conducted on Luke's parable of the "Prodigal" Son (Luke 15:11–32).[4] In the study, Powell asked one hundred Americans of diverse gender, race, age, economic status, and religious affiliation to read the parable carefully, close their Bibles, and then recount the parable as completely as possible.

All of the American respondents (100 percent) remembered the detail of the son squandering his father's wealth. This makes sense. What a loser! But, incredibly, only a small fraction (6 percent) were able to recall the detail of the famine. And this was not a run-of-the-mill famine—it was a "severe famine." Many were starving, and many were likely dying (see Luke 15:14). But the American readers Powell surveyed just didn't seem to take notice.

Powell then conducted the same study with fifty diverse respondents in St. Petersburg, Russia. In sharp contrast to their American counterparts, 84% of the Russian respondents remembered the detail of the famine. Interestingly, only 34% recalled the son squandering his father's wealth. Wow.

Powell presumes, rightly, I think, that the reason the Americans surveyed remembered the detail of the squandering and did not (except for a few) recall the famine is that they understood the son's squandering of his father's wealth as the only, or primary, cause of the son's plight. In other words, the narrative function of the squandering was just too essential to ignore, whereas the famine (the *severe* famine) was regarded as an ancillary detail that could be easily forgotten! In sharp contrast, the vast majority of the Russian respondents did not consider the detail of the famine superfluous, but essential to understanding why the son was in need.

This raises the question of why the American readers would focus on the son's squandering and the Russian readers on the famine. Powell proposes,

---

4. Powell, "The Forgotten Famine." I previously cited and discussed this study in *Having Words with God,* 118–20.

One probably does not need to look too far for a social or psychological explanation for this data. In 1941, the German army laid siege to the city of St. Petersburg (then Leningrad) and subjected its inhabitants to what was in effect a 900-day famine. During that time, 670,000 people died of starvation. Some of the current inhabitants of the city are survivors of that horror; more are descendents of survivors . . . In modern St. Petersburg, typical social issues (abortion, care of the elderly, imprisonment of lawbreakers, socialized medicine, and so on) are often considered through the lens of an important question: *but what if there is not enough food?* . . . It is, I think, not surprising that in *this* social location, more than four-fifths of the persons who read Luke's story of "the Prodigal Son" and then repeat it from memory do not forget that there was a famine.[5]

Here is the important point Powell's study illustrates. Reading the parable through lenses shaped in part by their experience and historical memory, Russian readers find it speaking to dimensions of God's character and provision quite differently than their American counterparts, whose lenses are shaped by other cultural and historical realities.

American readers understand the parable to be emphasizing the moral depravity of the son's squandering, the licentiousness of his pleasure-seeking lifestyle, and his repentance from his sinful ways. In contrast, Russian readers, who regard the famine as the primary cause of the son's suffering and attach less importance to the son's spending habits, see the parable as emphasizing God's gracious provision for and welcome of all the lost, alone, and famished into God's kingdom. In this reading, it is God's rescue of the needy *from matters beyond their control* rather than their moral transformation that takes center stage.[6] In Russia (and likely also in first-century Palestine where deadly famine was an all-too-common occurrence), it makes sense that that this reading of the parable would be far more common than in America, where resources are far more abundant for many and perhaps also more frequently squandered.[7]

5. Powell, "The Forgotten Famine," 266–67.

6. When Powell challenged the Russian students' focus on the famine as the primary cause of the son's plight, they replied that during a severe famine even the rich will die from hunger. In fact, the wealthy may be at a disadvantage since they have not cultivated the skills and networks to survive such desperate times.

7. Lest we quickly dismiss the reading of the parable favored by the Russian students as overly tendentious, Powell ("Forgotten Famine," 279–85) notes that several features of the parable as it appears in Luke's gospel could be marshaled to support it. He points out that the Greek terms that are commonly rendered "squandering" and "dissolute, "riotous," "loose," and "reckless" living in our English Bibles could just as

Sometime later, Powell had the opportunity to conduct a similar study on the parable with Tanzanian seminary students, in which he specifically asked them why it was that the prodigal son found himself in need. He eagerly awaited the results, wondering which of the two reasons held in opposition by the American and Russian students (squandering and famine, respectively) would be favored by the Tanzanians. The answer: neither! The majority of the responses, from a people who highly value the virtue of hospitality, identified as the chief cause of the son's hunger the fact that no one gave him anything to eat (see Luke 15:16).[8]

What we bring to a text *really* matters.

The Reading Glasses We Wear

Any act of discerning meaning is an act of interpretation (last time, I promise).

People interpret Scripture differently.

Our interpretation of Scripture is complicated by a host of factors, especially by what we bring with us to the biblical texts.

So far so good?

Excellent. We are now going to take this a step further by delving a little more deeply into epistemological and hermeneutical theory. Hang in there. This will not be as painful as it might seem. At least I hope not.

What is Your Hermeneutic?

A foundational assumption among many contributing to the study of epistemology (the study of how we know things), and the related discussion of critical thinking, is that all knowledge is conditioned by the commitments, experiences, and tendencies interpreters or researchers bring to their encounter with the world.[9] As stated above, this is no less the case with biblical

---

easily be translated in a far less pejorative sense, identifying the son not as "prodigal" (i.e., "recklessly wasteful") but more along the lines of "carefree spendthrift." He also argues that viewing the primary focus of the parable as God's salvation of the wayward and needy actually fits better with the two parables preceding it. Taken together, these three parables respond to the grumbling of the scribes and Pharisees (15:2), and portray "repentance" not so much as the moral transformation of the sinner but God's gracious act of welcoming home or "finding" those who would otherwise be lost (see 15:32).

8. Powell, "The Timeless Tale of a Prodigal Son."

9. The terms "point of view" or "frame of reference" are often used in these circles to identify this phenomenon. While the field of epistemology is home to many different theories of knowledge, the contextual nature of meaning has been one of the tenets of

interpretation. What we bring to the biblical text plays a significant role in what we get out of it.

In the fields of literary and biblical studies, we often refer to what one brings to their reading of the text as one's "hermeneutic."[10] One's hermeneutic—or interpretive approach—is shaped by a rich combination of realities that guides the way one reads a text. To repeat and expand on the list of things that influence our attempts to make meaning, a hermeneutic includes and is shaped by one's:

- state of mind

- culture

- historical context

- life experiences (such as family background, education, socioeconomic status, gender, sexual orientation, political affiliations, etc.)

- view of the world, or worldview

- view of the nature of the text they are reading (e.g., what Scripture is—its nature as the word of God and humans)

- goals for engaging that text (what I am looking to get out of it)

- assumptions of how to best engage that text (how I go about accessing what I want to get out of it).

Perhaps it will help to think of your hermeneutic as a set of reading glasses. The lenses of those glasses are shaped by the various tendencies, perspectives, commitments, and assumptions you bring to the biblical texts. And this is very important: we *all* need to wear such glasses to "see" anything, including Scripture. It these glasses that set the ground rules for how we view, how we interpret, the biblical writings. And the fact that Christians

---

postmodern thought to take hold in many modern discussions of how we know things. Moreover, deliberations on epistemological issues now commonly occur outside of traditional philosophical contexts within the natural and social sciences, including biblical studies. Researchers in many fields now feel compelled (and rightly so!) to address the complex nature of knowledge, even in disciplines that are often seen as dealing with "objective" facts.

10. Hermeneutics refers to the practice, or science, of interpretation. Most commonly, its focus is on written texts, but it also includes verbal and nonverbal communication. Accordingly, the term "text" is often employed in the field to refer to both written and verbal communication, as well as nonverbal action that has a communicative function. As a field of thought, it examines the practice of interpretation and critiques methods employed to discern meaning from texts. This book, in other words, and any conversation you might have on biblical interpretation, is part of the field of hermeneutics, which is a sub-discipline of the field of epistemology.

often read the Bible very differently is due to the reality that we come to Scripture wearing different reading glasses.

The Perspectival and Selective Character of Interpretation

That Scripture would be subject to disparate readings should not surprise us. Whenever any of us seek to understand an object or circumstance, our attempts to do so are always *perspectival*. This is simply to repeat what I have already stated: our understanding, our interpretation, is always conditioned by the reading glasses we use, which are in turn shaped by our experiences and commitments.

Relatedly, our attempts to understand are also commonly *selective*. We tend to cast our gaze on aspects of an object or circumstance we most readily relate to or understand. We look for the familiar. We start with what we know. When dealing with complex matters or situations, we often use what we know to help us make sense of the rest.

For example, if I am fishing a lake for the first time, I will start by focusing on techniques and patterns that have proven productive elsewhere. Or, if I am encountering the work of a philosopher that is new to me, I will often use parts of her discussion that make sense to me in order to help me figure out the parts that are unclear.

These two tendencies—the perspectival and selective—are natural and really unavoidable. In order for us to know anything, it has to mesh or intersect with the thought patterns and belief systems we already hold. Even if new information radically transforms our belief systems, it still has to gain a foothold in our psyches by connecting with at least some of the stuff that is already there. Our minds are not empty vessels. Zero times anything always equals zero. Raw materials are needed for any reaction to occur. And all of us have plenty of raw materials—plenty of perspective—lodged in our minds and hearts.

The selectivity with which we engage new objects or experiences in order to make sense of them can also be quite useful. Starting with what we know enables us to begin the process of feeling or thinking our way through a problem or situation. Gravitating to the familiar can give us the confidence we need to keep moving into uncharted territory. Conversely, when we lack any clear connection to an object or situation, it is easy to become overwhelmed or cognitively paralyzed: "I don't know where to begin!"

Being perspectival and selective interpreters can be a good thing! And that's good to know, because we really don't have any other choice.

Seeing Differently and Reading Badly

But being perspectival and selective interpreters also presents challenges. The fact we Christians read the Bible very differently from one another can be somewhat troubling, especially when those differences are about essential elements of our tradition. And if our understandings of Scripture and how to read it and the interpretations we take from it are so variable, what does it mean for us to claim these writings as the "inspired Word of God"?

This is not a trivial query. It is one we will return to in the pages to follow (see chapter 2). However, I would argue that our use of Scripture in the church is even more problematic than this. Not only do we as American Christians often read Scripture very differently than one another. We also tend it read it very badly.

The lenses we have crafted, consciously or not, often distort what Scripture seeks to show us about the will and ways of God. Some distortions are more severe than others. Some, as we noted above in the cases of slavery, Manifest Destiny, patriarchy, racism, Islamophobia, and homophobia, are downright tragic. Others are less extreme but still lead to the serious consequence of muting or misshaping the Bible's witness.

When paired with uncritical, biased, or unfaithful thinking, our perspectival and selective natures can lead to uncritical, biased, and unfaithful interpretations. The perspectival and selective character of our reading glasses are unavoidable and even valuable assets, but only if we are willing to recognize when our prescription needs to change, when the lenses we use are actually distorting rather than illuminating what it is we are trying to see.

Let's return to the example of me fishing a new lake. Suppose I fish that lake all day using the methods I found useful elsewhere but only catch a few fish. I return to the lake several more times, using the same methods, and end up with the same meager results. I conclude that problem *must* be with the lake—if there were fish here I (masterful fisherman that I am) would surely catch them! Or, to expand the analogy, I catch a bunch of fish but only of one species, and a species I really don't like. So, I conclude that there must not be many fish of more desirable species in the lake and decide to move on to the next.

Well, of course, you readily see the problem in my thinking. It is biased and irrational (and a bit arrogant). It assumes that I already possess all of the skills and knowledge I would need in order to catch any kind of fish I want in any lake. Sadly, I admit to falling victim to such silly thinking more than once, only to be corrected (and humbled) by the reports of other fisherfolk back at the dock.

But I think many of us fall into these patterns of thinking quite commonly. We think we know all that there is to know, or at least all that is worth knowing, about something. We fail to see the potential limitations in our perspectives, our ingrained modes of thought, our gravitation towards and preference for the familiar. Such biased, uncritical thinking is quite human of us. Yet in moments such as these we are at risk of living up to the title "duh-ciples."

It is just this mode of thinking, though here with more serious consequences than no fish for dinner, that Jesus is getting at when he tells the crowds "You have heard it was said in ancient times . . . but I say to you . . . !" and calls them to build their houses of faith on rock, not sand. This is what Paul is saying when he exhorts the believers in Rome "Do not conform any longer to the patterns of this world, but be transformed in the renewing of your minds!" This is what Isaiah cried out in his lament over Israel, and what Jesus proclaimed as taking place in his day:

> [14] With them indeed is fulfilled the prophecy of Isaiah that says:
> "You will indeed listen, but never understand,
>   and you will indeed look, but never perceive.
> [15] For this people's heart has grown dull,
>   and their ears are hard of hearing,
>   and they have shut their eyes;
>   so that they might not look with their eyes,
>   and listen with their ears,
> and understand with their heart and turn—
>   and I would heal them. (Matt 13:14–15; citing Isa 6:9–10)

The faith announced by the prophets, Jesus, and Paul is a faith rightly attuned to the perspectives of God. Unfortunately, it is a faith that does not (yet) come easily to us human creatures. Even Paul, years after his mind-transforming encounter with the risen Jesus, will admit to still seeing as if in a mirror, "dimly" (1 Cor 13:12) and not yet having attained full knowledge of Christ (Phil 3:7–16). Even the Spirit-filled followers of Jesus will disagree (see Acts 6:1, 15:1–21) and get it wrong (Gal 2:11–14) at times. We all struggle with the cost of duh-cipleship.

Adjusting our Lenses

So how do we do better?

The first step, I think, in becoming thoughtful and faithful interpreters of anything, including Scripture, is to recognize we view everything through a set of reading glasses. We have to get to the point where we can boldly proclaim:

"I don't just read Scripture, doggone it, I interpret it (fist pound)!"

The second, and perhaps more difficult step, is to acknowledge like Paul and many others that our reading glasses may need an adjustment from time to time.

It can be unsettling to recognize that we have not been seeing things clearly. We prefer when all is in order, when we are in command of our faculties, and confident in our views of reality. No one wants to hear that he or she has been mistaken. This is especially so when the things we have not been seeing clearly are very important to us, and when they play a central role in shaping our understanding of the world.

Scripture certainly plays this role for many people of faith. In many communities, Scripture holds a significant degree of authority and power. If some perspective or behavior is deemed "biblical," then it is seen as the will of God. These are matters of high stakes. It is important to be clear on what is of God, and what is not. It is important, Isaiah cries, to see and hear properly. So, yes, it is certainly understandable that we would resist any claim that we have been seeing and hearing God's word and will poorly.

Just like the Pharisees did.

Yet take note of this. Faithful recognitions of having misunderstood or neglected the ways of God fill the pages of Scripture. Recall the plea of the psalmist: "Make me to know your paths, O Lord!" In fact, I think we would be hard-pressed to find any major biblical figure that did not need a lens adjustment at some point during his or her life (and most needed several).

For this reason, *Jesus proclaims that few things are more righteous (and desperately needed) than humility and repentance!* He also makes it clear that few things are more foolish than pride and willful ignorance. Humility is about setting aside the arrogance, fear, and even hatred that is preventing us from seeing as Jesus sees. Repentance is about turning our hearts and heads in new directions, to perceive all things as persons attuned to the realm of God. According to Jesus, lens-adjusting is a necessary, even daily practice for his disciples:

⁹ Pray, then, in this way:

Our Father in heaven,
hallowed be your name.
¹⁰ Your kingdom come.
Your will be done,
on earth as it is in heaven.
¹¹ Give us this day our daily bread.

[12]And forgive us our debts,
    as we also have forgiven our debtors.
[13] And do not bring us to the time of trial,
    but rescue us from the evil one. (Matt 6:9–13)

Jesus makes it clear that we resist faithful lens-adjusting to our own peril: "The eye is the lamp of the body. So, if your eye is healthy, your whole body will be full of light; but if your eye is unhealthy, your whole body will be full of darkness. If then the light in you is darkness, how great is the darkness!" (Matt 6:22–23).

This book is about the lenses we use to read Scripture, especially those lenses that lead us to read the Bible badly. The maladjusted lenses I will discuss are common to American Christianity.

These lenses lead American Christians . . .

- to read the Bible's stories and instruction unaware of their historical and cultural settings, disregarding the testimony of their spiritual ancestors, and finding mostly a mirror image of their own values and selves in Scripture;

- to insist that the Bible must be the "inerrant word of God," historically factual in every way and doctrinally infallible, overlooking so much of what makes Scripture beautiful and relevant;

- to follow a lectionary that dices and splices Scripture into bite-size morsels for Sunday worship, divorces passages from their biblical settings, strikes verses deemed offensive, and undermines the literary artistry that is the lifeblood of Scripture's profound revelation;

- to read the Bible in fear, warping its witness to Jesus and tragically neglecting Scripture's ever-persistent call to compassion, hospitality, and love;

- to read the Bible looking for simple rules that affirm our sense of right and wrong, while missing the point of what true righteousness is about;

- to read the Bible as agents of heterosexual male privilege, using its enculturated patriarchy as a license to deny women's gifts and their call to leadership in the church, and to discriminate against members of LGBTQIA+ communities.

This book is also an invitation for us, like our ancestors in the faith, to discern those elements of our spiritual upbringing, psyches, and souls that cloud our vision. It is an invitation to seek our own lens adjustments, so that we can more faithfully embody and steward God's kingdom on earth as it is in heaven.

Reflection or Discussion Questions

1. How would you describe the reading glasses you use for interpreting the Bible? What experiences, beliefs, practices, and traditions shape the way you read Scripture?

2. What do you make of Powell's experiment with the parable of the "Prodigal" Son? How do *you* understand the parable? *Why* do you understand it in this way?

3. Are there elements of your "hermeneutic" (your lens for reading Scripture) that sometimes prevent you from seeing the Bible clearly? If so, where did they come from? Why do you still hold on to them?

4. Are there elements of your hermeneutic that you cannot do without, that are nonnegotiable for you?

CHAPTER ONE

Reading the Bible with Amnesia and Dishonoring Our Ancestors

FEW THINGS ARE MORE typical of the celebration of Christmas by American Christians than children's Christmas programs.

Shepherds, sheep, a donkey, the angelic host, three wise men. Center stage, underneath a glittering star and illuminated with a golden glow, nestle Mary, Joseph, and the baby Jesus. There may be variations in the sophistication of the set. The number of peripheral characters may change, depending on how many children are attending Sunday school that year or which costumes are easiest to fashion in haste (those angel wings can be a chore!). Perhaps the Little Drummer Boy joins the crowd (Pa-rum pum pum pum). Perhaps—and I cringe as I write this—Santa makes an appearance, dancing across the chancel and tossing out candy canes while screaming "Merry Christmas!" Understandably, this is the moment when babies start to cry.

Children's Christmas programs. What a strange rite of the church year to put ourselves through! Of all the burdens we place on our Sunday school teachers, this has to be one of the worst. The planning, the preparing, the props, the politics ("I was really counting on my Jimmy being Joseph this year! He was a shepherd *last* year!"). But in many congregations, this strange rite has become a sacred one. It has become central to their celebration of Christmas. Christmas would simply not be the same without it.

But perhaps this could actually be a good thing—to not have Christmas be the same, at least *our* Christmases.

What would it be like, I wonder, to celebrate and remember the birth of Christ in the way it was celebrated and remembered by his earliest followers and the Gospel writers? What would it be like to read the Christmas stories in Luke and Matthew's gospels mindful of the kinds of realities, experiences, and yearnings of those who first encountered them? What would it be like to honor the memory of these spiritual ancestors who composed, wrote down, and passed along these stories to us?

I think it would change the way we understand, and celebrate, the miracle of Jesus' birth.

Misremembering Christmas

Most of our children's Christmas programs, like our nativity scenes, Christmas cards, and many of the ways our culture observes Christmas, are clear manifestations of how we *mis*remember Christmas. This is not a new observation or complaint.[1] For years, Christians across the theological spectrum have decried the commercialized perversion that Christmas in America has become. We have seen the slogans: "Jesus is the reason for the season." "Keep CHRIST in CHRISTmas!" There is certainly some merit to this criticism and these tag lines.

The reason for the Christmas season, at least the *original* reason, is a far, far cry from shopping malls, ugly sweaters, Chia Pets, a new Lexus, and kneeling Santas. But the reason for the season is also quite different from the messaging of our children's Christmas programs (if they even have a message) and what many American Christians celebrate about Christmas. Two particular tendencies in how we tell the story of Jesus' advent serve as troubling examples of we misremember Christmas, of how our reading lenses do not allow us to see the story of Jesus' advent clearly.

First Tendency: Forgetting a Main Character

Keep Christ in Christmas. Yes, that would be a good thing. But it would also be a good thing to keep *Caesar* in Christmas.

Caesar? You mean the guy who ordered the census? What a bit role! We never even cast him in our Christmas programs.

Perhaps you should.

Our remembrances of Jesus' birth commonly include details from both Matthew's and Luke's accounts, the two Gospels that contain birth narratives.[2] But it is Luke's gospel that has the most extensive birth narrative

1. For a still relevant and thoughtful critique of how American Christians celebrate Christmas, see McKibben, *Hundred Dollar Holiday*.

2. Mark's gospel begins with John's arrival and Jesus' baptism as an adult, during which the divine voice proclaims Jesus as God's beloved son (1:1–15). John starts his

and provides the basic outline many of us follow when retelling the story of Jesus' birth. Beginning in Luke 2 we read:

> [1]In those days a decree went out from Emperor Augustus that all the world should be registered. [2]This was the first registration and was taken while Quirinius was governor of Syria. [3]All went to their own towns to be registered. [4]Joseph also went from the town of Nazareth in Galilee to Judea, to the city of David called Bethlehem, because he was descended from the house and family of David. [5]He went to be registered with Mary, to whom he was engaged and who was expecting a child. [6]While they were there, the time came for her to deliver her child. [7]And she gave birth to her firstborn son and wrapped him in bands of cloth, and laid him in a manger, because there was no place for them in the inn.
>
> [8]In that region there were shepherds living in the fields, keeping watch over their flock by night. [9]Then an angel of the Lord stood before them, and the glory of the Lord shone around them, and they were terrified. [10]But the angel said to them, "Do not be afraid; for see—I am bringing you good news of great joy for all the people: [11]to you is born this day in the city of David a Savior, who is the Messiah, the Lord. [12]This will be a sign for you: you will find a child wrapped in bands of cloth and lying in a manger." [13]And suddenly there was with the angel a multitude of the heavenly host, praising God and saying,
>
> > [14]"Glory to God in the highest heaven,
> > and on earth peace among those whom he favors!"

Note the setting at the start of Luke's account. We are in the throne room of Rome! Caesar Augustus, Sovereign of the Roman Empire (which includes all of the Mediterranean world and Israel) commands that "all the world be registered" (v. 1).

Many readers of this story, including some scholars, don't pay much attention to the mention of Caesar and the census, thinking that the role of these details is simply to provide a chronological marker for Jesus' birth. To be sure, this may be *one* reason Luke includes the reference to Caesar, as suggested further by v. 2. But it is not the only or even the main reason. There are several other details from these opening verses and the remainder of Luke's story that indicate that Caesar, and his rule, function as a counterpoint to Jesus and what God will accomplish through him.

---

narrative "in the beginning," prior to creation, with Jesus as the divine Logos through whom all of creation comes into existence (1:1–18).

In other words, one of the *main* reasons Luke tells this story is to draw a stark contrast between Jesus and Caesar, and between the two realms that each is seeking to establish. Luke wants to make clear to his readers that Jesus, *not* Caesar, is the true Lord and Savior of all. He wants to make clear that Jesus, *not* Caesar, rules on behalf of God.

If this description of Luke's birth story seems a bit strange to you, I understand. Luke's account of Jesus' birth is not the "Christmas Story" you have come to know. This is not a cozy up to the Christmas tree with a mug of hot chocolate, warm and fuzzy, feel good kind of story. This is not a "weren't those little angels just adorable and little Jimmy so cute in his shepherd out-fit" kind of story.

Rather, the story of Jesus' birth as told by Luke is a dangerous, even treasonous tale. It is about lords being unmasked as the frauds they really are before the one truly sent by God to rule and serve. It is a story that claims that the world you know is about to be turned on its head.

Lens Adjustment: The Realm and Rule of Caesar

But before we can appreciate the edgy and even dangerous character of this tale told in Luke 2, before we can experience it in the way it was likely intended to be experienced by those who first told it, we need a lens adjustment. We need to become acquainted with the world in which it is set: the Roman world. We need to become familiar with the real-life realities confronting those who first told and heard this tale. We need to understand, in other words, their *context*.

You may be familiar with the real estate maxim: "location is everything." When it comes to interpretation in general, and certainly interpretation of the Bible, this maxim applies: "context is (nearly) everything." When we are ignorant of the context in which the biblical writings are set, we simply limit our ability to understand what those writings actually intended to say.

So, what follows is a lens adjustment needed to delve deeply and faithfully into the story of Jesus' birth: a cursory, thumbnail sketch of Jesus' world, drawing out those features that are most relevant for understanding Luke's account (and really all of the New Testament).[3]

3. For more a more detailed account of the Roman world during the time of Jesus, please see Kuhn, *Kingdom*, 1–54, and the other resources listed in the notes to follow.

1. Caesar is a godly Lord and Rome a godly realm

One of the first things we need to get straight about the Roman world (though this is also true of most cultures throughout human history) is that within it, "religion" is inextricably intertwined with politics, economics, and social standing. Caesar, in other words, is not simply a "secular" ruler. The Roman empire was not a secular state. Rather, Caesar was a "religious" figure, and after his death he even became enshrined as one of the Roman deities. Temples were built in honor of him and the royal family. Sacrifices were offered to seek his ongoing patronage and blessing. Eventually, some Roman emperors, like Domitian (late first century CE), would claim to be divine even before their deaths.

A central profession of Roman religion and of the "Imperial Cult" divinizing the emperors was that the Roman state and its leaders both existed and ruled with the assistance and approval of the gods. They ruled with a "divine mandate." Caesar, in other words, enacted the will of heaven. Other Roman rulers, serving under Caesar's authority, also enacted the will of heaven. Roman military, political, legal, and economic policy enacted the will of heaven. Things were the way they were because this was the world mandated by heaven. At least that is what those Romans benefiting from the status quo enthusiastically proclaimed.

2. Elite Privilege to the Extreme

And it is not hard to figure out why. Roman political and economic policy was an extraordinary source of blessing for an extraordinarily small proportion of the population. As declared by the anthropologist, G. E. M. de Ste. Croix, the Roman economy was "a massive system of exploitation of the great majority by the ruling class."[4] This ruling class, consisting of only 2 to 5 percent of the population, enacted economic hegemony through aggressive taxation, a market system that "nickled and dimed" the underclass through rents and tariffs, lending policies that routinely resulted in the foreclosure of peasant land holdings, and cheap labor in the form of institutionalized slavery, artisans, and agricultural workers.

These policies, enforced by a bureaucratic system of officials, police and military who benefitted from their loyalty to the elite, ensured the flow of wealth and resources from the underclass to the very wealthy micro-minority. As a result, 2 to 5 percent of the population controlled about 60 to 65 percent of the empire's resources, leaving 95 to 98 percent of the population the difficult task of getting by with the remaining 35 to 40 percent.

4. de Ste. Croix, *Class Struggle*, 374.

3. The Brutal Realities of Roman Rule

Not surprisingly, for most within the Roman world, life was nasty, brutish, and short. In sharp contrast to the elite and the higher class officials keeping them in power, 75 to 85 percent of the population, consisting of peasants and slaves, oscillated near or below "subsistence." This means that they suffered irregular access to adequate nutrition, water, hygiene, and secure shelter. The consequences of perpetually living on the edge were devastating.

> For most lower-class people who did make it to adulthood, their health would have been atrocious. By age thirty, the majority suffered from internal parasites, rotting teeth, and bad eyesight. Most had lived with the debilitating results of protein deficiency since childhood. Parasites were especially prevalent, being carried to humans by sheep, goats, and dogs. . . . If infant mortality rates, the age structure of the population, and pathological evidence from skeletal remains can be taken as indicators, malnutrition was a constant threat as well (Fiensy, 1991, 98).[5]

Take note of these shocking figures offered by anthropologists: because of the way resources were distributed in the Roman world and the resulting poverty afflicting the overwhelming majority, the life expectancy of urban peasants was twenty-seven, and rural peasants thirty-two. Infant mortality rates were about 30 percent, and over half of all peasant children living past age one would fail to make it past age sixteen.[6]

I'll give you a second to absorb that.

In short, many of the underclass were struggling to survive, their days filled with worry about the next harvest, the next tax, tribute, rent, or loan payment, and often the next meal. This was the world mandated by Caesar, and by the gods. This was the world the elite zealously and often brutally protected with their military might, police forces, prisons, and crosses. This was the lived reality of most of the earliest followers of Jesus.

4. More of the Same Among the People of God

This very same exploitative economic and political system resulting in the tragically disparate distribution of resources was replicated within Israelite society. In reality, the rule and power of the Israelite elite was an extension of the rule and power of Rome. Herod the Great ruled over Israel from

---

5. Rohrbaugh, "Social Location," 154. The two studies cited by Rohrbaugh are Zias, "Death and Disease" and Fiensy, *Social History*.

6. Rohrbaugh, "Social Location," 150, 151.

37–34 BCE as a "client king" of the Roman emperors, and following him his descendants ruled in various capacities with the mandate of Rome. The Jerusalem temple was the center of the Judean economy until its destruction in 70 CE. It received tithes, offerings, and sacrifices from the populace, and also collected tribute for Rome, in exchange for its "brokerage" of divine forgiveness and blessing.[7]

The economic benefits for the temple priesthood were significant, establishing them as members of the elite. Just like the Roman upper class, this priestly aristocracy acquired much of the arable land in the region through its own onerous lending policies and peasant foreclosure.[8] And just like the Roman elite, the Israelite elite claimed that their rule and the current state of affairs were mandated by heaven, by God.

5. Yearning for the Kingdom of God

But many among the people of Israel living in Palestine and throughout the Mediterranean region did not buy into the elites' claim that elite rule and the status quo were in tune with the will of God. Remember, among the vast majority of Israelites, *half of their children who managed to live past age one would die before they reached age sixteen!* As we would expect, many Israelites found this state of affairs unacceptable. Many of them claimed that Caesar and the Israelite elite ruled not with a divine mandate, but a demonic one. Their children were starving.

In protest against their lived reality, many Israelites in Jesus' time, as did their ancestors, dared to hope for a day when Israel and all the world would become a realm governed by *God's* intentions for humanity. They dared to hope for the arrival of *God's* kingdom, in which the blessing God intended for humankind would finally be realized. To express such hope and to encourage one another, they told themselves "Kingdom of God Stories." While these stories took various forms and could be told in many different ways, they nearly always revolved around three essential claims, or story lines:

a. The God of Israel is Creator and Master of all

b. The current state of the world violates God's intentions for creation

c. God is coming to fix this, to save the faithful, and to return creation to a state of blessing

7. Horsley, *Jesus and the Powers,* 7.
8. Hamel, "Poverty and Charity," 314.

Within Israel's sacred traditions (including what Christians refer to as the Old Testament), the abuse of Israel by foreign leaders, and their own leaders, are manifestations of a world gone horribly wrong.[9] In the century leading up to the birth of Jesus, many within Israel were proclaiming Kingdom Stories in response to Roman rule and what they perceived as the corruption of Israel's own rulers, especially the temple elite and those allied with them.[10] Some Kingdom Stories, including those found among the Dead Sea Scrolls, regarded Roman and Israelite elite, and their followers, as the spawn of Satan. A day was arriving soon when these reprobates would be destroyed. God would establish a new Temple, a new people of Israel, who would share in God's abundance.[11]

So, as we prepare to rejoin Luke's infancy narrative, let's quickly summarize the main points from our whirlwind tour of the realm of Rome.

1. In the Roman world, religion and politics mix, all the time. Rulers claim a divine mandate to rule, appealing to and even creating sacred ritual and tradition to validate their control of the economic and political mechanisms of empire.

2. Rome, like most ancient civilizations and many still today, cultivates a grossly unequal distribution of resources. This results in a very wealthy upper class who hoard most of that society's resources.

3. The vast majority of the population suffers, and many suffer horribly, under the inequity and brutality of Roman rule.

4. Israelite elite are an extension of Roman rule. They are supposed to shepherd the people in ways of righteousness and be ministers of God's blessings, but many use their positions to abuse and oppress.

5. Most within Israel, well before and during the time of Jesus, know that the current state of affairs is *not* okay with God. They earnestly hope that God will do something about it, and soon, and tell Kingdom Stories to express that hope and encourage one another.

This information about Jesus' context is crucial for making sense of what Luke and the rest of the New Testament is trying to say about Jesus

---

9. Israel's prophetic tradition and numerous texts surviving from the "intertestamental period" (about 250 BCE to 50 CE) identify socioeconomic exploitation by the elite as an egregious violation of God's will for Israel and humanity in general. See, e.g., Amos 5:1–24; Micah 2:1–11; Isa 10:1–4.

10. See Kuhn, *Kingdom*, 43–44.

11. See Kuhn, *Kingdom*, 31–45.

and the significance of his birth. And if you approach the passage with this information as part of your interpretive lens, then you can't help but notice the significance of Caesar in this story. Allow me to repeat myself: most Israelites in the time of Jesus, knew that the current state of affairs was *not* okay with God, and earnestly hoped that God would do something about it, and *soon*. According to Luke and the other NT writers, that time has now come. Jesus is God's answer to Caesar, the Israelite elite, and all that has gone desperately wrong with this world!

Let's return to the story (perhaps go back and reread it before moving on).

Lord Caesar

Recall that as the passage opens, we are not in Israel. We are in Rome, in the palace of the emperor. We are likely meant to picture Caesar, menacing, seated on his throne.

For it is the one known throughout the Mediterranean region and beyond as Lord who speaks and moves "all the world" to action (2:1). Caesar Augustus orders a census to be taken. Caesar wants to take stock of his subjects and possessions, the objects of his rule and sources of revenue (think taxation). His word is spoken, his underlings such as Quirinius, Governor of Syria, make it happen. The rest of the world has no choice but to comply with this "penetrating symbol of Roman overlordship."[12] And "all went to their own towns to be registered" (v. 3). As the scene now shifts to the dusty roads of the Israelite countryside, we learn that the father of Jesus is no exception: "Joseph also went from the town of Nazareth in Galilee to Judea, to the city of David called Bethlehem" (v. 4).

Note these repeated references to Caesar's census in vv. 2–5. Nearly all the activity that occurs in this part of the story revolves around the need for people, including Joseph, to be registered. The Roman Emperor dominates the opening of the story. Caesar's command rules the cosmos, or so it seems.[13]

12. Green, *Luke*, 122. For a helpful discussion of how the census would be perceived by most Israelites as a particularly egregious instance of oppressive Roman hegemony, see Horsley, *Liberation of Christmas*, 33–38.

13. However, already in these opening verses Luke drops a subtle dig at Caesar and his mighty rule. By telling us that Joseph and Mary are headed to "the city of David, called Bethlehem" (v. 4), Luke calls to mind the prophecy of Micah 5:2–6 announcing a future leader who would come forth from Bethlehem, save Israel from its enemies, and "be great until the ends of the earth" (v. 4). Throughout his two-volume work, as he does here, Luke shows the proud and powerful seeking to control the lives of faithful

Lowly Lord Jesus

But then Jesus is born. In simple, unadorned prose, we are told that Jesus is wrapped in bands of cloth, and laid in a feedbox "because there was no place for them in the inn" (2:7). Luke goes out of his way to emphasize the impoverished circumstances of Jesus and his parents. The "inn" (*kataluma*)—a sparse, hostel-like room for guests or travelers adjoining a house—is full. None move aside so that the very pregnant and eventually laboring Mary can give birth in the security of even these very meager quarters. So the young couple squeezes into a dirty, cramped, and likely ramshackle stable, delivers their child, employs a crap-encrusted feedbox for a crib, and wraps their child in scraps of spare cloth.[14]

The repeated references to the bands of cloth and manger and their function as the "sign" that identifies Jesus (2:7, 12, 16–17) keep these lowly elements in view even as he is exalted by the heavenly host and found by the shepherds. Luke's recipients are confronted with an image of Israel's Messiah that could not be more incongruous with the pomp and might of Emperor Augustus on his throne, commanding the world at will. Caesar and Jesus. Roman Emperor and Israelite peasant infant. One at the very top of the political and economic hierarchy of Rome, and the other among those at the bottom struggling to survive.

To be sure, the claim that the birth of this Israelite, peasant infant, and his manifestation in this desperate setting so far removed from the center of elite power, poses any sort of meaningful challenge to Caesar's rule would be regarded by nearly all in first-century Rome as simply ludicrous. It is important that we appreciate this reality.

Yet, as the scene shifts again—from dark, dank stable to darkened field—it is this very claim that explodes into the night! The glory of God Most High engulfs a band of shepherds and a heavenly messenger stands among them to proclaim: "Do not be afraid; for see—I am bringing you good news of great joy for all the people: to you is born this day in the city of David a Savior, who is the Messiah, the Lord." Then, adding a massive exclamation point to this startling message and most unexpected scene, as if to affirm that this really is taking place (as the shepherds rub their eyes in disbelief), an angelic host suddenly appears to announce: "Glory to God in the highest heaven, and on earth peace among those whom he favors!" Here too we encounter another setting far removed from the domains of

---

and in doing so unwittingly advancing God's designs: here it is Caesar's census that gets Jesus to Bethlehem where he must be born!

14. Those of you who have spent time around farm animals know that "crap-encrusted feedbox" is no exaggeration.

elite power. Shepherds, along with other agricultural workers, were among the large peasant class whose servitude fueled the economy of empire and hegemony of Roman rule. Yet is to these favored ones—and not to the Israelite priestly elite in Jerusalem—that glory of God appears. "God's glory, normally associated with the temple, is now manifest on a farm!"[15]

Jesus, not Caesar, is Sovereign

The angelic proclamation about Jesus amplifies (in tandem with Luke 1:26–38) Jesus' divine identity. The use of the titles "Savior" and "Lord" for Jesus is striking, for they are the same titles Israelites use for God. At the same time, these titles and other elements of the angles' pronouncement compose a repudiation of Caesar and his reign. Luke shapes the angels' testimony so that many of the things celebrated about Caesar and his birth by those allied with Rome are now attributed to this infant lying in a feedbox. In their decision to honor Augustus by beginning the new year on his birthday, the Roman provincial assembly announced,

> Whereas the providence which divinely ordered our lives created with zeal and munificence the most perfect good for our lives by producing Augustus . . . for the *benefaction of mankind*, sending us a *savior* who put an end to war . . . and whereas the *birthday* of the god marked *for the world* the beginning of *good tidings* through his coming.[16]

The parallels to the angel's announcement in 2:10–11 are apparent:

> Do not be afraid; for see—I am bringing you *good news* of great joy for *all the people*: to you is *born this day* in the city of David a *Savior*, who is the Messiah Lord (my translation).

As Richard Horsley comments, "any reader or hearer of this story in the Hellenistic-Roman world, particularly in Palestine, would have understood here a direct opposition between Caesar, the savior who had supposedly brought peace, and the child proclaimed as the savior, whose birth means peace."[17]

In not so subtle challenge to the prevailing Roman propaganda of the day, Luke dramatically relays this incredible claim: Jesus—the Israelite infant lying in a crusty feed box among sheep, goats, cattle, and fowl—undermines

15. Green, *Luke*, 131.
16. Translation from Price, *Rituals and Power*, 54.
17. Horsley, *Liberation of Christmas*, 32–33.

the might and authority of Caesar and Rome. *Jesus* is the one who is really hailed by heaven as "Savior" and "Lord" of all. In his humility and lowliness, *he* is the one who truly manifests the identity and power of God. For this reason, Jesus' birthday, not Caesar's, is good news for all of humankind. His reign, not Caesar's, will lead the heavens to erupt in praise of God and the celebration of enduring peace: "Glory to God in the highest heaven, and on earth peace to those whom he favors" (vv. 13–14).

This, Luke shows, is how God's plan for the redemption of Israel, and even all of humanity, unfolds. In this peasant infant, not Caesar nor any other, divine identity and purpose comes into the world and turns it upside down. Thus, already near the start of his narrative, Luke puts the recipients of his Kingdom Story on notice that what God does in Jesus significantly undermines all other claims to mastery over humankind. The true Lord has been born and revealed. Unlike Caesar and the "massive system of exploitation of the great majority by the ruling class" that he zealously directs and protects, the Lord Jesus will teach the world what it truly means to rule with the mandate of heaven, to rule with justice on behalf of the meek of the earth.

Reimagining the Birth of Jesus

Imagine a children's Christmas program in which Caesar is a main character. Imagine a Christmas program that celebrates Jesus' birth as an end to the political and economic exploitation of the underclass, and the hoarding of resources by a select few. Imagine a Children's Christmas program which concludes not with "Away in a Manger" but with Mary's hymn (Luke 1:46–55), in which she cries:

> 51 He has shown strength with his arm;
>   he has scattered the proud in the thoughts of their hearts.
> 52 He has brought down the powerful from their thrones,
>   and lifted up the lowly;
> 53 he has filled the hungry with good things,
>   and sent the rich away empty.

Then imagine yourself as an impoverished Israelite (or for that matter, an impoverished American) who has borne four children, and watched two of them succumb to disease or malnutrition or violence or injustice. Imagine what this Kingdom Story—told as it was meant to be—might mean for you.

And for those of us who are not dirt poor, who benefit from the patterns of privilege and resource distribution safeguarded by our status quo—what does this story mean for us?

Second Tendency: Misremembering Three Wise Men

The story of the magi in Matthew's gospel (2:1–12) is one of the central narratives in the celebration of Jesus' advent and the holy day of Epiphany immediately following the short Christmas season in the liturgical year. It has come to symbolize for Christians important elements of who we proclaim Jesus to be and what it means to follow Jesus. Yet this story serves as another example of how American Christians often misremember Christmas and forget something important about the kingdom of God.

> [1]In the time of King Herod, after Jesus was born in Bethlehem of Judea, wise men from the East came to Jerusalem, [2]asking, "Where is the child who has been born king of the Jews? For we observed his star at its rising, and have come to pay him homage." [3]When King Herod heard this, he was frightened, and all Jerusalem with him; [4]and calling together all the chief priests and scribes of the people, he inquired of them where the Messiah was to be born. [5]They told him, "In Bethlehem of Judea; for so it has been written by the prophet:
>
> > [6] 'And you, Bethlehem, in the land of Judah,
> >   are by no means least among the rulers of Judah;
> > for from you shall come a ruler
> >   who is to shepherd my people Israel.'"
>
> [7] Then Herod secretly called for the wise men and learned from them the exact time when the star had appeared. [8]Then he sent them to Bethlehem, saying, "Go and search diligently for the child; and when you have found him, bring me word so that I may also go and pay him homage." [9]When they had heard the king, they set out; and there, ahead of them, went the star that they had seen at its rising, until it stopped over the place where the child was. [10]When they saw that the star had stopped, they were overwhelmed with joy. [11]On entering the house, they saw the child with Mary his mother; and they knelt down and paid him homage. Then, opening their treasure-chests, they offered him gifts of gold, frankincense, and myrrh. [12]And having been warned in a dream not to return to Herod, they left for their own country by another road.

Set in the opening pages of Matthew's narrative, the account foreshadows what will become clear as the Gospel unfolds. These magi are Gentiles from distant lands. Perhaps framed by Matthew as a fulfillment of Isaiah 60:1–6, which speaks of non-Israelites journeying to Israel to behold and even participate in its restoration, these magi recognize the importance of this child and who he will become. This story introduces recipients of Matthew's gospel to the profession that this child, Jesus, is to be Savior and Lord for *all* of humanity, Israelite and Gentile alike.

The magi also serve as an example of how to welcome the Christ child. The magi undertake an arduous journey from afar, compelled by their earnest desire to come before this new king. Upon seeing Jesus, they worship him and present him precious gifts. Their actions parallel those of others in the pages to follow who respond to Jesus with almost immediate trust and devotion.

And so, in their remembrance of this story, American Christians often emphasize that Jesus is Savior to all humankind, and celebrate those who embrace Jesus with eyes and hearts of faith. These are aspects of the story that are certainly good and faithful to remember. But they are not the whole story. Again, we need a lens adjustment in order to see this account more clearly.

Lens Adjustment: The Not So Three, or Wise, or Even Men

In our remembrance of the magi we tend to add several elements to their story that are actually not found in the Gospel of Matthew, the only Gospel which tells us about them. In Christian tradition, the magi are commonly regarded as kings: "We three kings of Orient are . . ." the carol goes. But there is nothing in Matthew's gospel to suggest this.

We also commonly remember the magi as being three in number, and several different sets of names throughout the centuries have been suggested for them. Again, there is nothing in Matthew's account that tells us that there were three magi or the names they were called. The magi's gifts being three in number simply does not indicate that there were three magi.

The gifts also do not, as many assume, necessitate that the magi were wealthy. Gold, frankincense, and myrrh were indeed valuable commodities, but Matthew does not indicate the amounts that were gifted to Jesus. The gifts could represent the collective wealth of this group of magi and further underscore the sacrifice implied in their journey.

Just as strangely, we (including the NRSV translators!) have commonly regarded the magi as *wise men*, even though there is nothing in Matthew's gospel that tells us that they were wise, or that they were all men.

Really.

From what we can piece together from surviving historical evidence, it appears that magi were astrologers and interpreters of dreams, especially in Eastern cultures that had been influenced by Persian customs.[18] They were not kings themselves, but some of them served in the courts of kings, functioning as advisors, like the "magi" (NRSV: "magicians") described in Daniel 2:1–11. It is likely that most such advisors were men, but some could have been women. After all, in ancient Persia women served as priests and astrologers, and even in Israelite tradition women served as prophets. There is also evidence suggesting that some magi may have been itinerant, traveling in large groups, including their families—like roaming gypsies.

By Gentile folk, some magi would have been regarded as wise. But to others, especially Israelite folk, this was not likely the case. We can find no ancient Israelite text that presents the magi as wise persons. In fact, in every surviving Israelite text of the time, including two that would have been widely known by Israelites in Jesus' day, the magi are regarded not as wise, but fools![19] As surprising as this may be, it makes perfect sense. How do you discern the will of God if you are a faithful Israelite? By reading the Torah and Prophets, not the stars, not by magic!

Accordingly, it is very likely that most recipients of Matthew's gospel—most of whom were likely Israelite Christians—would not have held the magi in high regard. Rather, they and most early Christians would have heard this story very differently than how many Christians hear and tell this story today. For first-century Jesus folk, this is not a story about the wisest, wealthiest, and most discerning among the Gentiles coming with great reverence to honor the Israelite King. Instead, they would have heard it as an almost comical, puzzling tale, about a bunch of silly, Eastern astrologers who are led by a star to see Jesus. "What was God up to?" many

18. For a helpful review and assessment of this evidence drawing on Greco-Roman literature, Jewish midrash (commentary on biblical traditions), and the Israelite Scriptures, see Powell, *Eastern Star,* 139–54.

19. The characterization of magi as foolish appears in Jewish midrash on Pharaoh's magicians in the Exodus story and on the foreign prophet, Balaam (see Num 22–24). Pharaoh's magicians are revealed to be ineffectual: their magical arts end up worsening the plagues against Egypt, in other moments their arts fail to produce any results, and in the end they become plague victims themselves. Balaam is characterized by Philo as the "most foolish of all men." As summarized by Powell (*Eastern Star,* 152), "Philo presents the magus as foolish in a broader sense: he is a ridiculous figure whose useless art is easily thwarted by God and exposed for the nonsense that it really is."

of the original recipients of Matthew's gospel would have asked. "Why, of all people, them?[20]

Note too that if we carefully attend to Matthew's account, we are not encouraged to regard the magi as all that astute. Just the opposite. While in the East, the magi see the star rising and follow it to Judea. Yet even with the guidance of the bright and luminous star, the magi still get lost! So they stop off in Jerusalem and ask for directions. Eventually, King Herod gets wind of this and secretly summons the magi (vv. 7–8). He sends them off to Bethlehem, saying "Go ahead, find the Christ child, and then come back and let me know where he lives, so that I too can go and worship him" (camera cue: focus in on Herod as he turns aside, rubs his hands, and laughs evilly under his breath). But the magi are oblivious to Herod's ulterior motives, and to the fact that he has just gained information from them that puts Jesus at great risk (see Matt 2:16–18). The magi then head off to Bethlehem and the star leads them to the very place where Jesus lives. Finally, the still clueless magi need to be warned in a dream not to return to Herod (v. 12).

The Magi as Faithful Fools

If we read this story *without* the assumption that the magi are three discerning, wise men, then we can see how this story may have been understood differently by those who first told it and first heard it. Then we too might ask concerning the silly magi, along with the earliest tellers and hearers of this tale, why these folk? What was God up to?

Asking these questions can help us to recognize another important element of Matthew's gospel that is in view here already in its opening

---

20. If magi were regarded by most Jewish folk as foolish, then it begs the question of why Herod and the inhabitants of Jerusalem would have been troubled by the magi's assertion that a king had been born among the Jews on the basis of observing his star. Herod was of mixed ethnicity, and though his family had converted to Judaism, many Israelites at the time (as do historians today) questioned Herod's allegiance to Jewish perspectives and traditions, despite the resources he devoted to the restoration and expansion of the Jerusalem temple. The fact that he finds the magi credible is consistent with the view of numerous Israelites that Herod subscribed to many foolish, Gentile notions. Likewise, Herod's fear and questioning of the magi in Matthew's story reveal his ignorance of Torah and his self-serving lack of interest in the arrival of God's kingdom. Moreover, Herod's irrational paranoia during the latter part of his reign compelled him to murder members of his own family (including his wife, Mariamne) and friends. Thus, it is entirely plausible that Herod would find the magi's query credible or at least worrisome enough to take action. And given Herod's inclination towards violence when he felt his reign was being threatened, it is not surprising that many within Jerusalem would also fear any perceived challenge to Herod's reign. Tragically, it turns out that their fear was justified (see Matt 2:16–18).

chapters. As we will see later on in the narrative, Jesus picks fishermen, sinners, rebels, and tax collectors—basically a bunch of nobodies and no-goods—to be his disciples (4:18–22; 9:9). For this he is upbraided by the Pharisees, to whom he responds: "I have not come to call the righteous, but sinners" (9:10–13). He commends a Canaanite woman for her great faith (15:21–28). He tells his disciples, "Whoever wishes to be first among you must be your slave" (20:27). He defines righteousness as concern for the least among us (25:31–46), and emulates that in his own miracles of healing.

Then at one point, Jesus proclaims regarding his followers, "I praise you Father, Lord of Heaven and earth, because *you have hidden these things from the wise and learned and revealed them to little children*" (11:25).

In short, through this story and others to follow, Matthew is concerned to tell us that those whom the world often finds silly, naïve, trashy, power-less, and childish are more likely to open their hearts and minds to Christ. The saving reign of God makes little headway among those who hoard their riches, who seek to preserve their privileged positions, who celebrate their status at the expense of others, who so trust in their own manner of "wisdom" that they are blind to the way of blessing God is making known in plain sight before them. The kingdom of heaven comes to the ones "foolish" enough to set the lies of this world aside, and rest their hearts in the truth and love of God made known in Emmanuel.

The Magi through the Centuries

Very few Christians throughout history have celebrated let alone remem-bered the foolish and childlike character of the magi as Matthew presents them. It seems likely that as the telling of the magi story moved from an Israelite to Gentile cultural context, those hearing it simply assumed that magi were wise. This interpretive tendency is still alive and well among American Christians today. Yet before discussing how the magi are most often viewed in our American context, it may be illuminating to explore how over the centuries Christians have told the magi story differently from how it is told by Matthew. In his book, *The Journey of the Magi: Meanings in History of a Christian Story*, Richard Trexler traces the various forms of the magi story as they appear in Christian literature and art from the open-ing centuries of Christianity until the beginning of the modern age. As we might expect, the story—and the magi themselves—have been presented in a number of different ways.

Early Christians of means often associated themselves with the magi in burial art adorning their tombs. A prominent motif in these settings was the generous gift-giving of the wealthy and wise magi and their subsequent reception of Christ's salvation. Presumably, the wealthy Christians interred in the tombs displayed this depiction of the magi to emphasize their own wise and generous giving to Christ's church and expectation of salvation. As Trexler summarizes,

> The Christians who paid for these representations wanted to show that, like the magi, they had made gifts to Jesus through his church. This fundamental association between what had launched the church—the magi's gifting of Jesus—and the salvational giving that was a consequence expected of all Christians will be one leitmotif of this work.[21]

Later, after Constantine's adoption of Christianity as one of the unifying forces of his empire, a new motif was added to the portrayal of the magi. Funeral art and other sources depict the magi as legates or client kings submitting themselves to the authority of Jesus. In some of these depictions, the magi seem to represent the devotion and submission of the Roman emperors and leaders to Jesus and the church. Others associate the authority of Roman and later Byzantine emperors with that of Jesus. In these scenes, the image or example of the magi is used to depict the powers of the world presenting themselves to Christ *and* to the Christian emperor. Some depict the magi as members of Jesus' royal court, as the child Jesus sits on a throne and receives the homage of foreign kings and the offerings of the nations. In both cases, the magi, Trexler points out, function as figures that legitimate not only the worship of Jesus, but also the authority of the emperor and empire, *and* their reception of tribute!

As we move into the early medieval period, many of these same depictions continue, including the use of the magi story to celebrate and legitimate elite power. It is also during this time that magi are first presented in Western art and literature as "the three kings" who pay homage to Jesus, and are assigned the names Balthazar, Caspar, and Melchior.[22] At the same time, the image of the magi was used not only to encourage allegiance to church and empire, but to cast emperors as faithful devotees to Jesus. The Emperor Justin and his wife, Theodora, are presented in a mosaic dating to 546–48 as "quasi-magi" offering gifts directly to Jesus.

Later, the characters of the magi would be used to promote and justify the church's attempts to reclaim Jerusalem in the first of the crusades. Trexler writes,

21. Trexler, *Magi*, 23–24.
22. Trexler, *Magi*, 35.

the crusading idea that gentiles (also from the west) might be heirs of Jerusalem, even as the eastern magi had been the first gentiles to recognize the truth of Christianity, would over time develop into the notion that the western crusading monarchs were indeed like veritable magi, returning to rescue Jerusalem from latter-day Herods."[23]

By still other writers and artists, the magi were cast as representative of humankind in general. Often, but not exclusively depicted as three in number (sometimes as many as twelve), the magi represented men in different stages of life, men of different dispositions, or different Gentile races or regions of the world.

READING THE STORY THROUGH ELITE-SHAPED LENSES

The way in which the magi have been cast by Christian artists and thinkers throughout these centuries has been variable. But the surviving depictions reviewed by Trexler overlook a critical component of Matthew's portrayal of the magi: their childlike simplicity that challenges the prevailing notions of wisdom, power, and access to God. Instead, the magi are frequently associated with elite gift-giving, faithful royalty, or submission to royalty. These depictions reflect a retelling of the magi story by the elite in promotion of elite values and the power of the state and church.

THE MAGI AS COLONIZED SUPPLICANTS

As we move into the modern period, elite and state interests continue to guide the framing of the magi story, and now in service of colonization. Columbus and others speculated that the Americas included the gold and wealth-laden homelands of the three kings.[24] Building on these assertions, artwork began appearing presenting at least one and sometimes all of the magi as native American, and numerous attempts were made to draw connections between the Americas and the fabled worlds of the magi. In the mind of the church-sanctioned state, this not only legitimated the exploration and eventually exploitation of native resources, but of the natives themselves.

Once established in a region of the new world, the colonizing Spaniards held a ceremony Trexler terms the "feast of the magi," and compelled their new subjects to play along. This was a ritualized drama in which

23. Trexler, *Magi*, 74.
24. Trexler, *Magi*, 138.

natives representing different communities dressed as magi and prostrated themselves before and offered gifts of their land not only to Jesus, but to their colonizing conquerors in exchange for the "salvation" they had received from their new lords.

> The feast of the magi was soon established in the so-called new world, since it facilitated exchanging the salvation of the Americans for the wealth of the Indies. It brought native peoples before the one altar of the child, and it allowed the dramatic union of different indigenous social configurations, from the calpullis, or neighborhoods, up to the various tribes. That was precisely what the Spaniards needed, for even if they would tolerate ethnic diversity at the representational level, they were concerned to show the union of all the American tribes at the feet of the infant, that is at the feet of the Spanish crown and the European clergy.[25]

Similar feasts and processions casting natives as suppliant magi took place in North America as well during the feast of Epiphany. In summary, Trexler states that these rituals "show cultures forced to play the magi within paradigms and effects prescribed by the spiritual conquerors of those regions. Not surprisingly, missionaries loved to write home about how docile and childlike such people were."[26]

Now, finally, the magi are portrayed by the elite in ways that have some semblance to their appearance in Matthew! They are childlike! But this is a far cry from the childlikeness that Matthew had in mind.

Tragically, the native Americans forced to play the role of the magi in these propagandizing spectacles actually had more in common with the slaughtered children of Matthew 2. These colonizing leaders and missionaries not only radically reconfigured Matthew's portrayal of the magi, they themselves—through exploitation, enslavement, and disease—took on the role of Herod.

Our Magi Stories Today

Allow me to restate the summary of the magi story as read within the context of Matthew's narrative I provided above:

> In short, through this story and others to follow, Matthew is concerned to tell us that those whom the world often finds silly, naïve, trashy, powerless, and childish are more likely to open

25. Trexler, *Magi*, 147.
26. Trexler, *Magi*, 208.

their hearts and minds to Christ. The saving reign of God makes little headway among those who hoard their riches, who seek to preserve their privileged positions, who celebrate their status at the expense of others, who so trust in their own manner of "wisdom" that they are blind to the way of blessing God is making known in plain sight before them. The kingdom of heaven comes to those who set the lies of this world aside, and rest their hearts in the truth and love of God made known in Emmanuel.

This summary, of course, reflects a very different understanding of the story of the magi than we see reflected in our history. Throughout the centuries, the story of the magi has often been framed in self-congratulatory and self-serving ways that reflect elite objectives: recognition by God and others for their generous patronage, maintenance of elite power, promotion of the crusades and later colonization, and subjugation of native peoples.

Recent readings of the magi within our American context have shifted away from the most exploitative of these retellings. But as noted earlier, the magi are still commonly regarded by Christians today as wise and admirable exemplars of how one finds his or her way to Jesus. The countercultural, even revolutionary, dimension of their story in Matthew, and its focus on God's initiative in leading the magi to Jesus, is often overlooked. In other words, instead of experiencing the story as the surprising, disorienting tale which challenges our conceptions of who truly welcomes the kingdom of God—instead of experiencing the tale as Matthew likely intended—we often read it as a tale that affirms our sense of what it takes to be a believer, or perhaps the kind of believers we consider ourselves to be: wise, learned, and discerning. Here is a sampling of such readings readily found online.

> The three wise men, also known as magi, were men belonging to various educated classes. Our English word magician comes from this same root. But these wise men were not magicians in the modern sense of sleight-of-hand performers. They were of noble birth, educated, wealthy, and influential. They were philosophers, the counselors of rulers, learned in all the wisdom of the ancient East. The wise men who came seeking the Christ child were not idolaters; they were upright men of integrity. They had apparently studied the Hebrew Scriptures and found there a clear transcript of truth.[27]

> They were certainly men of great learning . . . The magi would have followed the patterns of the stars religiously. They would have also probably been very rich and held in high esteem in

27. Bible Info, "Three Wise Men."

their own society and by people who weren't from their country or religion. They had seen an unusual new star in the sky,
and knew that it told of the birth of a special king in Israel . . .
The Magi would have known about the prophesies of a special Jewish Savior (also known as the Messiah) from when the
Jews had been held captive in ancient Babylon several hundred
years before.[28]

Magoi were experts in such astral phenomena. But what
about *this* star drew them to Jerusalem? The most plausible
explanation lies in Israel's Scriptures. As learned men who interacted with various religious literature, the *magoi* would have
been familiar with Jewish political or messianic oracles. And
one of the central political prophecies in the Hebrew Scriptures
is Balaam's oracle.[29]

These foreigners, the first Gentiles to see the Light, recognize
what Herod and the Temple priesthood cannot: the newborn
Savior. The wealthy, learned, alien Magi of St. Matthew's Gospel
complement the poor, ignorant, local shepherds of St. Luke's
Gospel. Foreshadowing the universality of the Church, these
Gentiles and Jews worship God Incarnate to show that salvation
is offered to all men.[30]

A common theme in these descriptions of the magi and their devotion
to Jesus is the assumption that they would have been men of great learning
familiar with the Israelite Scriptures. I guess this is possible, but there is absolutely no evidence to support this contention. Indeed, there was likely a sharing of religious thought between Israelites and Persians starting around the
late sixth century BCE and continuing on for at least the next hundred years.
But we do not know how long such interreligious dialogue lasted or its extent,
and we simply cannot validly assume (1) that it continued into the first century BCE and that (2) it was occurring among this particular group of magi.
Even more telling, if it was the case that the magi were led by Israel's Scriptures
to await the birth of the messiah and rightly interpret the significance of the
star, then why wouldn't Matthew—who emphasizes that Jesus' birth fulfills
the Israelite Scriptures—have included that information?

28. WhyChristmas.com, "All About the Wise Men."
29. Lanier, "We Three Kings."
30. Miesel, "Wise Men."

Celebrating the Magi as Matthew Did

As I stated at the start of our discussion of the magi, when reflecting on this story American Christians do well to emphasize that Jesus offers God's salvation to all humankind, and celebrate those who like the magi embrace Jesus with eyes and hearts of faith. But we also tend to cast the magi as characters we find admirable: Scripture-reading, prophecy-discerning, wealthy, wise men.

But such readings undercut the story's original intent to challenge our notions of wisdom, power, and self-sufficiency. After all, it is the wise and wealthy and powerful ones in this story who recoil with fear and hatred when hearing the news about Christ. They plot to encounter Jesus on their terms. And eventually, they kill him.

The magi didn't come to Jesus because they were wise. They came because they were led by God, and had just enough sense to keep following the star. The magi came not representing royal elite. They came because they were infantile enough to know goodness when they saw it, even if they didn't fully comprehend yet what it was all about and the implications of their actions.

> "I praise you Father, Lord of Heaven and earth, because you
> have hidden these things from the wise and learned and re-
> vealed them to little children" (11:25).

What would it mean for us to truly identify with those the world finds silly, naïve, trashy, powerless, and childish? Rather than reading this story through a self-gratulatory set of lenses, as if the magi are discerning wise people just like us, what if we grasped that the saving reign of God makes little headway among those who hoard their riches, who seek to preserve their privileged positions, who celebrate their status at the expense of others, who so trust in their own manner of "wisdom" that they are blind to the way of blessing God is making known in plain sight before them?

Remembering our Roots, and Honoring our Ancestors

When it comes to biblical interpretation, context is (nearly) everything. At least that is the case if one is interested in reading biblical passages in a way that is similar to how many of the first recipients of these texts would have heard them. I hope my discussion of Luke's account of Jesus' birth and Matthew's story of the magi illustrates the importance of engaging three different contexts when it comes to reading the Bible well.

The Worlds of the Text

Many interpreters refer to these contexts as the world behind the text (so-cial and historical contexts), the world of the text (the literary context of the surrounding work or narrative), and the world in front of the text (the context of the readers themselves). What follows is a very brief description of each. For illustration purposes, I also summarize how engaging each of these worlds may enable us to become more faithful readers of Luke 2 and Matthew 2 (and by extension, most other biblical texts).

The World Behind the Text: how our reading of the text makes sense with respect to the time and place in which it was written. What historical, politi-cal, economic, and cultural realities are reflected within the text and must be addressed in order to understand the text more fully?

- Understanding what life was like in the first-century world, including grossly inequal distribution of resources, widespread poverty, Roman propaganda casting Caesar as Savior and Lord, and Israelite hopes for deliverance, helps us to discern the revolutionary character of Luke's story and the contrast he dramatically depicts between Caesar and Je-sus, between the Roman world and the Realm and rule of God.

- Understanding that most Israelites in Jesus' day would have regarded magi as silly and foolish helps us to see the ways in which Matthew's portrayal of the magi leans on and exploits these popular conceptions in order to say something startling about the kingdom of God and what it means to be part of it.

The World of the Text: how our reading of this text fits with its immediate context, and the tendencies of the rest of the biblical work in which it ap-pears. How does this passage or story contribute to the interests of the work as a whole?

- Luke's portrayal of Jesus' birth builds upon Luke's characterization of Jesus in the preceding narrative as the divine savior whose advent will upend prevailing patterns of power and right the wrong of gross inequity (recall Mary's hymn in 1:47–55). It also further prepares us to recognize the ongoing manifestation of these themes in the narrative to follow.

- Matthew's frequent characterization of Jesus' followers as marginal-ized members of society, even "infants," and Jesus' consistent critique of wealth, power, and those who wield them for their own selfish pursuits, reaffirms our sense that Matthew also intended to present the magi as marginalized characters who had the humility and faith to receive God's call.

The World in Front of the Text: how our own biases, limitations, and interests shape our reading of the story. What parts of our lenses might not be well-suited to engaging this text faithfully, and how can we adjust our lenses to allow the text to speak on its own terms?

- It is important for us to be aware of our tendency as American Christians to sentimentalize the story of Jesus' birth and overlook its political, social, and economic dimensions—the parts of the story that make many of us uncomfortable. As American Christians, we often resist the integration of religion, politics, economics, and social stratification, and yet Luke's gospel, like the other Gospels, consistently presents Jesus as addressing such matters as integral to the arrival of God's kingdom.

- We also do well to be aware of the tendency throughout the ages and even today of Christians and Christian authorities casting the magi according their own interests and biases. Christians have often characterized the magi in ways that reflect their own self-image or selfish objectives, and in doing so have skewed Matthew's witness to what it means to embrace Jesus as Emmanuel.

Reading with Respect

Not only does being mindful of these different contexts help us to become better, more critical readers of the Bible, it can also help us to be more respectful and faithful ones.

The Bible preserves the gathered testimonies of our spiritual ancestors, spanning over a millennium, to their experience and understanding of God, their history, and sense of what it means to be God's people. We are the privileged—very privileged—heirs of these sacred traditions. But if we read this holy testimony without any concerted interest or effort to hear it as it was originally intended to be heard, then whose voice are we hearing as we encounter it? Are we truly engaging the testimony of our ancestors, or just our own voices?

Moreover, Christians have also commonly regarded this very same testimony as inspired by God, and an important resource that God has provided us to discern who God is and what it means to live rightly with God and one another. This belief began with our spiritual ancestors' sense that these texts provided such inspired, faithful witness. But if we read this holy testimony without any concerted interest or effort to hear it as it was heard by our ancestors, who heard in these stories the voice of God, then we could rightly ask if we are actually reading the same "Bible" our ancestors gathered together, wrote down, and passed down to us. Are we truly engaging the "Word of God"? In other words, are we coming to the Bible to be entertained by a quaint tale, or to affirm the rightness of our own views and interests, or to be transformed?

Two Clarifications

I hope my logic here is straightforward. But as I close this chapter, I will offer a couple points of clarification.

> *Does this mean that all is lost if we have trouble discerning the historical context of a biblical passage, or we do not do so perfectly?*

Not necessarily. Even if we don't have all the information we need to reconstruct the specific features of every historical setting we encounter, just having a general sense of prevailing political and economic patterns and cultural norms in particular periods can often be very helpful. We also do well to keep in mind that interpretation of any sort is rarely an exact science and is more about probabilities than perfection. This is also the case with biblical interpretation. For this reason, ongoing study and research is important, and even more so, humility, self-awareness, and dialogue. We won't always get it right. But we will almost never get close to the intended meaning and objectives of biblical texts if we don't try to read them with these contexts in mind.

> *Does this mean that more "spiritual" or devotional readings that don't critically engage the contexts behind the texts, of the text, and in front of the text, are worthless?*

Not at all. I believe that the Spirit has the capacity to connect with us and guide us through a variety of avenues. The devotional reading of biblical passages is one of those rituals through which many—including myself—encounter the presence and instruction of God.

But I also believe that such practices should not be the sole avenue through which Christians engage Scripture. Our tendency to hear in the text what we want to hear, our tendency to shape our lenses in ways that mirror back to us our own preconceived notions, is a strong one. Remember, we are by nature and necessity perspectival and selective interpreters!

Our devotional reading of Scripture should be informed by and in conversation with those readings that try to hear the witness of our ancestors as they testify to God and God's will in their times and places.

The key, I think, is that we don't fall into the trap of engaging Scripture in isolation from other believers, or through only one approach. The narrower our lenses, the more narrow our encounter with Scripture, and the more narrow our understanding of God and God's will. We must be self-aware and humble enough to realize that faithful reading the Bible will sometimes, perhaps even often, lead us to read against the grain of our own biases and our own self-interests, at least as those are often defined by our world. We must strive for a way of reading that honors our ancestors' testimonies to the often-revolutionary, always-transforming, real life-relevant work and word of God.

To do otherwise is to dishonor our ancestors. To do otherwise is to read the Bible badly.

Reflection or Discussion Questions

1. Do you agree with the author that there is a major disconnect between the way in which Luke and Matthew present the stories surrounding Jesus' birth and how we remember and celebrate these stories as American Christians? If so, what manifestations of this disconnect do you recognize? Why do you think this disconnect exists?

2. It seems strange to many American Christians to consider the political and economic dimensions of the Gospel traditions, along with the rest of the biblical writings. How do you feel about this? How does attending to these dimensions help or complicate your understanding of Scripture?

3. In your mind, how might we faithfully honor the testimony of our ancestors in the faith as we read and reflect on Scripture today?

CHAPTER TWO

Reading the Bible as Inerrant and Making It Much Less Relevant

The Bible is the God-breathed,
sharper than a double-edged sword,
light unto our path,
saving Good News,
Word of God.

Therefore, it must be true. It must be without error. It must be *inerrant.* Makes sense.

This simple train of logic is basic to many, even most, Christians' understanding of Scripture. For good reason. The logic is clear, compellingly straightforward. For many, this formula has become an integral piece of their hermeneutic, the lens they use to read the Bible. It leads them to expect, and to find and even to fight for the unity, consistency, infallibility (without falsehood), and inerrancy of Scripture.

For many, if the Bible could be shown to contain *any* error of any type, then *everything* it says is suspect. The Christian faith itself is then suspect. It is an all-or-nothing sort of thing. The Bible is the inerrant Word of God. Must be. Has to be.

But. And this is a big but. What if upon closer inspection we find that the Bible does contain inconsistencies and inaccuracies? What if upon closer inspection we find that the Bible even contains portrayals of God and others that don't seem to square with how God and others are portrayed elsewhere in Scripture? What if the character, or nature, of Scripture is not nearly as straightforward as "it is the Word of God and therefore it must all be true" formula that many Christians claim for it?

What do we do with that?

The Case for the Inerrancy of Scripture

Before considering this issue, let's pause to explore in more detail what defenders of "biblical inerrancy" say about Scripture and why they find this belief so important. To do this, we are going to dip back in recent history to consider the "Chicago Statement on Biblical Inerrancy," composed during an international conference sponsored by the International Council on Biblical Inerrancy (ICBI) in the fall of 1978.[1] The Chicago Statement was signed by nearly 300 noted evangelical scholars and has served as a touchstone for the conservative view of Scripture over the last several decades.[2] This excerpt comprises the "short summary" of the position articulated in the document. If you find the language overly technical and a bit stiff, don't worry. We will unpack its essential claims in just a moment.

1. God, who is Himself Truth and speaks truth only, has inspired Holy Scripture in order thereby to reveal Himself to lost mankind through Jesus Christ as Creator and Lord, Redeemer and Judge. Holy Scripture is God's witness to Himself.

2. Holy Scripture, being God's own Word, written by men prepared and superintended by His Spirit, is of infallible divine authority in all matters upon which it touches: it is to be believed, as God's instruction, in all that it affirms: obeyed, as God's command, in all that it requires; embraced, as God's pledge, in all that it promises.

3. The Holy Spirit, Scripture's divine Author, both authenticates it to us by His inward witness and opens our minds to understand its meaning.

4. Being wholly and verbally God-given, Scripture is without error or fault in all its teaching, no less in what it states about God's acts in

1. The Chicago Statement is easily accessible on the web, including on the Dallas Theological Society's website where the records of the ICBI are archived (http://library. dts.edu/Pages/TL/Special/ICBI.shtml). The document containing the statement consists of a preface, the short statement cited above, followed by nineteen articles and an exposition.

2. Smith (*Bible Made Impossible,* 10–16) labels the 1978 Chicago Statement as a landmark example of "biblicism," and further details how this interpretive perspective is currently represented in the faith statements of numerous evangelical universities, seminaries, parachurch organizations, and denominational bodies such as the Southern Baptist Convention.

creation, about the events of world history, and about its own literary origins under God, than in its witness to God's saving grace in individual lives.

5. The authority of Scripture is inescapably impaired if this total divine inerrancy is in any way limited or disregarded, or made relative to a view of truth contrary to the Bible's own; and such lapses bring serious loss to both the individual and the Church.

By my reading, this summary and other assertions contained in the Chicago Statement echo four foundational claims common to defenders of biblical inerrancy.

God is the Author

Repeatedly, the summary emphasizes that Scripture is "God's own Word." Though "written by men," these same men were "prepared and superintended by His Spirit," to the degree that that it is the Spirit who is truly "Scripture's divine Author," yielding a text that is "wholly and verbally God-given." What this means for many conservative readers is that God directed the composition of the biblical texts down to the level of word choice. For it is the patterning of its very words that creates the infallible meaning that the texts convey. Even though later sections of the statement affirm that "God utilized the distinctive personalities and literary styles of the writers he had chosen and prepared," the stress always falls back to the divine authorship of Scripture: the inspiration God provided "guaranteed true and trustworthy utterance on all matters which the biblical authors were moved to speak and write." In this sense, then, conservatives see Scripture as a "monological" witness to God and God's will. It was God and, ultimately God only, who crafted these texts into the revelation that they are. Human writers were involved, but only as instruments or mediums of divine authorship.[3] When we hear Scripture, we are hearing the voice of God alone.

On what basis do conservatives claim the divine authorship of the Bible? The summary affirms that the Holy Spirit "authenticates it to us by His inward witness," and the statement later adds that "the Holy Spirit bears witness to the Scriptures, assuring believers of the truthfulness of God's

---

3. Some conservative scholars have offered several different suggestions on the "mode of inspiration": i.e., how, exactly, such inspiration took place. Many conservatives, however, do not attempt to explain this phenomenon, and the framers of the Chicago Statement concur: "The mode of divine inspiration remains largely a mystery to us."

written word." This, conservatives claim, is why so many believers possess an intuitive sense of Scripture's divine origin and truthfulness.

In addition to the inward testimony of the Spirit, conservatives claim that Scripture itself testifies to the divine origin of Israel's Scriptures (our Old Testament). Numerous narrative and prophetic texts in the Old Testament clearly indicate God as the source of faithful prophecy. In some New Testament texts, Jesus also cites Old Testament passages as if they are direct statements of God, even when they are not in the form of divine direct speech or prophetic oracles (e.g., Matt 19:4-5, citing Gen 2:24). This leads Millard Erickson, a prominent evangelical theologian, among others to conclude that "evidently, in Jesus' mind anything that the Old Testament said was what God said."[4] Statements within the New Testament claim divine authority for some their writings as well. For example, in 2 Peter 3:16, the writer appears to associate Paul's letters with "the other scriptures." The writer of 1 John claims that the instruction he conveys is divine truth received from God, and Rev 22:18-19 indicates the apocalypse's status as divinely conveyed prophecy to which nothing should be subtracted or added. By implication then, conservatives argue that *all* Scripture—both the Old and New Testaments—originate from God.

Fully Inspired Means Fully Inerrant and Infallible

According to conservatives, the full, verbal inspiration of the biblical texts necessitates their inerrant (without error in terms of fact) and infallible (true and reliable in terms of teaching about God and salvation) nature. Some conservatives allow that the biblical authors used approximations, reporting techniques common in the authors' times, and made grammatical errors.[5] Conservatives, like other Christians, also understand that there is a progressive dimension to God's revelation, so that later revelation can qualify the relevance of earlier commands (such as with Christian understandings of the dietary and purity codes, and other OT laws).[6] But the text that must result from God's full inspiration is a completely accurate and truthful representation of everything it addresses. Erickson offers a representative articulation of this position:

> If God is omniscient, he must know all things. He cannot be ignorant of or in error on any matter. Further, if he is omnipotent,

4. Erickson, *Christian Theology*, 239.
5. Chicago Statement, article 13.
6. Chicago Statement, article 5.

he is able to so affect the biblical author's writing that nothing erroneous enters into the final product. And being a truthful or veracious being, he will certainly desire to utilize these abilities in such a way that man will not be misled by the Scriptures. Thus, our view of inspiration logically entails the inerrancy of the Bible. Inerrancy is a corollary of the doctrine of full inspiration.[7]

In short, God said it (or led the biblical authors to say it), so therefore all of Scripture must be true.

The Authority of Scripture Depends on its Inerrancy

The full inspiration, inerrancy, and infallibility of Scripture is, for many conservatives, the basis on which they trust its witness to God and what it means to be God's people. If the Bible cannot tell the story of Israel or Jesus accurately, if it can be shown that Scripture is in error or inconsistent on any particular matter, then on what basis could its witness to God and God's salvation embedded in those reports also be trusted? As Erickson summarizes this position: "false in one, uncertain in all."[8] Or, as the framers of the Chicago Statement argue, "The authority of Scripture is inescapably impaired if this total divine inerrancy is in any way limited or disregarded, or made relative to a view of truth contrary to the Bible's own."

Inerrancy Ensures Doctrinal Fidelity

Relatedly, conservatives such as Erickson observe that "where a theologian, a school, or a movement begins by regarding biblical inerrancy as a peripheral or optional matter and abandons this doctrine, it frequently then goes on to abandon or alter other doctrines which the church has ordinarily considered quite major, such as the deity of Christ or the Trinity."[9] I think it is fair to say that for conservatives the full inspiration, inerrancy, and infallibility of Scripture is both the basis and guardian of Christian doctrine.

---

7. Erickson, *Christian Theology*, 251.

8. Erickson, *Christian Theology*, 253.

9. Erickson, *Christian Theology*, 252.

Assessing Conservative Attempts to Defend the Inerrancy of Scripture

In summary, according to conservatives the inerrancy of Scripture is *necessary*. It is logically necessary, and it is necessary to the integrity and legitimacy of Christianity. The inerrancy of Scripture cannot be rejected "without grave consequences both to the individual and to the Church."[10]

On the one hand, this claim to necessity is the conservative view's greatest strength. It employs a logic that, as I mentioned at the start of the chapter, is compellingly straightforward for many Christians. It also fuels a passionate commitment to promoting and defending this doctrine, as reflected in many conservative statements of faith. Biblical inerrancy is essential to what most conservatives mean when they speak of being a "Bible-believing Christian."

Yet this claim of necessity, the conservative view's greatest strength, is also its greatest weakness.

This brings us back to the "But . . ." I identified earlier. But . . . what if the Bible clearly does contain "errors" and contrasting views of God and God's ways?

It is not as though conservative theologians are unaware of this possibility.

Making a Choice

Some conservatives, such as Erickson, thoughtfully acknowledge that in arguing for the full inspiration and inerrancy of Scripture they are privileging one of two available sets of information.[11] One approach in formulating a view of Scripture is to place primary emphasis on what the biblical writers appear to communicate or imply about the inspiration of Scripture in passages that suggest God's authorship of Scripture. This is the approach favored by most conservatives, including Erickson, and as we just saw leads them to the conclusion that the Bible is fully inspired by God and thus inerrant and infallible. Again, one following this approach would assert, "Scripture states and implies that God inspired its content, and therefore it must be fully truthful, since God is fully truthful." So what about the apparent inconsistences and inaccuracies we find in Scripture? They are simply not deemed significant enough by conservatives to overcome the otherwise

10. Chicago Statement, Article 19.
11. Warfield, "Inspiration," 223–26.

substantial evidence they find supporting their belief that God authored the
Scriptures (we will say more on this later).

The other approach is to put primary emphasis on a careful analysis of
the biblical writings to determine if these texts actually appear to be completely consistent with one another. Those who opt for this "phenomeno-
logical approach," Erickson points out, often find enough inconsistencies
between biblical accounts to call into question the inerrancy of Scripture.[12]
Proponents of this approach might retort, "Hey, wait a minute, the Bible
doesn't actually seem to be inerrant, so how can we say that it is?"

I think this question makes a lot of sense.

Conservatives argue that "the authority of Scripture is inescapably
impaired if this total divine inerrancy is in any way limited or disregarded,
or made relative to a view of truth contrary to the Bible's own." But what
if the doctrine of inerrancy itself is a "view of truth contrary to the Bible's
own"? What if the nature of Scripture is not as simple and "monological" as
conservatives claim?

Scripture is Best Viewed as Inspired Testimony

Many Christians falling outside of the conservative camp do not view Scripture as a divine monologue, but more as a dialogue, a community of voices.
To them, Scripture is a gathering of testimonies to God's character as Creator
and Savior, to God's will for humanity and the rest of creation, and to God's
attempts to reclaim them. As helpfully stated by Rachel Held Evans,

> While we may wish for a clear, perspicuous text, that's not what
> God gave us. Instead, God gave us a cacophony of voices and
> perspectives all in conversation with one another, representing
> the breadth and depth of the human experience in all its com-
> plexities and contradictions.[13]

Many who believe this about the Bible also believe that these sometimes cacophonous testimonies are called forth by and inspired by God.
But not to the degree that God merely used the biblical writers as scribal
automatons. Each biblical text is a Spirit-*inspired* witness to God and God's
ways, but it is not a Spirit-*controlled* witness. God graciously allowed God's
Word to become incarnate in human minds and hearts, in particular social
and historical contexts, in times of triumph but mostly times of tragedy,
and then called for the faithful to speak with conviction, pain, and joy out

12. Erickson, *Christian Theology*, 233–34.

13. Evans, *Inspired*, 103.

of their experiences. What resulted is a rich, compelling, passionate, profound, and variegated witness to the relationship between Israel and God, and God's love for all of humanity.

By allowing God's word to become incarnate in human minds and hearts, by allowing it to become truly human words as well, God allowed these testimonies to God and God's ways to be subject to the same limitations affecting all human communication: limitations of context, limitations of perspective, limitations of insight. The resulting witness, then, is not a sterile, perfect, flawless, infallible, inerrant revelation. It is a much more messy, uneven, earthy, complicated, yet also, I think, a much more real and relatable testimony to what it means to struggle with God and the community claiming to be God's people—what it means to be Israel and eventually the church.[14] As Peter Enns explains,

> When we try to squish the Bible's diverse voices into one voice,
> we are no longer reading the Bible we have—we are distorting it
> and cutting ourselves off from what it has to offer us. The Bible
> *shows* us how normal and expected it is for all people of faith to
> be part of the same sort of process, the same spiritual journey,
> of living, reflecting, changing, growing in our understanding of
> God, ourselves, the world, and our place in it.[15]

The Phenomenon of Scripture

Many non-conservative readers of Scripture share with conservatives an intuitive sense that Scripture provides a faithful testimony to who God is and what it means to be God's people. I think that they would agree with conservatives that the Spirit has led them to embrace the broad contours of Scripture's testimony as true. But for many non-conservative readers of Scripture, this simply does not necessitate that all of Scripture is inerrant or infallible. As Christian Smith observes, "There is no reason whatsoever not to openly acknowledge the sometimes confusing, ambiguous, and seemingly incomplete nature of Scripture."[16] He goes on to argue that a faithful, genuinely evangelical approach to the Bible

> can be content simply to let the apparent tensions and incon-
> sistencies stand as they are. God is not shaken from heaven.
> Christ is not stripped of authority. The gates of hell do not

14. See Genesis 32:22–32!
15. Enns, *The Bible Tells Me So*, 136.
16. Smith, *Bible Made Impossible*, 131.

prevail against the church. The Bible, understood as what it actually is, still speaks to us with a divine authority, which we need not question but which rather powerfully calls *us* and our lives into question.[17]

Consider this illustration. Think of someone you greatly admire and trust. Someone you look to as a guide, teacher, or mentor. Because of your relationship and experience with that individual, you are likely to trust as good and sound wisdom most things that they say to you or others. But would you consider *everything* they say to be inerrant or infallible? Would you really go that far? And if you are not willing to grant their utterances the status of inerrant revelation, shouldn't you then treat with suspicion anything they say? False in one thing, uncertain in all?

My hope is that you responded in the negative to each of the questions in the illustration. What I am trying to point out is that *the inspired and faithful character of Scripture as a witness to God and God's ways and our heritage as God's people is not dependent upon it being wholly inerrant and infallible.*

It simply isn't.

And this is a good thing. The straightforward, even compelling, train of logic promoted by conservatives—it's God's Word so it must be perfectly true—can't help but eventually run off the tracks when one carefully considers the kind of testimony that Scripture actually provides.

For when we carefully consider the phenomena of Scripture, we find that there are inconsistencies and inaccuracies. We find that the biblical authors felt comfortable revising earlier scriptural tradition, or retelling stories with a new slant or focus. We find that the biblical authors were more concerned with making their testimony to God relevant for their recipients than with factual precision. We even find that, collectively, the Bible as a whole contains some incompatible and contested understandings of God's will. Much of what follows will explore these features of Scripture.

Inconsistencies within Scripture

In this section, I arrange the inconsistencies or tensions many find in Scripture into three different categories: inconsistencies and tensions between parallel accounts, the New Testament's use of Old Testament traditions, and contrasting views of God and God's will. I hope this will help us work through the relevant material efficiently.

17. Smith, *Bible Made Impossible*, 134.

Inconsistencies Between Parallel Accounts: the Historical Books and the Gospels

There are several traditions within the Bible that offer parallel accounts of the same events or periods of history. Careful readers have long noticed when comparing these parallel accounts that some contain inconsistencies between them. For the sake of brevity, I will focus here on only two specific sets of parallel traditions. One set is the record of Israel's history during the monarchy as portrayed by 1 Samuel–2 Kings (these works are commonly regarded as part of the "deuteronomistic history" that includes Joshua–2 Kings, excluding Ruth) and the treatment of that same period by the writers of 1 and 2 Chronicles, likely written some fifty to one hundred years after the deuteronomistic history reached its near final form. The second set of parallel traditions we will consider is the four Gospels.

DISCREPANCIES IN ISRAEL'S HISTORICAL TRADITIONS

Let's begin with some specific differences in detail between 1 Samuel–2 Kings and 1 and 2 Chronicles. To these examples several others could be added.

- In reporting on David's battle with King Hadadezer, 2 Samuel 8:4 indicates that the Israelite forces consisted of 1,700 horsemen and 20,000 foot soldiers, whereas 1 Chronicles 18:4 indicates 7,000 horsemen and 20,000 foot soldiers.

- In reporting on Israel's battle with the Arameans, 2 Samuel 10:18 speaks of 700 Aramean chariot teams, and 1 Chronicles 19:18 lists 7,000.

- In recounting David's ill-advised census of the people, 2 Samuel 24:9 reports totals of 800,000 men of Israel and 500,000 men of Judah, while 1 Chronicles 21:5 reports 1,100,000 men of Israel and 470,000 men of Judah.

Indeed, these are not earth-shattering differences, and some conservatives would simply write them off as due to different methods of approximation. This raises the issue, however, of how much of a difference in detail can be attributed to "approximation." Note that 2 Sam 8:4 lists 1,700 horsemen and 1 Chronicles 19:18 lists 7,000. That is a difference of 5,300 soldiers, or over 300 percent. The writer of 1 Chronicles 19:18 overshoots the figure provided by 2 Samuel by 1000 percent! That is some pretty shoddy estimating on someone's part.

But note this discrepancy, from two different accounts of the story of David's rash and sinful census of the people. 2 Samuel 24:1 tells us that "the anger of Yahweh was kindled against Israel, and he incited David against them, saying, 'Go, count the people of Israel and Judah.'" Yahweh, due to his anger with Israel (reason unspecified), incited David to order the census. However, 1 Chronicles 21:1 tells us: "Satan stood up against Israel, and incited David to count the people of Israel."

Who or what "Satan" (literally, "*Adversary*") is at this point in Israel's traditions is not altogether clear. This figure is likely undergoing a significant development in Israelite thought during the post-exilic period in Israel's history and in the years to follow (539–200 BCE). The writer may have in view a character like "the adversary" in Job, who appears to be a member of the heavenly court who goads God into putting his faithful servant to the test. But the use of "Satan" as a formal name here in 1 Chronicles is unique to the Old Testament, and may indicate that in the mind of the author Satan is the demonic, tempting figure who only becomes clearly known to us in later Israelite tradition.

Also take note of this. We know that later Israelite writers attribute to Satan actions that had been previously attributed to God. For example, The *Book of Jubilees* provides a parallel account of Genesis and Exodus 1–20, and is dated by most to sometime about the second century BCE. For the writer of *Jubilees*, it was Satan (Mastema), not God, who tempts Abraham to kill Isaac (17:15–18:13), provokes the Egyptians to pursue the Israelites (48:12), and was the one who sought to kill Moses on the way to Egypt (48:2). The account in 1 Chronicles appears to be taking a similar approach, attributing to Satan actions that seemed to this author not very God-like.

Yet whoever or whatever Satan is in the mind of the writer of 1 Chronicles, he is clearly not Yahweh. And there is absolutely no indication that Satan is present in the mind of the writer of 2 Samuel 24 when he tells us that it was Yahweh who incited David. This is a pretty glaring discrepancy.

Scholars also find clear differences in emphasis and perspective between 1 Samuel–2 Kings and 1 and 2 Chronicles. First Samuel–2 Kings and 1 and 2 Chronicles both seek to explain why it was that Israel found itself an exiled and beleaguered people in the sixth century BCE. Yet 1 and 2 Chronicles, composed after the deuteronomistic history, also seems concerned to help the post-exilic Israelite community in the late fifth or fourth centuries BCE reclaim its liturgical practices as God's people once they were able to return to the land and rebuild the temple. Unlike the deuteronomistic historians, the writers of 1 and 2 Chronicles ignore the history of the Northern Kingdom and focus nearly exclusively on Judah. Receiving much attention is David and Solomon's faithfulness as model kings, their endorsement of the priesthood, and the unity of the people in embracing the rule of the kings and priests. Accordingly, many of David's and Solomon's failings are omitted (such as David's affair with Bathsheba) or downplayed, as are the power struggles surrounding their reigns. First and 2 Chronicles, unlike 2 Samuel, records David's extensive preparation for the building of the temple, and emphasizes the importance of worship for the people of Israel, celebrating the temple and the customs surrounding it.

In the estimation of most scholars, the writers of 1 and 2 Chronicles are, in effect, retelling this history in such a way that it speaks to the concerns of its writers to reestablish the central role of the temple cult once many had returned to Jerusalem and the rebuilding of the temple had begun. For this reason, not only do 1 and 2 Chronicles deviate from 1 Samuel–1 Kings on numerous specifics, they also tell this part of Israel's story very differently.

Discrepancies in the Gospel Traditions

Similarly, in many Gospel passages, the reporting of events or Jesus' words differ to the extent that it is difficult to see how the comparable accounts could both be regarded as fully accurate. Some may argue that Jesus could have taught his disciples the same lesson more than once, using slightly different wording. This could certainly apply to similar passages with different or unspecified narrative settings. But several discrepancies occur in the reporting of what are clearly the same events. Here are a few examples.

- The accounts of Jesus' trial, crucifixion, and resurrection differ in so many details (including dialogue, chronology, characters, and setting) that it seems impossible to many readers that all of the specific features of each account can be combined into a consistent whole.

- Mark 6:8 reports that Jesus told his disciples to take a staff and sandals, while in Matthew 10:9–10 he prohibits it, and in Luke 9:3 Jesus prohibits a staff but does not mention sandals.

- In Mark 14:30, Jesus tells Peter that before the cock crows *twice*, Peter will have denied Jesus three times. Matthew 26:34, Luke 22:34, and John 13:38 have Jesus telling Peter that before the crock crows once, the threefold denial will have occurred. Accordingly, Mark 14:72 presents the second crowing taking place immediately following Peter's third denial, while the others (Matt 26:74; Luke 22:60; John 18:27) report only one crow immediately following Peter's third denial.

- Jesus' cleansing in the temple is presented by Matthew, Mark, and Luke as occurring at the tail end of Jesus' public ministry, but John places it at the beginning of Jesus' ministry.

Other differences include parallel passages that either omit or add details or dialogue that has the effect of significantly altering the character of a passage. Consider this comparison of Mark 8:27–29 and Matthew 16:13-20. Both of these passages occur in the same narrative setting, and there can be little doubt that they are parallel accounts of the same event.

Mark 8:27–30	Matthew 16:13–20
27 Jesus went on with his disciples to the villages of Caesarea Philippi; and on the way he asked his disciples, "Who do people say that I am?" 28 And they answered him, "John the Baptist; and others, Elijah; and still others, one of the prophets." 29 He asked them, "But who do you say that I am?" Peter answered him, "You are the Messiah."	13 Now when Jesus came into the district of Caesarea Philippi, he asked his disciples, "Who do people say that the Son of Man is?" 14 And they said, "Some say John the Baptist, but others Elijah, and still others Jeremiah or one of the prophets." 15 He said to them, "But who do you say that I am?" 16 Simon Peter answered, "You are the Messiah, the Son of the living God." 17 And Jesus answered him, "Blessed are you, Simon son of Jonah! For flesh and blood has not revealed this to you, but my Father in heaven. 18 And I tell you, you are Peter, and on this rock I will build my church, and the gates of Hades will not prevail against it. 19 I will give you the keys of the kingdom of heaven, and whatever you bind on earth will be bound in heaven, and whatever you loose on earth will be loosed in heaven."
30 And he sternly ordered them not to tell anyone about him.	20 Then he sternly ordered the disciples not to tell anyone that he was the Messiah.

A readily observable difference between these accounts is their respective lengths. Indeed, Matthew contains a considerable amount of material that Mark lacks. The very large "gap" in Mark's account I illustrate above signals most of the missing material. Everything that Jesus says in Matthew 16:17–19 is found only in that Gospel. Note too that Peter's response in Matthew 16:16 in comparison to his response in Mark 8:29. In Mark, Peter says,

"You are the Messiah."

But in Matthew, Peter says

"You are the Messiah, *the Son of the living God*."

Now here are some additional insights that are helpful to keep in mind as you assess these differences. Many years ago readers of the Gospels noticed that the Matthew, Mark, and Luke are very similar. They share a lot of the same stories about Jesus, many of those stories occur in the same order, and many accounts also share the very same wording.[18] As a result of these similarities, many scholars have for centuries concluded that there must have been some type of literary relationship between these three Gospels. In other words, someone must have copied material from someone else, or they shared a common source.

The majority of New Testament scholars today conclude that both of these scenarios are true. If you take a course on the New Testament or the Gospels, you will likely learn that most scholars believe that Mark was the first of the New Testament Gospels to have been written, and that both Matthew and Luke use Mark as a source when composing their own.[19] In addition, because both Matthew and Luke share material that is not in Mark, and because there is not strong evidence that either Matthew and Luke copied from one another, most scholars posit that Matthew and Luke must have shared a common source. This source is commonly termed "Q," after the German word *quelle,* which means "source." While John shares with the synoptic Gospels a similar outline of Jesus' ministry (except for the cleansing of the temple), most of the stories that John contains about Jesus are simply different from what we find in Mark, Matthew, and Luke. It appears that John's material came from a completely separate trajectory of tradition. If we were to diagram out the relationship of the four gospels to one another, it could look something like this.

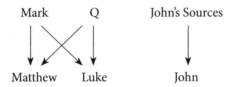

Why is all of this so important? It matters because when we compare parallel accounts between Matthew, Mark, and Luke, this understanding of

---

18. For this reason, Matthew, Mark, and Luke are commonly called the "synoptic" gospels, since they offer a similar (*syn*) view (*optic*) of Jesus and his ministry.

19. About 90 percent of Mark is contained in Matthew, and about 60 percent in Luke.

their literary relationship guides how we assess and make sense of the differences and similarities between them. In fact, these insights are integral to the analysis of the Gospels practiced by most scholars and many clergy today. When, for instance, we examine these parallel accounts in Mark 8 and Matthew 16, with the understanding that Matthew used Mark as a source, we are poised to ask, "Why did Matthew make these changes to Mark's account, and why did he keep the other material the same?" This mode of thinking is often termed "redaction criticism," because it critically (or thoughtfully) examines the way in which one biblical writer "redacts," or edits, the material he or she used to compose his or her account.

Hang in there. One more piece to put into place before we get back to Mark 8 and Matthew 16.

Redaction criticism is not only applied to parallel passages. It is also applied to biblical books as a whole. Scholars not only notice differences and similarities between individual accounts. They also catalogue the characteristic tendencies in the ways a particular writer redacts sources throughout his or her narrative. These compiled tendencies in how an author uses his or her sources enable us to discern the primary interests or concerns the author is addressing in the work as a whole.

A key assumption of this approach is that the biblical writers are not simply automatons compelled by the Spirit, or reporters woodenly replicating their sources. Instead they are creatively shaping the material at their disposal in ways that resonate with their experience of God and in ways they think will be compelling for the recipients of their work. They are, in other words, giving testimony. They are bearing witness. They are speaking the Word, as they discern it, to their context. Like good preachers still today, the Gospel writers knew their "congregations" and how the story of Jesus should be shaped to speak powerfully and faithfully to their real-life needs and struggles.

So now, back to Mark 8 and Matthew 16.

As we noted above, in Matthew 16:13–20, the wording of Peter's declaration about Jesus contains an important difference to its counterpart in Mark 8:27–29: Peter declares Jesus as both Messiah and (unlike Mark) the "Son of the living God." Scholars often point out that this difference is consistent with Mark's refusal to have any human character recognize Jesus as the Son of God until he breathes his last on the cross (15:39). This is often called the "messianic secret" or "secrecy motif" in Mark, and it seems to fit with Mark's interest in emphasizing over and over again that Jesus' identity as the divine Son of God cannot be understood before and apart from his death on the cross. Elemental to Mark's account is his paradoxical portrait of Jesus as both the exalted and divine Son of God (see 1:1–15), and Jesus as the one who "came not to be served, but to serve and give his life as a ransom for many" (10:45). On the other hand, Matthew's "addition" to Peter's testimony, signaling Peter's recognition of Jesus as "Son of the living God," is consistent with Matthew's interest in showing that Peter and the other disciples demonstrate a much fuller understanding of Jesus' identity and the kingdom while he is with them. In Mark, the disciples repeatedly struggle to make sense of Jesus and the culmination of his paradoxical ministry at the cross.

As we also noted above, Matthew's account greatly expands Jesus' response to Peter, emphasizing Peter as the foundation of Jesus' new community and the disciples' authority to interpret Mosaic law. Scholars have long noted that the inclusion of this additional material, which is unique to Matthew, is one of several indications that Matthew is very concerned to present Peter and the other disciples as those who are authorized by Jesus and God to interpret Torah and carry on Jesus' witness to the kingdom after he is crucified and resurrected. As Jesus' disciples, they will eventually bind and loose the law of God guided by the insight of heaven. This will enable them to fulfill the mission Jesus grants them at the close of the Gospel: to go forth and make disciples of all nations, baptizing them and teaching them to obey everything that Jesus has commanded them (see Matt 28:16–20).

Let's consider one more example of Matthew significantly expanding Mark's account, turning our attention to the story of Jesus walking on water.

Mark 6:45–52	Matthew 14:22-33
[45] Immediately he made his disciples get into the boat and go on ahead to the other side, to Bethsaida, while he dismissed the crowd. [46]After saying farewell to them, he went up on the mountain to pray. [47] When evening came, the boat was out on the lake, and he was alone on the land. [48]When he saw that they were straining at the oars against an adverse wind, he came towards them early in the morning, walking on the lake. He intended to pass them by. [49]But when they saw him walking on the lake, they thought it was a ghost and cried out; [50]for they all saw him and were terrified. But immediately he spoke to them and said, "Take heart, it is I; do not be afraid."	[22] Immediately he made the disciples get into the boat and go on ahead to the other side, while he dismissed the crowds. [23]And after he had dismissed the crowds, he went up the mountain by himself to pray. When evening came, he was there alone, [24]but by this time the boat, battered by the waves, was far from the land, for the wind was against them.[25]And early in the morning he came walking towards them on the lake.[26]But when the disciples saw him walking on the lake, they were terrified, saying, "It is a ghost!" And they cried out in fear. [27]But immediately Jesus spoke to them and said, "Take heart, it is I; do not be afraid."

[28] Peter answered him, "Lord, if it is you, command me to come to you on the water." [29]He said, "Come." So Peter got out of the boat, started walking on the water, and came towards Jesus. [30]But when he noticed the strong wind, he became frightened, and beginning to sink, he cried out, "Lord, save me!" [31]Jesus immediately reached out his hand and caught him, saying to him, "You of little faith, why did you doubt?"

[51]Then he got into the boat with them and the wind ceased.

[32]When they got into the boat, the wind ceased.

And they were utterly astounded, [52]for they did not understand about the loaves, but their hearts were hardened.

[33]And those in the boat worshipped him, saying, "Truly you are the Son of God."

Note again Matthew's insertion of a major chunk of material, and again focused on Peter who takes the lead in following Jesus (admirably though not perfectly!). Note again the disciples' inability to comprehend fully what was going on in Mark (see v. 52, referring back to the previous episode of Jesus' feeding the five thousand). But not so in Matthew! Matthew omits Mark's reference to the disciples' confusion, and in the end instead shows them worshipping Jesus and professing him as the Son of God.

The inclusion of such extensive, additional information by Matthew in these two stories may not be seen by some as an overt contradiction between them and their counterparts in Mark. Some may argue that no "error" has occurred. Matthew simply adds material that Mark does not include.

But such an explanation fails to address what is really going on within these parallel accounts. To argue that Mark's and Matthew's versions are both truly "inerrant" when Mark fails to include so much of the material crucial to Matthew's account—and material that is to play a key role in shaping our understanding of Peter and the disciples—seems to stretch the meaning of "inerrant" past its breaking point. If Mark and Matthew are both supposed to be providing inerrant accounts of the same event, then how is Mark not committing an "error of omission"? Recall too that in the second example Matthew omits Mark's reference to the disciples' confusion and hard heartedness, and instead shows them worshipping Jesus and professing him the Son of God. Matthew actually *changes* Mark's account to have it say something *very* different about the response of the disciples! Matthew is not simply supplementing Mark's version of the same story, he is altering it.

Simply put, the information about Peter and the church that Matthew conveys is seeking to accomplish a very different rhetorical objective than what Mark intends in his versions of the same story. The evangelists are telling very different versions of the same stories for very different reasons. And these are only two examples among many! Such retellings that include significant degrees of recasting along with some contradictions are characteristic of the Gospel traditions. This simply does not fit into the inerrantist paradigm of the Bible's nature championed by conservatives.

The New Testament's Use of Old Testament Traditions

A second type of discrepancy that challenges the characterization of Scripture as inerrant are irregularities in the New Testament writers' use of the Old Testament. We find that the New Testament writers felt free to make use of the Israelite Scriptures in quite creative and rhetorically charged ways. Here are three types of examples.

- Occasionally (but not often) New Testament writers will attribute to an Old Testament source a citation that is actually a combination of several Old Testament traditions or not present in the cited source at all. For example, Matthew 27:9–10 identifies a quotation as coming from Jeremiah, but it appears nowhere in that work and has its closest parallel in Zechariah 11:12–13. Similarly, Mark 1:2–3 attributes a citation to Isaiah that most regard as a "conflated quotation" combining Isaiah 40:3 (Mark 1:3) with Malachi 3:1 and possibly Exodus 23:20 (Mark 1:2b). In contrast, the parallel passages in Matthew 3:3 and Luke 3:4–6 provide different forms of the citation, and do not include the material from Malachi. Since, as we noted above, the majority of scholars believe that Matthew and Luke used Mark as a source, it is assumed by many that Matthew and Luke noticed this discrepancy in Mark's account and corrected it when incorporating this material into their own.

- The New Testament writers will at times alter the wording of an Old Testament passage or disregard the meaning it has in its original context in order to show more clearly how Jesus fulfills the promises God made to God's people. Returning to Mark 1:2–3, we find that Mark (or someone before him) slightly altered the Isaian text in v. 3 so that "make *his* paths straight" replaces "make straight in the desert a highway for our *God*" (Isa 40:3). The use of the personal pronoun "his" rather than "God" allows Mark (and also Matthew and Luke) to apply the Isaian text to Jesus. Similarly, in Mark 1:2 the *"your* way" of v. 2 replaces the *"my* way" of Malachi 3:1.

- In Matthew 2:16–18, the evangelist applies Jeremiah 31:15 to Herod's massacre of infants in Bethlehem. Within the context of Jeremiah, the verse clearly refers to the devastation Israel suffered at the hands of the Babylonians, and is followed by the prophetic promise that God will restore Israel and bring the Israelites out of exile to their own land. By applying the passage from Jeremiah to Herod's murderous, myopic rage, Matthew weaves together these two eras of Israel's history and further strengthens the connection between God's long-standing promise to redeem Israel and the arrival of Jesus. But it seems clear to many readers that the text in Jeremiah is not fulfilled in any direct and obvious sense by Herod's massacre.[20]

- Similarly, Paul can also be quite creative in his use of Old Testament traditions: he alters wording, treats certain Old Testament passages out of context, and employs interpretive techniques such as allegory (e.g., see Gal 3:15–18; 4:21–31) that clearly go beyond the "plain sense" of Scripture that conservatives often claim is the vehicle for God's revelation. In doing so, Paul and other New Testament writers were simply drawing from their own interpretive models for biblical interpretation, employing exegetical procedures common to Israelite interpreters. But these techniques differ significantly from interpretive methods advocated by most scholars and theologians today, including conservative readers.

Contrasting views of God and God's will: the reality of "counter-testimony" within the Bible

This category is a bit less straightforward than the previous two. And the perspective one brings to the Bible can make all the difference in terms of one's acknowledgment or denial of this alleged characteristic of Scripture. For those readers open to the idea that Scripture can contain contrasting perspectives on God and God's will, there are several examples that will likely be convincing. For those readers who tend not to be open to this idea, the evidence provided may not be strong enough to shift their thinking on

---

20. The same critique would apply to Matthew's citation of Hosea 11:1 in Matthew 2:14–15.

this issue. As is so often the case, our lenses guide what we are able to see. But consider the following examples, and see what you think.[21]

Faithfulness to God Leads to Blessing—Or Does It?

From Genesis 1 onwards, much of the Old Testament directly states, implies, or assumes as fundamental to a "biblical worldview" the notion that those who live in right relationship with God and one another will participate in the abundant blessing God intends for humanity, and those that reject God and God's ways will not. For a clear example of this perspective, take a look at Moses' sermon in Deuteronomy 30:11–20 ("I set before you today life and prosperity, death and adversity . . .") or Psalm 1 ("Blessed are those . . . The wicked are not so . . .").

Yet the wisdom traditions of Job and Ecclesiastes, and many of the lament psalms, provide a sharp *counter-testimony* to this fundamental claim.[22] They bear witness to the inescapable reality of unjust human suffering, even for the faithful. Some of these traditions, especially the lament psalms, also dare to challenge, rail against, even blame God for the injustices that the faithful suffer. Consider these anguished words from Psalm 88.

> [1]O Lord, God of my salvation,
>   when, at night, I cry out in your presence,
> [2] let my prayer come before you;
>   incline your ear to my cry.
>
> [3] For my soul is full of troubles,
>   and my life draws near to Sheol.
> [4] I am counted among those who go down to the Pit;
>   I am like those who have no help,
> [5] like those forsaken among the dead,
>   like the slain that lie in the grave,
>
> like those whom you remember no more,
>   for they are cut off from your hand.
> [6] You have put me in the depths of the Pit,
>   in the regions dark and deep.
> [7] Your wrath lies heavy upon me,
>   and you overwhelm me with all your waves.
> [14] O Lord, why do you cast me off?

21. We will also discuss the significant tension among New Testament traditions addressing the role of women within the Christian community in chapter 6.

22. For more on the Bible's embodiment of a dialectical testimony–counter-testimony dynamic, see Brueggemann, *Old Testament*, 317–403.

> Why do you hide your face from me?
> [15] Wretched and close to death from my youth up,
>   I suffer your terrors; I am desperate.
> [16] Your wrath has swept over me;
>   your dread assaults destroy me.
> [17] They surround me like a flood all day long;
>   from all sides they close in on me.
> [18] You have caused friend and neighbor to shun me;
>   my companions are in darkness.

For many people of faith, including those whose testimonies are pre-served in the Bible, their lived reality does not always or often square with the way the universe is supposed to work. There is another side to the story. Those putting together and preserving the writings of Scripture were wise enough to notice and include witnesses to this truth, even if it conflicted with a dominant pulse of Scripture.

All the Nations shall be Blessed (or Slaughtered) through You

We also learn, again from the very first pages of the Bible, that God seeks blessing for all of humanity. To be sure, according to the Old Testament, God selects a particular people to be God's own—Israel, the descendants of Abraham through Isaac and Jacob. But at the inauguration of this rela-tionship, and repeatedly throughout Genesis, Abraham and his descendants who become Israel are told that the ultimate purpose of this relationship is so that "all the nations of the earth shall be blessed through you" (see Gen 12:1–3). Blessing, abundant life, the Old Testament teaches us, is what God intends not only for Israel but all peoples everywhere.

But when it comes time for Israel to take possession of the land prom-ised to Abraham and his descendants, there's a problem. Other people are already living in the land of milk and honey. These are—as Moses warned years before—pagan, idol-worshipping, dangerous people who would surely entice Israel to worship false gods. So, in order to displace the Canaanites and others and take possession of the land for themselves, Israel invades and goes to war. And not just war against able-bodied soldiers. Israel, as told in the Old Testament, slaughters everything and everyone they encounter. Man, woman, child, livestock—"all that breathed" we read over and over again—are put to the sword. Israel, shockingly, commits genocide.

Just as shocking, according to writers of Joshua and other texts within the deuteronomistic history (see also Exod 34:11–16; Deut 7:1–6; Josh 23:1–13),

Israel is told to do this by Yahweh. Consider this passage, deeply troubling to many Jews and Christians today, from Joshua 11:16–20:

> ¹⁶ So Joshua took all that land: the hill country and all the Negeb and all the land of Goshen and the lowland and the Arabah and the hill country of Israel and its lowland, ¹⁷from Mount Halak, which rises towards Seir, as far as Baal-gad in the valley of Lebanon below Mount Hermon. He took all their kings, struck them down, and put them to death. ¹⁸Joshua made war a long time with all those kings. ¹⁹There was not a town that made peace with the Israelites, except the Hivites, the inhabitants of Gibeon; all were taken in battle. ²⁰For it was the LORD's doing to harden their hearts so that they would come against Israel in battle, in order that they might be utterly destroyed, and might receive no mercy, but be exterminated, just as the LORD had commanded Moses.

According to this witness, extermination, not blessing, is what God ordained for the Canaanites and others unfortunate enough to have settled in the land God selected for Israel.[23]

Some readers work hard (too hard!) to justify God's genocidal command as reported by Joshua. I have often heard or read some version of the following rationale: Yes, the elimination of the Canaanites and others was unfortunate. But it was necessary for God to cleanse the promised land of pagans and their deities. This provided a clean slate for Israel to prosper materially and spiritually. And remember, in the end Israel's prosperity would enable it to fulfill its destiny to bring blessing to all of humanity.[24]

It saddens me that so many Christians find this rationale a satisfying explanation of the genocide Joshua says God commanded Israel to commit. For we can also find a very similar version of the same logic at work in Nazi propaganda justifying the extermination of Jews and others. We also find it in the sermons of those Christian leaders who supported the physical and cultural genocide of Native Americans, sermons that sometimes turned to the conquest story in Joshua to justify their "manifest destiny" to overtake a new Promised Land for the sake of Jesus and country. Here is that logic in a nutshell: humans that (from our perspective) are irredeemably depraved are expendable for the sake of the common good (as we define it).

But even within the account of Joshua's bloody, genocidal conquest of Canaan we get glimpses of another side of the story. The Gibeonites,

23. For thoughtful, in-depth discussions on the challenges the conquest narrative poses for Christian theology and biblical inerrancy, see Evans, *Inspired*, 59–79, and Enns, *The Bible Tells Me So*, 29–72.

24. For examples of this rationale with some variations, see Stewart, "Destruction of the Canaanites"; Currid, "Destruction of the Canaanites;" Koukl, "The Canaanites."

through their own cunning, manage to trick the Israelites into making a treaty with them (see Josh 9). Once the ruse is discovered, it is too late for Joshua to undo the oath. The Gibeonites are made subservient to Israel, but their lives are spared because Israel sealed the treaty by swearing in the name of Yahweh (9:19).

Moreover, the examples of the Gibeonites and that of Rahab—the Canaanite prostitute who shelters the Israelite spies in Jericho (Josh 2)—also counter the notion that the pagan inhabitants of the promised land are simply degenerates, unable to recognize the sovereignty of Yahweh. Hear the testimony Rahab speaks to the Israelite spies:

> [8] Before they went to sleep, she came up to them on the roof [9]and said to the men: 'I know that the LORD has given you the land, and that dread of you has fallen on us, and that all the inhabitants of the land melt in fear before you. [10]For we have heard how the LORD dried up the water of the Red Sea before you when you came out of Egypt, and what you did to the two kings of the Amorites that were beyond the Jordan, to Sihon and Og, whom you utterly destroyed. [11]As soon as we heard it, our hearts failed, and there was no courage left in any of us because of you. The LORD your God is indeed God in heaven above and on earth below. (Josh 2:8–11)

Rahab's help and testimony move the Israelite spies to honor her request that she and her family be spared the doom to befall her city. But note that her testimony is descriptive of "all the inhabitants of the land" (v. 9). She is not alone in her recognition of Yahweh as sovereign, which is just what Yahweh wanted the Israelites and all inhabitants of the land to realize with the Exodus (see Exod 9:13–21)! Similarly, the Gibeonites also acknowledge Yahweh's defeat of the Egyptians and others, and Yahweh's power to fulfill Yahweh's purposes for Israel (9:9–10, 24).

The text of Joshua itself, which presents the genocide of Canaan as commanded by Yahweh, does not allow us simply to dismiss the Canaanites as irredeemably corrupted, idol-loving souls. In fact, every Canaanite we hear speak in Joshua testifies to Yahweh's sovereignty, and Rahab reports that other Canaanites believe the same! This reality is made all the more poignant by the fact that thus far into the biblical story, and in the pages to follow, the Israelites themselves often neglect to remember the things Yahweh has done for them in their past and promises to do for them in their future. In fact, the reason why the Israelites just spent the previous forty years wandering around in the wilderness was because they refused to trust in God's promise to establish them in the promised land and actually tried to go back to their captors in Egypt (see Num 13–14)! Was genocide really the only option for these Canaanites, some of whom come across as more faithful than many within Israel?

No. It wasn't. At least not according to other Old Testament and New Testament witnesses.

Many years later, following Israel's destruction by Babylon and ensuing exile, Israelites are allowed by the Persians to return to Jerusalem and begin rebuilding the temple and city (539 BCE). Some time after, a crisis erupts among the restored community in Jerusalem. Many Israelites among the returned exiles have taken non-Israelite wives. Two leaders of the community, Ezra and Nehemiah, among others rail against this practice and forbid its continuation. To justify their position, Ezra and Nehemiah cite the earlier Torah traditions from Exodus and Deuteronomy calling upon Israel to show the inhabitants of the land no mercy and to avoid them at all costs (see Ezra 9:10–14). Under Ezra's leadership, the returned exiles in Jerusalem who have taken non-Israelite wives are forced to divorce them and their own children (see Ezra 9–10).

The prophet whose words are preserved in the latter chapters of Isaiah 56:1–8 directly opposes this perspective, as do the books of Ruth and Jonah, which were likely composed during this same period. In their view, repentant non-Israelites (and even their animals!) are indeed cherished by God (Jonah), and are to be included among the faithful of Israel (Isaiah and Ruth). Hear these words from Isaiah 56:

> ¹Thus says the LORD:
>   Maintain justice, and do what is right,
> for soon my salvation will come,
>   and my deliverance be revealed.
> ² Happy is the mortal who does this,
>   the one who holds it fast,
> who keeps the sabbath, not profaning it,
>   and refrains from doing any evil.
> ³ Do not let the foreigner joined to the LORD say,
>   "The LORD will surely separate me from his people";
> and do not let the eunuch say,
>   "I am just a dry tree."
> ⁴ For thus says the LORD:
> To the eunuchs who keep my sabbaths,
>   who choose the things that please me
>   and hold fast my covenant,
> ⁵ I will give, in my house and within my walls,
>   a monument and a name

> better than sons and daughters;
> I will give them an everlasting name
>   that shall not be cut off.
>
> [6] And the foreigners who join themselves to the LORD,
>   to minister to him, to love the name of the LORD,
>   and to be his servants,
> all who keep the sabbath, and do not profane it,
>   and hold fast my covenant—
> [7] these I will bring to my holy mountain,
>   and make them joyful in my house of prayer;
> their burnt-offerings and their sacrifices
>   will be accepted on my altar;
> for my house shall be called a house of prayer
>   for all peoples.
> [8] Thus says the LORD God,
>   who gathers the outcasts of Israel,
> I will gather others to them
>   besides those already gathered.

Note how the language employed by the prophet or group producing these oracles invites us to hear its instruction with Ezra and Nehemiah's practices in mind: "Do not let the foreigner joined to the Lord say, 'The Lord will surely *separate* me from his people." Here the Hebrew verb for "separate" (*badal*) is the same as that used in Ezra 10:11 in reference to the Israelites separating themselves from foreign wives and their children, and in Nehemiah 13:3 in reference to their separation from all those of foreign descent. Verse 8 strengthens the likelihood of an intended connection as it specifically holds in view the congregation of returned exiles and those "others"—namely, the foreigners and eunuchs—whom God will gather to join them: "Thus says the LORD God, who *gathers the outcasts of Israel*, I will *gather others to them besides those already gathered*." Note too the all-encompassing embrace God offers to faithful foreigners: "these I will bring to my holy mountain and make them joyful in my house of prayer; their burnt offerings and their sacrifices will be accepted on my altar" (v. 7). They are to fully partake in the life of God's people and in the worship of Yahweh.[25]

The contrasting perspectives on non-Israelites embedded in these post-exilic traditions are part of a persistent tension evident throughout the entire Old Testament. Coursing through the Israelite Scriptures is an inclusive trajectory of tradition that repeatedly bears witness to God's concern and Israel's blessing for Gentiles. Yet there is also an exclusive trajectory of tradition that

---

25. For a fuller account of this debate within second temple Judaism on the place of non-Israelites within Israel, see Kuhn, *Insights from Cultural Anthropology*, 72–87.

regards non-Israelites as degenerates and enemies of God's people. As we transition to the New Testament, we see that the inclusive perspective wins out in dramatic fashion among Jesus' followers: the blessing God intends for all humanity announced in Genesis and reclaimed by Isaiah, Ruth, Jonah, and others is embraced as an integral part of God's purposes for creation. In the Gospels and Acts, in the epistles and Revelation, we see non-Israelites recognize the sovereignty of God and trust in Jesus, and we see them welcomed by Jesus and his followers into the kingdom.

One of the most powerful testimonies to God's intentions for all of humanity is the pointed counter-testimony to Joshua's conquest spoken by Jesus.[26] At the culmination of his Gospel, Matthew presents Jesus as the new Moses, ordering a very different kind of conquest and promising a very differing kind of realm. This is Matthew's understanding of how God's promise to bring blessing to all of humanity comes full circle. The resurrected Jesus gathers his disciples, and leaves them with these final words:

> [7]When they saw him, they worshipped him; but some doubted. [18]And Jesus came and said to them, "All authority in heaven and on earth has been given to me. [19]Go therefore and make disciples of all nations, baptizing them in the name of the Father and of the Son and of the Holy Spirit, [20]and teaching them to obey everything that I have commanded you. And remember, I am with you always, to the end of the age." (Matt 28:17–20)

Go, Jesus says. Make disciples *of all nations*. Bring them into your community and share with them the blessings of God's kingdom. Teach them to obey my command—the Torah that leads to true righteousness. Go into the dark world before you and sow sacrificial love for all, and then let God do the rest. And know that no matter what befalls you, I am with you. I will not fail to bring you and all my followers into the true promised land.

Conservative Strategies for Dealing with Inconsistencies

Erickson and many other conservatives acknowledge that these apparent inconsistencies present a challenge to the conservative position. Erickson goes on to enumerate several different strategies conservatives have employed to resolve the challenges raised by these problem texts.[27]

The first strategy, as dubbed by Erickson, is the *abstract approach* (we briefly touched on this above). Utilized by conservatives such as B. B.

---

26. On this point, see Sparks, *Sacred Word*, 69.

27. See Erickson, *Christian Theology*, 255–59.

Warfield, adherents claim that the internal and external evidence demonstrating the full inspiration and consequent inerrancy of Scripture is so considerable that the weight of such problem texts is insignificant in comparison.[28] Little effort is thus made to address these supposed inconsistencies. They simply do not present a viable challenge to what most conservatives know to be true through the testimony of the Spirit.

A second strategy is the *harmonistic approach*, which takes up the task of trying to resolve the apparent discrepancies in parallel biblical accounts. The way harmonization works in most cases is to construct scenarios that can account for these alleged inconsistencies. In doing so, each of those conflicting accounts are treated as *partial* representations of the circumstance or activity in view, and a fuller account is conjectured that resolves the conflict.

For instance, Matthew 27:5 tells us that Judas committed suicide by hanging himself, while Acts 1:18 reports that Judas "falling headlong, he burst open in the middle and all his bowels gushed out." These two passages are, on the face of it, in conflict with one another. One way conservative scholars have resolved this apparent discrepancy is to conjecture a scenario that would be consistent with the circumstances underlying these two (partial) accounts of Judas' death: Judas hung himself, and after the body began to decay, it fell to the ground and burst open.[29]

To take another example, recall that in Mark 14:30, Jesus tells Peter that before the cock crows twice, Peter will have denied Jesus three times. But Matthew 26:34, Luke 22:34, and John 13:30 have Jesus telling Peter that before the cock crows once the threefold denial will have occurred. Accordingly, Mark 14:72 presents the second crowing taking place immediately following Peter's third denial, while the others (Matt 26:74; Luke 22:60; John 18:27) report only one crow immediately following Peter's third denial. To resolve this inconsistency, Harold Lindsell proposes that what actually happened was not a threefold, but actually a sixfold denial, with three preceding the first crowing (as in Matthew, Luke, and John) and another set of three denials preceding the second crowing (as in Mark).[30] In this way, so the reasoning goes, we can see how both scenarios reported in the Gospels can be, in a partial sense at least, correct.

A third approach sometimes utilized by conservatives, especially in regard to the discrepancies between in the historical books, argues that the biblical authors did not necessarily correct mistakes in the uninspired

28. Warfield, "Inspiration," 214–26.

29. This example is attributed by Erickson (*Christian Theology*, 256) to Louis Gaussen, *Inspiration*, 214–15.

30. Lindsell, *Battle for the Bible*, 174–76.

sources they utilized when composing their accounts. So, in the case of the Chronicler or writer of 1 and 2 Samuel who at times provide counts of battle participants that disagree, it is possible that one or both sets of writers were simply drawing from inconsistent sources. Erickson does not provide a label for this view, but perhaps it could be termed the *inconsistent sources* approach.

An approach not addressed by Erickson but sometimes employed to account for irresolvable discrepancies is to claim that the Bible's full inspiration and inerrancy applies only to the original autographs of Scripture. We could call this the *appeal to the original autographs* approach. Returning to the Chicago Statement, the framers announce "we affirm that inspiration, strictly speaking, applies only to the autographic text of Scripture, which in the providence of God can be ascertained from available manuscripts with great accuracy."

The framers thus here posit two related but separate claims: 1) that the science of textual criticism has (providentially) advanced to the point that it can reproduce with a high degree of reliability the original biblical text; and yet 2) only the original manuscripts produced by the biblical authors are truly inerrant. This important qualification leads some conservatives to claim that irresolvable inconsistencies could be explained by errors in copying or other factors impacting transmission (such as damaged manuscripts) over the long course of Scripture's history. At the same time, conservatives can trust in the overall, high degree of correspondence between our present texts and their originals.

The Problems with Biblical Inerrancy

I think it is undeniable that the conservative position works for a significant number of Christians. If I had to guess, in light of what I know about the character of Christianity in America and around the world, I'd say that the conservative position (or something very like it) is embraced by more Christians than not. I think there are at least two reasons for this.

First, most Christians hold the perspective—as informed by their life experiences and the testimony of the Spirit—that the view of reality they encounter in Scripture is true. And for many of these Christians, as we noted above, it thus logically (or even intuitively) follows that if Scripture is from God then it can be trusted on all matters it addresses. There is a basic logic to this that many Christians find appealing, or simply accept as common sense. The Christian practice of referring to the Bible as "God's word," and the repeated appeal to Scripture as the authoritative source for Christian thought and practice, both enact and reinforce this essential claim for many Christians.

Second, in light of the intuitive and straightforward character of this perspective, it is easily communicated and comprehensible to a wide array of believers. I think it has also been the "default" view of Scripture embraced by many Christians even in non-conservative traditions. My students from mainline denominations are frequently surprised at the possibility of discrepancies in Scripture and unaware of alternative understandings of its nature. Moreover, many Christians do not have the resources or take the time to engage in detailed discussions on the nature of Scripture. While hard to believe, such an activity is not high on the priority list for most Christians (if only they knew what they were missing!). Believers are inclined, in the absence of compelling reasons to the contrary, to stick with what works. And, frankly, the conservative view works for many Christians.

Yet, as we have seen, there are some serious deficiencies with the conservative view of Scripture commonly identified by its critics and sometimes by its own adherents.

Inadequate Attempts to Explain Discrepancies in the Bible

Perhaps first and foremost, there are simply too many indications that Scripture does *not* provide an absolutely consistent witness to God, Israel's history, or the story of Jesus to ignore or explain away. Despite this evidence, conservative scholars insist on Scripture's full inerrancy, claiming that there is stronger evidence supporting inerrancy than challenging it. But note that a fundamental piece of the counter-evidence they cite is the inward testimony of the Spirit. As I argued above, the Spirit can testify to the inspired nature of Scripture without leading us to believe that it is inerrant.

Conservative attempts to address discrepancies through harmonization also fail to be convincing. These efforts lead to forced and sometimes even bizarre readings of biblical texts that no one would offer unless they were motivated to defend the Bible's inerrancy. Such attempts end up positing "hybrid" scenarios that are not actually presented by either of the conflicting texts in view. To take the examples offered above, note that there is no biblical text reporting that Judas hung himself and became disemboweled as his decaying corpse fell to the ground. Nor is there any text that tells us that Peter denied Jesus six times—in fact, all four Gospel texts tell us that Peter denied Jesus three times! Harmonization often leads to readings of conflicting texts that are less biblical than the conflicting texts themselves. It is hard to see how this exegetical practice elucidates and respects the plain meaning of the text that conservatives claim to value.

The appeal to inconsistent sources or original autographs as a means of explaining discrepancies that cannot be harmonized away is equally problematic. Both amount to an unverifiable argument from silence, and thus have little probative force. Such appeals also create self-defeating co-nundrums. On what basis could one assure us that errant sources were used only for such minor details as the number of chariots and participants in battle, or the number of years one reigned as king? Most scholars argue that the framers of the Pentateuch drew from a variety of sources to compose these traditions, and that even Mark made use of sources for the teach-ings and stories of Jesus. What if *those* sources got some of the information wrong, and we simply have no way of knowing? Moreover, if we only have access to errant autographs, then one could argue that all of the benefits we might ascribe to an inerrant and infallible Scripture are lost to us. If the manuscripts we possess are no longer fully inspired, then on what basis do we claim inerrancy and infallibility for the Bibles we are actually using? False in one thing, uncertain in all, right?

In response, conservatives have argued that God's guiding hand en-sured that any revelation within Scripture related to Christian faith and practice would not be compromised. But note that when conservatives make this move, they are now offering a different argument than the one they claim is at the heart of their view of Scripture. The argument that Scripture's full inspiration necessitates its nature as inerrant and infallible revelation that can be fully trusted has now become the qualified claim that Scripture's (almost) full inspiration has led to a (mostly) inerrant and (when it comes to matters relevant to doctrine) infallible Bible. But conservatives offer these qualifications while at the same time claiming that the Bible is fully inspired, inerrant, and infallible, and when they do so the logical consistency of their view is severely compromised.

Commitment to Inerrancy Does Not Ensure Doctrinal Consistency

In a similar vein, the benefits conservatives would claim for an inerrant and infallible Scripture are also seriously undermined by the reality that a shared understanding of the full inspiration of Scripture does not yield uniformity of beliefs among evangelicals. Conservative theologians and members of their communities commonly tangle with one another over such important matters as justification, free will, predestination, church polity, charismatic gifts, keeping the Sabbath, wealth, poverty, just war, homosexuality, and engagement with the wider culture.[31] The simple truth is that conservative agreement on the Bible as an infallible guide for faith and practice has not resulted in conservative agreement on what the Bible actually says about many areas of Christian faith and practice. For this reason, the conservative claim that their view of Scripture is needed to prevent doctrinal deviation is simply not convincing.

Muting the Voices of Scripture

Beyond these shortcomings, what I find most problematic about a lens that treats the Bible as inerrant and infallible is that it fails to acknowledge what appears so obvious to other readers: that the biblical writers felt free to interact dynamically and creatively with their sacred traditions—even the ones they thought came from God—in order to emphasize certain dimensions of their encounters with God. They felt free, in other words, to make their encounters with God and the testimonies of their spiritual ancestors their own. Really their own. In doing so, the writers, redactors, and compilers of Scripture join their ancestors in offering their own voices to the choir of witnesses that God calls into being and compels to sing. Through this sacred oration, God repeatedly encourages the primary themes and melodies, and even some counter-melodies, but allows the singers the freedom to contribute to the song in ways that capture their hearts and imaginations.

I struggle to express adequately how wondrous a thing Scripture is, this messy gathering of testimonies that God invites. Throughout the ages, God reveals God's self to humans and then allows humans to take God's self-disclosure to heart, to get themselves and their worlds caught up in this epic witness to what is most blessed and right. The miracle of Scripture is not that God so controlled the humans who composed it that it inerrantly entombs the voice of God alone. The miracle of Scripture is that as our ancestors and we join our complicated, context-bound, biased, even sinful lives to our sacred story we capture glimpses of our true home and are compelled to discover more about our true selves. The miracle of Scripture is that it is one more instance of God allowing God's word to become incarnate in our times and places, in our varied hearts and minds and voices, in both the good and evil parts of our communities and souls, so that our ancestors and we may emerge from darkness and cultivate eyes that see and ears that hear.

---

31. For helpful and cogent discussion of the reality of pervasive interpretive pluralism and theological diversity among conservatives, see Smith, *Bible Made Impossible*, 27–54.

Reflection and Discussion Questions

1. How does your own view of Scripture compare with the different perspectives presented in this chapter? What points did you find convincing, and why?

2. Some argue that those who defend the inerrancy of Scripture risk "divinizing" the Bible, treating it as the foundation of Christian faith and practice. (This is sometimes called "Bibliolatry"—turning the Bible into an idol). What do you think Christians should identify and pursue as the foundation of their faith?

3. What do you make of the author's claim that the Bible presents conflicting views of God and God's will, or at least perspectives that are in tension with one another? If this were true, would it undermine or change your sense of the Bible's authority and usefulness?

CHAPTER THREE

Reading the Bible in Fear: The Tragedy of a Broken-hearted Hermeneutic

FEAR CAN LEAD PEOPLE to believe and do some downright nonsensical and tragic things.

When people are afraid or burdened with anxiety, their ability to think clearly and compassionately can be severely undermined. If left unchecked or encouraged, such fear can even morph into hate.

The Mind of Terror

Take extremism and terrorism, for example. There is still much we do not know about the origins of extremism. But according to several recent studies focusing on former and current terrorists, those joining extremist groups and committing terrorist acts frequently share three perceptions, three ways of seeing the world around them.[1]

First, they perceive a threat to their physical security. They claim "We are not safe!" Others are threatening their well-being.

Second, they perceive that they are victims of economic exploitation. They claim "We are getting shafted!" Others are depriving or threatening to deprive them and their families of the resources they need to live well.

Third, they perceive a dissolution of their way of life. They claim "The way the world should be is under attack!" Others are undermining their values, sense of identity, and place in the world.

---

1. See Staub, "Evolution of Hate," 51–66; Cottee, "What Motivates Terrorists"; DeAngelis, "Understanding Terrorism"; Stern, "What Motivates Terrorists?"

Mark Juergensmeyer, Professor of Sociology and Director of Global and International Studies at the University of California, has interviewed numerous terrorists and examined the cases of many others. In his book, *Terror in the Mind of God: The Global Rise of Religious Violence*, Juergensmeyer claims that contrary to popular opinion, the vast majority of terrorists or militant extremists are not insane.

> I know of no study that suggests that people are terrorist by nature. Although some activists involved in religious terrorism have been troubled by mental problems, other are people who appear to be normal and socially well adjusted, but who are caught up in extraordinary communities and share extreme world views.[2]

Terrorists speak, strategize, and act, Juergensmeyer argues, with a clear sense of purpose: to terrify the public and undermine their confidence in their government and safety. It is not terrorists' *ability* to think that is at issue. Rather, their thinking is warped by fear, and eventually hate. They want others to experience the world as they experience it:

We are not safe. We are not getting our fair share. Our way of life, the way the world should be, is under attack.

Welcome to the darkened mind of a terrorist.

The Fear We Feel

But it is not just those committing terrorist acts that harbor such dark thoughts towards others and the world. In fact, the same fears that energize violent extremism echo throughout our public discourse and energize rather extreme and violent speech.

From President Donald Trump:

> We have people coming into the country or trying to come in, we're stopping a lot of them, but we're taking people out of the country. You wouldn't believe how bad these people are. These aren't people. These are animals.[3]

From the promotional description of a recent book, *Open Borders*, by Michelle Malkin:

> In the name of compassion—but driven by financial profit—globalist elites, Silicon Valley, and the radical Left are conspiring to

2. Juergensmyer, *Terror*, 8.
3. Korte and Gomez, "Trump Ramps Up Rhetoric."

undo the rule of law, subvert our homeland security, shut down free speech, and make gobs of money off the backs of illegal aliens, refugees, and low-wage guest workers. Politicians want cheap votes or cheap labor. Church leaders want pew-fillers and collection plate donors. Social justice militants, working with corporate America, want to silence free speech they deem "hateful," while raking in tens of millions of dollars promoting mass, uncontrolled immigration both legal and illegal.[4]

From a recent essay written by Ann Coulter:

The U.S. is one of the rare countries that makes citizens of people *who can't speak the language*—along with the masochistic Swedes. (How did they terrorize the world 800 years ago?) The United Kingdom, Canada, Germany, Australia, Norway and the Netherlands all have the crazy idea that citizens should be able to communicate with one another. We have a language requirement on the books but, it turns out, that too is merely a suggestion.[5]

From an interview with Lou Dobbs, criticizing the leadership of the Department of Homeland Security for their failure to implement stricter border control measures:

If this is what we have come to, if the quality of people in leadership in DHS from the secretary of the department on down I mean lets, you know, just literally put out welcome wagons. Pile them high because we're just going to consign tens of thousands perhaps millions of Americans to their deaths.

From President of FAIR (Federation for American Immigration Reform), Dan Stein,

Immigrants don't come all church-loving, freedom-loving, God-fearing . . . Many of them hate America, hate everything that the United States stands for. Talk to some of these Central Americans.[6]

---

4. Description of Malkin's book, *Open Borders Inc.*, provided on the Christian Broadcasting Network's website (https://shop.cbn.com/product/openbordersinc/). See also the video clip featuring Malkin at https://www1.cbn.com/cbnnews/us/2019/october/whos-behind-americas-immigration-crisis-michelle-malkin-follows-the-money-to-find-the-truth.

5. Coulter, "Suckers on Immigration."

6. Carlson, "Nativism."

We are not safe. Immigrants—many of them at least—are animals. Current levels of immigration will lead tens of thousands if not millions of Americans to their deaths.

We are getting shafted. Follow the money. Unchecked immigration is a ploy of the left and liberals and churches and social justice militants and corporations to rake in billions of dollars, while these immigrants steal our jobs and trash our economy.

Our way of life, the way the world should be, is under attack. They hate America, hate *everything* America stands for. They refuse to speak English.

These statements strike me as rather extreme. But, in reality, concerns about the place of immigrants within our society are pervasive among Americans. In a 2014 Reuters/Ipsos poll, 63 percent of Americans indicated that immigrants place a burden on the economy. A whopping 70 percent indicated that undocumented immigrants threaten traditional American beliefs and customs.[7]

More recent polls have shown that these concerns are less pervasive, and that the majority of Americans now hold favorable views of immigrants. But this is not a strong majority. In one 2018 poll, a significant minority, 38 percent, do not believe that immigrants are a benefit to America, and in another, only 53 percent said that immigrants make America better.[8] As one might guess, our disparate views on immigrants fall pretty closely along partisan lines.

In varying degrees, we think immigrants are a threat to our safety, our prosperity, and our way of life.

And not just immigrants. In varying degrees we also think this about Muslims, African Americans, Jews, and members of the LGBTQIA+ communities. The resurgence of white supremacist groups and activity in America, the rise in hate crimes, including mass shootings,[9] the growth of Islamophobia into a multi-billion dollar industry,[10] testify to the collective sense of many that we are not safe, we are not getting our fair share, our way of life is under siege—and that others who look and believe and love differently from most of us are to blame for it.

Many of those saying such things, and committing such acts, claim to be Christians.

7. Bell, "Americans Worry."

8. National Immigration Forum, "Polling Update."

9. Anti-Defamation League, "With Hate in their Hearts;" USA Facts, "Hate Crime Data"; U.S. Department of Justice, "Hate Crime Statistics."

10. CAIR, "Islamophobia and its Impact in the United States"; Beinart, "Islamophobia"; Chapman University Survey of American Fears, "Fear of Muslims."

This is painfully tragic yet true. Many Americans think about others, and read the Bible, with fear-filled hearts.

Many read the Bible like terrorists.

Faithless

That many Americans, including Christian Americans, regard others with severely compromised compassion is not a novel claim. In fact, some of the most strident criticisms of American Christianity of late have come from within its own ranks. Here are just a few examples among many.

In a *Sojourners* article from 2017 entitled, "American 'Christianity' has Failed," Stephen Mattson argues that the predominant theme of Western-ized Christendom is to advocate for the influence of Christianity in contemporary society while neglecting its core teachings. He states:

> While the gospels instruct followers of Christ to help the poor, oppressed, maligned, mistreated, sick, and those most in need of help, Christians in America have largely supported measures that have rejected refugees, refused aid to immigrants, cut social services to the poor, diminished help for the sick, fueled xenophobia, reinforced misogyny, ignored racism, stoked hatred, reinforced corruption, and largely increased inequality, prejudice, and fear.[11]

Charles Mathewes, who identifies as an evangelical Christian, published an op-ed in the *Washington Post* titled, "White Christianity is in Big Trouble. And it has itself to blame." In the article, he writes:

> White Christians seem unwilling to be guided by the plain truth of our shared faith . . . White evangelical Christians like guns, for example, and do *not* especially like immigrants. Compared to other demographics, we're excited about the death penalty, indifferent to those who are impoverished or infirm, and blind to racial and gender inequalities. We claim to read the Bible and hear Jesus' teachings, but we think poor people deserve what they (don't) get, and the inmates of our prisons deserve, if anything, worse than the horrors they already receive. For believers in a religion whose Scriptures teach compassion, we're a breath-takingly cruel bunch.[12]

11. Mattson, "American 'Christianity.'"
12. Mathewes, "White Christianity."

How did this happen to white Christians in America? Mathewes argues:

> There are many factors—historical, social and political—that have helped shape white American Christianity into what it is today. But when it comes to keeping us away from the core truths of our faith, I suspect this one error is key: Christians today seem governed by fear.

Historian John Fea, also a white evangelical, offers a similar assessment in his book *Believe Me: The Evangelical Road to Donald Trump*. In the introduction, he claims that

> For too long, white evangelical Christians have engaged in public life through a strategy defined by the politics of fear, the pursuit of worldly power, and a nostalgic longing for a national past that may have never existed in the first place. Fear. Power. Nostalgia.[13]

If fear is a critical factor shaping white Christians' perception of the world and politics, they are not alone. A number of voices, including those from the fields of psychology, social psychology, neuro-science, and sociology, are helping us to become more aware of just how anxious we Americans are.

The Prevalence and Power of Fear

According to the annual Chapman University survey of American Fears, Americans are more afraid than ever, with government corruption, the state of the environment, finances, and personal health topping the list. In 2018, all of the top ten fears identified in the survey were held by more than half of Americans, showing a notable increase over the last two years.[14]

Hyping Fear

Why is fear so prevalent in America?

In short, the experts tell us, because it sells. In our country, as in nearly all others throughout human history, fear is an *extremely* powerful motivator. It influences the way people pursue material resources, and cede

13. Fea, *Believe Me*, 7.

14. Chapman University Survey of American Fears, "America's Top Fears of 2018."

political power. It influences what we buy and how we vote. Those with stuff for sale and those running for office know this very well.

Sociologist Barry Glassner, in his essay "Narrative Techniques of Fear Mongering," explores the question of why fear—especially misplaced fear— is so prevalent in America despite the unrivaled safety experienced by most Americans.

> I suggest that the answer to these and related questions lies, in large measure, in the immense power and money that await individuals and organizations who can tap into Americans' moral insecurities for their own benefit. By fear mongering, politicians sell themselves to voters, TV and print newsmagazines sell themselves to viewers and readers, advocacy groups sell memberships, quacks sell treatments, lawyers sell class action lawsuits, and corporations sell consumer products.[15]

In the essay and his book, *The Culture of Fear: Why Americans Are Afraid of the Wrong Things*, Glassner explains how some media and politicians misrepresent isolated incidents as pervasive trends that threaten the well-being of average Americans. Things like child abductions, combustion during surgery, youth violence, terrorist attacks, plane crashes—all of these are certainly horrific when they do occur. But these tragic occurrences are not nearly as prevalent as the major causes of preventable injury, death, and financial stress suffered by Americans, such as suicide, poverty, gun violence, income inequality, and inadequate health insurance coverage.

As a result, Glassner argues, we end up afraid of the wrong things.

> One of the paradoxes of a culture of fear is that serious problems remain widely ignored even though they give rise to the dangers that the populace most abhors. Poverty, for example, correlates strongly with child abuse, crime, and drug abuse. Income inequality is also associated with adverse outcomes for society as a whole. The larger the gap between rich and poor in a society, the higher its overall death rates from heart disease, cancer, and murder.[16]

Similarly, psychologist Deborah Serani, in a *Psychology Today* essay, "If it Bleeds, it Leads: Understanding Fear-Based Media," writes,

> Fear-based news programming has two aims. The first is to grab the viewer's attention. In the news media, this is called the teaser. The second aim is to persuade the viewer that the solution for reducing the identified fear will be in the news story. If a teaser

15. Glassner, "Narrative Techniques," 819.
16. Glassner, *Culture of Fear*, xviii.

asks, "What's in your tap water that YOU need to know about?" a viewer will likely tune in to get the up-to-date information to ensure safety.

She goes on to explain,

> The success of fear-based news relies on presenting dramatic anecdotes in place of scientific evidence, promoting isolated events as trends, depicting categories of people as dangerous and replacing optimism with fatalistic thinking. News conglomerates who want to achieve this use media logic, by tweaking the rhythm, grammar, and presentation format of news stories to elicit the greatest impact . . . Often, these practices present misleading information and promote anxiety in the viewer.[17]

Neil Strauss offers a well-researched *Rolling Stone* article exploring sociological and psychological explanations on "Why We're Living in the Age of Fear."[18] He too points out the discrepancy between the fears commonly promoted by the media and politicians, and the reality of what actually threatens the well-being of most Americans. He argues that the media gravitates towards the new, the aberrant, and the spectacular in its reporting, such as terrorist attacks, mass shootings, and plane crashes.

> But far more prolific, and thus even less news-worthy, are the 117 suicides in the U.S. each day (in comparison with 43 murders), the 129 deaths from accidental drug overdoses, and the 96 people dying a day in automobile accidents (27 of whom aren't wearing seat belts, not to mention the unspecified amount driving distracted). Add to these the 1,315 deaths each day due to smoking, the 890 related to obesity, and all the other preventable deaths from strokes, heart attacks and liver disease, and the message is clear: The biggest thing you have to fear is not a terrorist or a shooter or a deadly home invasion. You are the biggest threat to your own safety.

Strauss points out that if Americans were really choosing politicians based on their own safety, "they would vote for a candidate who stresses seat-belt campaigns, programs for psychological health to decrease suicide, and ways to reduce smoking, obesity, prescription-pill abuse, alcoholism, flu contagion and hospital-acquired infections."

But fear is not often logical.

17. Serani, "If it Bleeds it Leads."
18. Strauss, "Living in the Age of Fear."

The Character and Origin of Our Misplaced Fear, or "Anxiety"

According to neuroscientist Joseph LeDoux, and drawing on a long-recognized distinction among psychologists, what the media and politicians are stimulating among Americans today is better understood as *anxiety*. Anxiety is a worry about something that hasn't happened and may never happen. Whereas fear is about a danger that seems certain, anxiety is, in LeDoux's words, "an experience of uncertainty."[19] Or as Neil Strauss summarizes, anxiety is a more complex and highly manipulable response to something one anticipates might be a threat in the future.

And, it seems, we are filled with anxiety and ripe for manipulation. In a 2017 essay published in the *New York Times Magazine*, Nitsu Abebe insightfully observes,

> We've reached a weird, quiet agreement that the most potent force in our politics is, for the moment, a stew of unease, fear, rage, grief, helplessness and humiliation. Anxiety, after all, need not be rational, need not be coherent, can contain multitudes. It's possible to be anxious about things that will almost certainly never affect you; it's possible for anxiety to prevent you from accurately assessing danger and making plans to address it. (This is how we remain more panicked by terrorism than medical bankruptcy.) Americans are acknowledging, more openly than we're used to or comfortable with, that the life of the nation may not take place in a realm of issues and policy and consensus-building but someplace more disordered, irrational and human.[20]

If this is true, that our collective life together is characterized by community that is "disordered and irrational," and if it is true that this is what it means to be "human," how do we make sense of this?

What is it about the human psyche that leads to such anxious, irrational disorder?

Limited good: we never have enough

A few insights from the realm of cultural anthropology may be of some help. First, anthropologists have long recognized that much interaction between humans, and between humans and their environments, is driven by the perspective that there is a limited amount of the resources that humans

19. Cited in Strauss, "The Age of Fear."
20. Abebe, "'Anxiety' Disorder."

need to survive and thrive. Anthropologists call this the perception of "limited good." As described by Bruce Malina,

> Thus extensive areas of behavior are patterned in such a way as to suggest to one and all that in society as well as in nature—the total environment—all the desired things in life, such as land, wealth, prestige, blood, health, semen, friendship and love, manliness, honor, respect and status, power and influence, security and safety—literally all goods in life—exist in finite, limited quantity and are always in short supply.[21]

Humans throughout history have behaved as though there is only so much of all good things to go around, and it is never enough. Life is a zero-sum game. If you have more, then I have less.

This perception of essential resources in short supply—whether the perception is true or not—has been an extremely powerful motivator of human behavior and impetus of much human conflict. Between societies, competing "national interests" have led to war, colonization, arms races, and border disputes. Within communities, any apparent relative improvement in someone's or some group's access to resources or social position may be viewed by others as a threat to themselves, and even the entire community, for it could upset the current balance of how goods are distributed and threaten the social and economic status of privileged groups. Defamation, ostracization, and in some cases, violent reprisals targeting the "offenders" occur in response. Consider in our own country the violence against African Americans, including lynching and the passage of Jim Crow laws, during and after Reconstruction. Or note the vicious reprisals in rural India against shudras and untouchables who develop successful businesses and begin to gain access to more of their society's resources.

Tribalism: defining our folk

The perception, or reality, of limited resources is also what likely led to another essential trait of human behavior: we are social creatures. Like other species, we formed groups to facilitate our access to safety and the other things we need to survive and thrive. But as we formed these groups, we also developed norms on how group membership is to be determined, and how we view our group in relation to others.[22] These norms, once estab-

21. Malina, *New Testament World*, 89.
22. For a helpful summary of recent social-scientific work on group formation driven by the need for resource acquisition, see Baumeister and Butz, "Roots of Hate."

lished, became an integral part of our cultures. We created complex and sometimes overlapping, sometimes conflicting systems of "in-groups" and "out-groups." Another term for this is "tribalism."[23]

The criteria we humans develop to determine group membership have been quite variable, and can shift over time. But family lineage, ethnicity, race, and gender have been common determinants of group membership, and personal status within groups, across many cultures. In our own day, we can add political affiliation and polarization as another important determinant of group membership and our perception of others.[24]

These norms, and the categories between groups and within groups we create, play an integral role in determining access to various goods that are in limited supply. It is nearly always the case that some groups have more of the coveted resources of a society than others. Not surprisingly, when a culture grants particular groups privileged access to these resources, including political power, these groups do everything they can to hold on to that access. They develop narratives, sacred traditions, interpretive strategies, propaganda, and rituals to legitimize their elevated status or at least to reinforce the cultural norms that grant them power and privilege.[25] They also zealously protect the political and economic mechanisms that ensure their prosperity at the expense of others. Interestingly, many within a society who do not benefit materially from the status quo will still defend it if they share with the privileged group a desire for stability and order over change.[26]

Change is not good (for us)

As anthropologists and social psychologists tell us, anxiety increases for dominant groups during times of social change and upheaval, when the "rules to the game" are being challenged or rewritten. To draw once again from the insights of cultural anthropology, "social movements" occur when a significant number of people within a society advocate for changes in social norms or how status, honor, or resources are distributed. When such movements emerge, there is nearly always a "countermovement" that seeks to re-establish the cultural norms and patterns of power distribution under threat, the world that is under attack.[27]

---

23. For a concise account of social-scientific, psychological, and neuro-scientific insights into tribalism and prejudice, see Fiske, "Look Twice."

24. See Iyengar and Westwood, "Fear and Loathing."

25. Fiske and Taylor, *Social Cognition*, 286–89.

26. See Fiske and Taylor, *Social Cognition*, 289.

27. Zald and McCarthy, *Social Movements*, 20.

A Fight for America

Accordingly, just as many have observed that Americans of late have become noticeably more anxious, many have also pointed out that this anxiety may be driven in part by a notable transformation taking place within American society. To draw from the language coursing through our media, we now find ourselves embroiled in a "culture war," a "fight for the soul of America," a battle between those who "hate America" and those who want to "protect our freedom and way of life." Or, to use the less rhetorically charged lingo of cultural anthropology, we find ourselves in a moment of tension between an American "social movement" and "countermovement."

Social Movement: The Changing Values and Faces of America

Robert P. Jones, CEO of the Public Religion Research Institute and author of *The End of White Christian America,* has documented a number of trends within America over the last thirty years that reflect notable changes in our social, political, and cultural landscape.[28] Three of the more salient trends he identifies are 1) shifting values among Americans, especially as it relates to homosexuality and gay marriage; 2) the disaffiliation of many American youth from organized religion (but especially Protestantism); and 3) the changing demographic makeup of America itself. As the title of his book indicates, Jones argues that these trends signal the decline of white Christian influence in American society and politics.

Jones chronicles the dramatic rise in support for same-sex marriage from 1988 to 2014. In 1988, only 11 percent of Americans supported allowing gay and lesbian couples to marry legally. When Massachusetts became the first state to legalize same-sex marriage in 2004, those supporting gay marriage had climbed to 32 percent. By the time the Supreme Court declared all bans on same-sex marriage unconstitutional in 2015, a solid majority of Americans (54 percent) supported allowing gays and lesbians to marry. As Jones points out, this represented "an astounding leap of 22 percentage points over the last decade and 43 percentage points since the late 1980s."[29]

This major cultural shift occurred despite the concerted efforts of white evangelicals during that period to oppose the legalization of gay marriage. As Jones stresses, "The Supreme Court's decision to legalize same-sex marriage nationwide was a nuclear event for the evangelical wing of White

28. Jones, *White Christian America.*
29. Jones, *White Christian America,* 124.

Christian America, which has for decades staked its identity on opposing this issue."[30] It also signaled that the tremendous political power wielded by white evangelicals throughout the 1980s and well into the new millennium had waned considerably.

The number of Americans who claim an affiliation with organized religion, and Protestant Christianity in particular, has also slipped over the last twenty years. In 1994, 60 percent of the population identified as Protestant. By 2014 that number had dipped to 47 percent. A large share of that loss was among white Protestants. As recently as 1993, 51 percent of Americans identified as white Protestants. By 2014 that number stood at a startling 32 percent. Both mainline and evangelical white Protestants are losing younger members, but this decline has been especially sharp among white evangelicals. Twenty-seven percent of American seniors (aged sixty-five plus) identify as white evangelical Protestants. Only 10 percent of white Americans ages eighteen to twenty-nine identify as evangelicals. Altogether, according to Jones, "these numbers point to one undeniable conclusion: white Protestant Christians—both mainline and evangelical—are aging and quickly losing ground as a proportion of the population."[31]

Demographically, as America becomes more ethnically diverse due to immigration and birth rates, the percentage of white Christian (not just white Protestant) voters continues to decline. In 1992, when Bill Clinton was elected to his first term, 73 percent of the electorate was white and Christian. By 2020, that number will have dropped to 52 percent of the population, and by 2024, white Christians will no longer constitute a majority of voters in America.[32]

Countermovement: Make America Afraid Again

The MAGA movement set in motion by Donald Trump's 2016 presidential campaign and reinforced throughout his presidency, and the overwhelming support for Trump and his policies by white evangelical Christians, has been understood by many observers as largely a response to the decline of white Christian influence in our culture. Some see this as the primary factor in white evangelical support for MAGA, even more relevant than the financial insecurity of white Americans following the decades long-decline of several blue collar industries.[33]

30. Jones, *White Christian America*, 145.

31. Jones, *White Christian America*, 56.

32. Jones, *White Christian America*, 105.

33. Khazan, "People Voted for Trump;" Sewer, "The Nationalist's Delusion."

It is difficult to argue against this assessment. The MAGA motto, the calls to rescue our American values in tandem with the fear mongering language that saturates the speeches and tweets of Trump, conservative media, and his supporters, the relentless attacks against those who symbolize the "liberal agenda"—collectively, these features of the MAGA campaign indicate that it is a countermovement, trying to reclaim an America that is slipping away.

It is not at all surprising that America would be experiencing a serious countermovement at this point in its history in response to the dramatic cultural shifts taking place over the last few decades. What many have found surprising, and deeply disturbing, is what they see as the xenophobic, racist, and dehumanizing character of the rhetoric and policies used by Trump and his supporters to empower the MAGA countermovement. As noted near the start of the chapter, many have also found it deeply disturbing that white evangelical Christians would so readily support such a candidate and participate in such a movement, with 81 percent of white evangelicals voting for Trump in 2016 and close to that number still supporting his policies.[34]

Michael Gerson, who served as a policy adviser and the chief speechwriter to President George W. Bush, published a lengthy article in the April 2018 edition of *The Atlantic* titled "The Last Temptation." The article puzzles over and laments support for Donald Trump and his policies by white evangelicals. This excerpt captures one of his main points:

> Trump supporters tend to dismiss moral concerns about Trump's behavior as squeamishness over the president's "style." But the problem is the distinctly non-Christian substance of his *values*. Trump's unapologetic materialism—his equation of financial and social success with human achievement and worth—is a negation of Christian teaching. His tribalism and hatred for "the other" stand in direct opposition to Jesus's radical ethic of neighbor love. Trump's strength-worship and contempt for "losers" smack more of Nietzsche than of Christ. *Blessed are the proud. Blessed are the ruthless. Blessed are the shameless. Blessed are those who hunger and thirst after fame.*[35]

White evangelical support for a candidate whose lifestyle, demeanor, prejudices, and policies conflict with basic elements of Jesus' teaching and ministry is indeed puzzling. That is, until you consider the level of white evangelical anxiety over an America they fear is slipping away.

In 2015, the Public Religion Research Institute conducted a poll in response to the question, "Since the 1950's, do you think American culture

34. Schwadel and Smith, "Evangelical Approval of Trump."
35. Gerson, "The Last Temptation."

and way of life has mostly changed for the better, or has it mostly changed for the worse?" White evangelicals along with Tea Party members led the way in expressing their concern with the erosion of American culture: 72 percent of each group concluded that the American way of life has changed for the worse.[36]

John Fea points out that politicians who successfully appeal to white evangelicals intentionally stoke these fears.

> To win the evangelical vote, these political candidates knew that they would have to convince the faithful that the Christian fabric of the country was unraveling, the nation's evangelical moorings were loosening, and the barbarians were amassing at the borders—ready for a violent takeover. Fear is the political language conservative evangelicals know best.[37]

We are not safe. We are not getting our fair share. The way the world should be is slipping away.

Limited good and tribalism . . . American style.

Led by such anxiety-inducing stimulants, many white evangelicals have adopted the mind-set that the ends of once again having a seat at the tables of power, a supreme court aligned with their values, and a political movement forceful enough to reverse the tide of liberalism, justify the means of supporting the presidency and policies of Donald Trump.

Desperate Readings of Donald Trump and the Bible: a Ruler Like Esther, David, and Cyrus

To rationalize their embrace of the MAGA countermovement and support of Donald Trump, evangelicals have drawn parallels between candidate and then President Trump to biblical characters and narratives. On the more extreme end, some Trump staffers and evangelical devotees profess that the president has been sent by God to save America and it allies during their dark hour of need.[38]

36. Jones, *White Christian America*, 86.
37. Fea, *Believe Me*, 15.
38. Restuccia, "Sanctification of Donald Trump."

For a Time Like This: Queen Esther

For example, during a visit to Israel in April of 2019, Secretary of State Mike Pompeo was asked by a Christian Broadcasting Network reporter, "Could it be that President Trump right now has been sort of raised for such a time as this, just like Queen Esther, to help save the Jewish people from the Iranian menace?" [39]

Pompeo took the bait, "As a Christian, I certainly believe that's possible."

The facile comparison between Israel's conflict with Iran today and the situation of ancient Israel under Persian rule two and a half millennia ago (fifth century BCE) is by itself deeply problematic. It reflects a lack of an even elementary understanding of ancient Israel's history.

As mentioned earlier, the Israelites were invaded and nearly destroyed by the Babylonians in 587 BCE, after repeatedly rebelling against them. Many Israelites were killed, the temple was demolished, the king was dethroned and imprisoned, and survivors were exiled in various parts of the Babylonian empire. The Israelites were expected by their Babylonian captors to assimilate and to live as Jews no more. But many Israelites remembered who and whose they were, and never gave up hope that someday they would return to Israel. When the Persians defeated the Babylonians about fifty years later, the Persian king, Cyrus, gave permission and material support for Israelites to return to Jerusalem, reclaim it, and rebuild the temple and city.

It is indeed possible that Israelites were subject to periods of oppression under Persian rule, but this seems to be the exception to the norm, as the story of Esther itself suggests. While Persian support for the returned exiles and the rebuilding of Jerusalem waned under King Artaxerxes (465–424 BCE) and the Jews were forced to stop their restoration of the temple and city walls, Persian permission and patronage for the rebuilding effort resumed under King Darius (423–404 BCE), who committed the protection and resources needed to complete the work (see Ezra 5–6).

The Persians, in other words, often served as the Israelites' patrons and benefactors. The CBN reporter's comparison of ancient Persian policy towards Israelites with Iranian aggression towards Israel today, and Pompeo's validation of that comparison, is simply fallacious.

So too is the comparison between Trump and Esther.

The story of Esther is set in the time of King Xerxes, also known as Ahasuerus, who ruled Persia from 486–465 BCE. When Xerxes's wife, Queen

39. Restuccia, "Sanctification of Donald Trump."

Vashti, refuses the king's summons to display her beauty before guests gathered for a feast, she is deposed of her royal title. Esther is among one of scores of virgins rounded up to participate in a contest to determine who would be the new queen, based on who pleased the king the most (2:4). In light of the repeated attention the story gives to the beauty of the virgins and the extensive cosmetic treatments the women received (2:2, 3, 7, 9, 12), their value to the king and the kind of pleasure they are to provide him is clear. Esther has no choice but to comply. She begins her adult life as an unmarried, disenfranchised woman of a refugee people. At the very bottom of the social scale, she is forced to become the object of an elite male's sexual appetite.

Esther humiliates herself and dutifully serves her role in Xerxes's harem, while hiding her Israelite identity as Mordecai, her kinsman, warned her to do. When Esther is finally summoned, she pleases the king and we are told that Xerxes "loved her more than all the other women." Against all odds, Esther—the secret Israelite refugee—is made queen.

But soon all is not well. Mordecai, apparently a low-status member of the royal court, infuriates Haman, Xerxes's right-hand man and second-in-command. Haman possesses a megalomaniacal god-complex and demands that in his presence everyone bends the knee and does obeisance to him. But Mordecai repeatedly refuses to do this, for "he was a Jew" (3:4). In retaliation, Haman goes into attack mode—he schemes to destroy Mordecai and his people.

This is the plot that Esther eventually foils to save her kinsman and scores of other Israelites. The deliverance she sets in motion includes a dramatic and bloody reversal: Haman and his family are executed on the gallows that he had built to kill Mordecai, and faithful Mordecai takes Haman's place as second-in-command.

The book of Esther is a compelling rags-to-riches story. Esther is a sex-slave heroine beating all odds as she eventually summons the courage and cleverness to outwit patriarchal power at its most degenerate and risk all for the sake of her beleaguered, displaced people who are viewed with suspicion by the elite members of Persian society.

But of all the characters in this powerful tale, I can't imagine one less suited as an analogue to Donald Trump than Esther.

God Uses Flawed Leaders: King David and King Cyrus

More common among evangelicals has been the attempt to use biblical characters to explain and justify their qualified support of Trump and toleration of his less than Christian proclivities. Just as God has used flawed leaders in the past; the reasoning goes, so too can God use a flawed leader like Donald Trump. King David, the second and most celebrated king of ancient Israel, and the Persian King Cyrus, who supported Israel's resettlement of Judea after their exile under Babylon, are two precedents that evangelists lift up to validate this claim.

I find this mode of reasoning problematic for several reasons. First, this is an argument that could be made for *any* human ruler, even the most faithful ones. All human leaders are flawed. The reason evangelicals make this argument for Trump is that his behavior and views force them to acknowledge serious deficiencies in his character. Somehow the spectacle of Donald Trump and his administration, and their support of both, needs to make sense within a biblical worldview. I find their line of argument an instance of special pleading.

Second, it is indeed the case that the biblical tradition shows God using flawed, even downright despicable, human rulers to forward God's saving intentions for humanity. But this does not mean that God engineered their rise to prominence and validated the vile things they did to achieve it. What God does, rather, is work within the situation at hand, and at times even uses the narcissism and fear of leaders to lead them to their own downfall or to unwittingly advance God's designs. In Scripture we see God do this with Pharaoh, Pilate, the Sanhedrin, several Roman Emperors, and even Satan. Just because God can use such rulers doesn't mean that it is God's will that deeply flawed humans (or demons!) achieve power.

Third, the evangelicals who voted for Trump and continue to support his presidency have chosen to do so despite him manifesting and endorsing racist, misogynistic, xenophobic, and narcissistic behaviors during his campaign and afterwards as president. Trump was elected because evangelicals voted for him. They had a choice. They are the ones who decided that restoring an America they fear is slipping away validated their election of Donald Trump. At the very least, evangelicals should soberly acknowledge that despite the gains they believe they have made with Trump in the White House, those gains have also come at a cost to our constitutional principles and to the character of American society. At the very least, they should join their fellow Christians lamenting this reality, rather than excusing it or ignoring it.

Finally, just as with Esther, neither King David nor King Cyrus provide the analogous examples to Donald Trump that some evangelicals claim they do.

King David

David is described by God and extolled by the biblical writers as a man after God's own heart. But, like Esther, his rise to power was extremely unlikely. Though born into a prominent family, he was the youngest of Jesse's sons. When the prophet Samuel told Jesse to have his sons pass before him to see which one God would select to establish a new dynasty over Israel, David was not even invited to the gathering (1 Sam 16). But God, "who does not see as humans see," didn't select the tallest, the boldest, or the strongest, but the ruddy-looking youth, highly gifted at protecting sheep. God was after a shepherd.

In the years that followed, we see David growing into the role that Samuel said he would one day fulfill. Through all sorts of hardships and toil, he perseveres. He also reveals himself to be a man of incredible faith in God, unfailing integrity and compassion, guided by a keen sense of justice. When David finally assumes the throne and unites the tribes of Israel, and God makes an everlasting covenant with David and his heirs forever establishing his house as a dynasty over Israel (2 Sam 7), we are at a most blessed moment in the story of the monarchy, and one of the high points in the story of ancient Israel. So much promise awaits David and all of Israel.

But a few chapters later into 2 Samuel, all of that changes.

David sleeps with Bathsheba, wife of Uriah, while Uriah is off fighting for Israel. Then, when David learns that Bathsheba is pregnant, and can't get the faithful Uriah to abandon his duty as a soldier and return home to sleep with his wife so that David can cover up the affair, David arranges to have Uriah killed. David, a man after God's own heart, a paragon of integrity and justice, commits adultery and murder. The shepherd has become a ravenous wolf.

From this point on, the story of David and Israel weaves around two essential plotlines. One is God's enduring faithfulness to David despite David's deplorable transgressions, and God's faithfulness to David's descendants despite their even more deplorable transgressions. The other is the dire consequences that David, his descendants, and all of Israel suffer because of their neglect of God's Torah and transgressions against others.

When the prophet Nathan appears before David to deliver God's condemnation of David's adultery with Bathsheba and his murder of Uriah, he cries, "Now, therefore, the sword will never depart from your house for you have despised me" (2 Sam 12:10). As we would expect, Nathan's words are prophetic. Absalom, David's son, rebels against him, seizes the throne, and plunges Israel into a civil war, during which many are killed.

David regains the throne, but it soon becomes clear that he is a shell of the ruler he once was. Strife continues to undermine his reign. His relationship with God becomes simply dysfunctional. Death, not blessing, is now the fruit of his rule. He satisfies "the blood guilt" that Saul incurred for killing Gibeonites by offering Saul's descendants as a human sacrifice to God (2 Sam 21). He is compelled by God to conduct a sinful census of the people, and when God gives David a choice as to the judgment for his sin, David chooses the option less painful to him but most devastating for Israel: 70,000 are killed by disease (2 Sam 24). When we last encounter David on his deathbed, his parting words are instructions to Solomon on who he must kill to secure his reign and to avenge his father. Painfully, tragically, the very last word we hear David speak is "Sheol" (1 Kgs 2:9), the realm of the dead.

What is critical to appreciate about David's story (and this is also true of the story of Solomon) is that it is really the tragic story of the monarchy as a whole. It is not only about the rule of David; it establishes a pattern that we will see play out again and again in the centuries to follow through the rule of David's descendants.

David's story begins with so much promise for blessing, for David, his house, and all of Israel. It reveals that when Israel's kings and people follow in the ways of God the land overflows with abundance, and Israel stands as a beacon of righteousness and justice and bears witness to God's sovereignty. But eventually with David and Solomon—and the monarchy as a whole— faithfulness gives way to self-serving indulgence and unfaithfulness to God and those they are called to serve. The inevitable result is the decline of their relationship with God, the decline of their rule, and the decline of Israel. Eventually, after centuries of such decline under the kings to follow, after years of rulers and people despising God and God's ways, the covenant God makes with David and his descendants is stretched past the breaking point. First Israel falls to Assyria, and then Judah falls to Babylon. Temple, king, and land—nearly all that defines Israel—are swept away. From that point on, no Davidic heir rules on the throne of Israel.

So, when evangelicals draw a comparison between Donald Trump and King David to argue that despite the deficiencies of Trump's character he can still serve God's purposes just as David did, they are apparently forgetting or choosing to ignore the devastating consequences of David's own self-serving indulgence on his own soul, his household, his reign, and all of Israel. They are forgetting that David's decline foreshadows the tragic decline of the monarchy in the centuries to follow and Israel's steady march towards devastation.

Please do me a favor. Pull out your Bible and read Isaiah 5.

Take note of its description of Israel's embrace of indulgence and injustice, and the terrible consequences this "fruit" has produced for its victims and Israel itself. God lovingly planted Israel as one plants a vineyard, expecting the produce of justice and righteousness. But instead he finds bloodshed and hears the cries of victims (Isa 5:7)! The elite have run roughshod over the poor, they have recklessly feasted and drunk, they have bribed, they have acquitted the guilty and defrauded the innocent, they have rejected God's ways (Isa 5:8–24).

> Therefore, the anger of the Lord was kindled against his people,
>   and he stretched out his hand against them and struck them,
>   the mountains quaked,
> and their corpses were like refuse in the streets.
> For all this his anger has not turned away,
>   and his hand is stretched out still (Isa 5:25).

If white evangelical leaders truly see the self-indulgences of Donald Trump like those of King David, they should not be comforted. Frankly, such parallels should scare them like hell.

King Cyrus

As mentioned earlier, the Persian King Cyrus, also known as Cyrus the Great, defeated the Babylonian Empire in 539 BCE. He then established the Persian Empire as the greatest realm that part of the world had yet seen. Shortly into his reign, as part of a larger strategy for dealing with subjected peoples, he issued a decree allowing Israelites to return to Jerusalem to rebuild the temple and the city, and mandated that parts of the empire that are home to Jewish exiles financially support their efforts (see Ezra 1:1–11). While the rebuilding was interrupted during the reign of Artaxerxes, it resumed under Darius and the Israelites were able to complete their work on the temple and the city walls before the end of the fifth century BCE.

Shortly after the release of the Access Hollywood tapes recording Trump boasting of his sexual assault of women, evangelicals used the example of Cyrus to justify their belief that God could even use a vessel as imperfect as Trump to achieve God's purposes for America. Later, when President Trump announced in spring of 2018 that the US would move its embassy in Israel to Jerusalem and recognize it as the Israeli capital, Israeli Prime Minister Benjamin Netanyahu made a similar comparison.

> We remember the proclamation of the great King Cyrus the
> Great—Persian King. Twenty-five hundred years ago, he

proclaimed that the Jewish exiles in Babylon can come back and rebuild our temple in Jerusalem . . . And we remember how a few weeks ago, President Donald J. Trump recognized Jerusalem as Israel's capital. Mr. President, this will be remembered by our people throughout the ages.[40]

From a white evangelical perspective, just as Cyrus, a non-believer, could be used as an instrument of God, so too is God now using Donald Trump. Tara Isabella Burton explains the objective of this "vessel theology."

> This framing allows for the creation of Trump as a viable evangelical candidate regardless of his personal beliefs or actions. It allows evangelical leaders, and to a lesser extent ordinary evangelicals, to provide a compelling narrative for their support for him that transcends the mere pragmatic fact that he is a Republican. Instead of having to justify their views of Trump's controversial past, including reports of sexual misconduct and adultery, the evangelical establishment can say Trump's presidency was arranged by God, and thus legitimize their support for him.[41]

One glaring problem in this line of thinking is the assumption that Trump's personal indiscretions and deficiencies of character are analogous to Cyrus being a pagan, or non-Israelite believer: "Despite the fact that Cyrus was a pagan, heathen king . . ." the reasoning goes.

In fact, if we carefully attend to what the biblical writers say about Cyrus, it is hard to find anything wrong with his conduct or religious sensibilities. The writer of Ezra presents Cyrus as attributing his victory over Babylon to "The LORD," or "Yahweh," the God of Israel. Then in the same breath, Cyrus identifies Yahweh as sovereign over the entire earth. Cyrus also claims that Yahweh specifically commanded him to restore the temple in Jerusalem (Ezra 1:2).

We might be justified in wondering if Cyrus was simply couching his edict in language that would appeal to his Israelite subjects. But there is nothing in Ezra's account to support this suspicion. In fact, Ezra tells us that "the LORD stirred up the spirit of King Cyrus" to compose and announce the edict (1:1), using the same language Ezra will later employ to describe God "stirring the spirits" of the Israelites who returned to Jerusalem to rebuild (1:5).

Moreover, the prophet whose words are preserved in Isaiah 45 appears to adopt a similar perspective of Cyrus as a truly righteous leader. Though Cyrus had not known God (vv. 4, 5), God has selected Cyrus as

40. Burton, "Biblical Story."
41. Burton, "Biblical Story."

the "anointed" king who will restore God's people. Through Cyrus, the world shall come to know that Yahweh, and no other, is the one true God (vv. 5–6). God will also arouse within Cyrus righteousness, and will make his paths straight (v. 13).

The prophet thus applies to Cyrus attributes of mission and character that Israelite tradition has applied to the ideal Israelite king from generations past and will continue to apply to the ideal Israelite king for centuries moving forward: deliverance and protection of God's people, bearing witness to the sovereignty and righteousness of Yahweh, and walking in God's ways. The implications are clear. According to this oracle, one who has not known God has been chosen by God to serve as God's messiah (anointed), to deliver God's people, and to walk in God's ways of righteousness. In short, the two biblical texts that most directly speak to Cyrus and his character present him as the ideal king who confesses faith in Yahweh's sovereignty and walks in God's ways. He is not much of a heathen. It is difficult to see how his character and actions serve as a precedent validating evangelical support of Donald Trump.

Godly and Ungodly Rule

But as long as we are on the subject of kings and what the Bible expects of them, note this critique from Daniel Block, an evangelical also not convinced that the comparison between Trump and Cyrus holds up. Block points out that the biblical expectations surrounding the character and priorities of a righteous king presents an alternative to the Ancient Near Eastern exercise of kingship. According to Moses's "charter for kingship" as recorded in Deuteronomy 17:14–20, kings are to "function as servants of their people." Block goes on to state,

> To guard against the predominant megalomaniacal paradigm, Moses focused on the personal character of the king. They were not to use their position of authority in self-interest (multiplying horses, women, and silver and gold *for himself*). Rather, Israel's kings were to read the Torah for themselves and then embody the righteousness the Torah called for in all of Yahweh's people: fearing Yahweh, walking in the ways of Yahweh, and walking humbly among their fellow Israelites (vv. 18–20). In short, the Israelite king's primary function was to be a model citizen, so that people could look up to him and declare, "I want to be like that person!"[42]

42. Block, "Is Trump Our Cyrus?"

Block warns that despite the reality that many of our leaders past and present are flawed, and some deeply so, we must never allow ourselves to become blind to those flaws. We must hold them to a higher standard.

> According to the Bible, leadership is more than effectiveness; it's also (and, in fact, primarily) a matter of character. Jesus modeled perfectly the righteous standard of which he spoke: "I am the good shepherd; the good shepherd lays down his life for the sheep" (John 10:11; cf. Eph 5:25b).

More pointedly, while speaking at a private meeting of evangelical leaders, Mark Labberton, President of Fuller Theological Seminary, described the "central crisis" facing American evangelicalism: "the gospel of Jesus Christ has been betrayed and shamed by an evangelicalism that has violated its own moral and spiritual integrity." He explains,

> This is not a crisis imposed from outside the household of faith, but from within. The core of the crisis is not specifically about Trump, or Hillary, or Obama, or the electoral college, or Comey, or Mueller, or abortion, or LGBTQIA+ debates, or Supreme Court appointees. Instead the crisis is caused by the way a toxic evangelicalism has engaged with these issues in such a way as to turn the gospel into Good News that is fake. Now on public display is an indisputable collusion between prominent evangelicalism and many forms of insidious racist, misogynistic, materialistic, and political power. The wind and the rain and the floods have come, and, as Jesus said, they will reveal our foundation. In this moment for evangelicalism, what the storms have exposed is a foundation not of solid rock but of sand.[43]

Similarly, in a *Christianity Today* editorial following the impeachment of Trump by the House of Representatives, editor Mark Gali calls for the removal of Trump, and pleads,

> To the many evangelicals who continue to support Mr. Trump in spite of his blackened moral record, we might say this: Remember who you are and whom you serve. Consider how your justification of Mr. Trump influences your witness to your Lord and Savior. Consider what an unbelieving world will say if you continue to brush off Mr. Trump's immoral words and behavior in the cause of political expediency. If we don't reverse course now, will anyone take anything we say about justice and righteousness with any seriousness for decades to

43. Labberton, "Political Dealing."

come? Can we say with a straight face that abortion is a great
evil that cannot be tolerated and, with the same straight face,
say that the bent and broken character of our nation's leader
doesn't really matter in the end?[44]

Ignoring what Matters Most: Jesus' Call to the Church

Block's, Labberton's, and Galli's insider critiques point to one of the glaring, even tragic consequences of white evangelical support for Trump. In
anxiously and even desperately lining up behind Donald Trump and the
countermovement he leads, white evangelicals have overlooked critical
parts of their tradition, and undermined their witness to Jesus. Not only
does anxiety lead evangelicals to misapply biblical characters and periods to
Trump's rise to power, it also leads them to neglect what should be basic to
their collective character and ministry. It's a heartbreaking example of the
warping of biblical tradition when refracted through a fear-filled lens.

Cold, Hard, Fearful Hearts

To offer a concrete example, let us return to the fear-filled rhetoric about
immigration with which this chapter began. Republican strategists, like
Stephen Miller and Steve Bannon, have intentionally used the issue of immigration to strengthen white evangelical support for Republican candi-
dates.[45] John Fea, helps us understand why such a strategy was bound to
be effective.

> Evangelicals have worried about the decline of Christian civiliza-
> tion from the moment they arrived on American shores in the
> seventeenth century. The have celebrated American values such
> as "freedom" and "liberty" while simultaneously building exclu-
> sive communities that do not tolerate dissent. They have revealed
> their fear in the ways that they have responded to the plight of the
> people who do not share their skin color. White evangelical fear of
> newcomers—those who might challenge the power and privilege
> that evangelicals have enjoyed in a nation of Protestants—has
> been present in every era of American history.[46]

44. Galli, "Trump Should be Removed."
45. PBS, "Zero Tolerance."
46. Fea, *Believe Me*, 75–76.

True to form, in January 2018, a Washington Post/ABC poll found that 75 percent of white evangelicals in the US described "the federal crackdown on undocumented immigrants" as a positive thing, compared to just 46 percent of Americans overall. And according to a Pew Research Center poll in May 2018, 68 percent of white evangelicals say that America has no responsibility to house refugees, 25 points over the national average.[47]

To be sure, the realities of immigration and illegal immigration are complex, with a host of variables that are extremely challenging to untangle and manage. Thoughtful, faithful people are likely to disagree on this issue and advocate for different solutions to address the economic and political challenges immigration poses for our nation.

But the vilification and inhumane treatment of immigrants, the lack of compassion many political and evangelical leaders have manifested for asylum seekers, and the anxiety of scarcity that warps much of white Christian thinking on these issues, all dash against two bedrocks of Jesus' teaching: to not give in to fear, and to treat all with generosity and love.

Jesus: Don't Worry!

Recall the realities of life for most living within the Roman world that we discussed back in Chapter 1. Most lived on the precarious edge of subsistence and were struggling to survive.

And yet a common theme of Jesus' teaching was for his followers not to be anxious about the very things that they had every reason to worry about. Consider, for example, Jesus' words as recorded in Matthew 6.

> [25]Therefore I tell you, do not worry about your life, what you will eat or what you will drink, or about your body, what you will wear. Is not life more than food, and the body more than clothing? [26]Look at the birds of the air; they neither sow nor reap nor gather into barns, and yet your heavenly Father feeds them. Are you not of more value than they? [27]And can any of you by worrying add a single hour to your span of life? [28]And why do you worry about clothing? Consider the lilies of the field, how they grow; they neither toil nor spin, [29]yet I tell you, even Solomon in all his glory was not clothed like one of these. [30]But if God so clothes the grass of the field, which is alive today and tomorrow is thrown into the oven, will he not much more clothe you—you of little faith?

47. Burton, "The Bible Says to Welcome Immigrants."

> [31]Therefore do not worry, saying, "What will we eat?" or "What will we drink?" or "What will we wear?" [32]For it is the Gentiles who strive for all these things; and indeed your heavenly Father knows that you need all these things. (Matt 6:25–32)

Why would Jesus say this to his fellow Israelites, to those who were often desperate for food, drink, clothing, and shelter? Most of them would not live into their mid-thirties! Half of their children who managed to live past age one would be dead by age sixteen!

Don't worry? Jesus, are you serious?!

Jesus: Seek God's Kingdom and Righteousness

The answer to this quandary comes in the next verse. But Matthew 6:33 is one of the most commonly, and tragically, misunderstood verses of the New Testament, at least by American Christians: "But strive first for the kingdom of God and his righteousness, and all these things will be given to you as well."

Throughout history and still today, many Christians take Jesus' words here to mean that if we live faithfully, God will grant us, reward us—individually—with the material resources we need to survive and thrive. The "Prosperity Gospel" movement is one of the more extreme manifestations of this misguided misreading of Scripture, but I think it is held in varying degrees by many American Christians today.

Yet this misreading completely misses the point of what Jesus was getting at. It is an example of reading individual passages of Scripture against the grain of its dominant impulses and the central contours of Jesus' ministry. It is an example of reading Scripture through lenses shaped by our individualistic and commodity-driven cultural mind-set. And the case of Matthew 6:33, it is another example of taking a verse completely out of its context, here Jesus' Sermon on the Mount extending from 5:1 to 7:29.

Jesus was not telling his disciples to live rightly so that God would provide them with the material resources they need to survive, as if God operates according to some divinely mandated quid pro quo. Jesus was telling them that if they truly embrace the kingdom of God, if they truly seek the right kind of treasure (Matt 6:19–21), if they truly see the world with sound eyes (6:22–23), if they set aside the misguided quest for wealth (6:24) and do God's will "on earth as it is in heaven" (Matt 6:9–13)—they would begin to create the kind of *community* in which *all* of God's children would share in God's abundance. This is to be the work of the followers of Jesus in every age. This is basic to what it means to be disciples of Jesus.[48]

Anxiety is the enemy of the kind of trust needed to live out this vision. Anxiety is that which believers must address and overcome if they are to be followers of Jesus. Jesus teaches this over and over again, as does much of the rest of the New Testament. This is why the word "faith," often better translated as "trust," is so central to biblical thought. It is also why "trust"/"faith"/"believe" is so commonly paired with "repent," "humility," and "love."

Lens (and Heart!) Adjustment: Trust and Compassion

So here too is another crucial lens adjustment that can make all the difference in terms of getting or not getting at what the Bible, and Jesus, are all about. Those who read Jesus' words here in Matthew 6 through a lens shaped by a self-centered individualism or tribalism stimulated by anxiety are very likely to hear Jesus say to them "Make sure that you are righteous so that God gives you and our own what you need to survive." But that is a perversion. It is, as Jesus warns, the wide and easy road that leads to destruction (Matt 7:13–14).

Those who read Jesus' words here shaped by an other-centered kinship grounded in trust and stimulated by compassion are very likely to hear Jesus say to them "Earnestly strive for the kind of kingdom I have come to establish, for that is the way God's gift of abundant life for you and all God's children will be achieved."

And once we come to terms with that, once we shift from the anxious, self-serving, broken-hearted hermeneutic peddled by the false—ravenous wolf—prophets among us (7:15), to a trust-filled vision molded by a savior that came not to be served but to serve and to give his life as a ransom for many, nearly everything we see and hear and in Scripture is cast anew in its proper light. We begin to see and hear the ongoing, nearly overwhelming cascade of images and instruction bearing witness to the central truth of our sacred tradition that "in everything, do unto others as you have them

---

48. I am not advocating here for a view of the kingdom, or reign of God, known as "realized eschatology," as though we are able to make God's kingdom fully present in the here and now. My view is a form of "inaugurated eschatology," which I and many other biblical scholars find reflected in the New Testament writings. That is, Jesus *inaugurated* the arrival of God's saving reign, and called his followers to do all that they can to embody and establish the ways of the kingdom in their midst as they await its fulfillment. The particular forms of that work will (and should!) vary from context to context, but it is *always* to be characterized by justice, integrity, humility, and compassionate love for all people (see chapter 5).

do to you" (6:12). We begin to see and hear that those "others" of whom Jesus speaks really does mean *all* others, even our enemies (5:43–48). We begin to see and hear that in living out this essential calling we are truly living by "the law and the prophets" (6:12) and embracing our true identity as righteousness-seeking, mercy-wielding, peace-making (5:1–11) children of God (5:45).

With this clearer vision, we can also see our anxious, self-serving tribalism and broken-heartedness as the sandy, shifty, untenable foundation that it surely is. We can faithfully seek and reclaim the true bedrock of our shared faith. And then, even now, we can withstand and repel the forces that beat against American churches from within and without, causing them to list alarmingly, threatening their great fall.

We can once again trust in God, and the future that we and God will shape together.

Reflection or Discussion Questions

1. Do you agree that anxiety has the potential to undermine our ability to love others? If so, how have you seen this manifested in American society or in your community?

2. What things cause you to feel unsafe, insecure, and angry?

3. Why do you think that Christians have such markedly different perspectives on current social and political issues?

CHAPTER FOUR

Reading the Bible Into Pieces

In the introduction, we talked about how all of our encounters with Scripture are unavoidably selective and perspectival. We focus on what resonates with us, and we bring to our reflection on the Bible all that makes us who we are. We all come to Scripture wearing lenses.

Our goal as faithful interpreters, it seems to me, is to do the best we can to make sure that our lenses are in tune with the kind of phenomenon Scripture is, and what our ancestors who contributed to it intended their writings to say. This is why it is important for us not to try to force Scripture into categories that it doesn't fit (such as "inerrancy"). It is also why it is important for us to try to honor the intentions of our ancestors who offered and passed down the testimonies preserved in Scripture.

In short, we should try to engage Scripture in ways that honor what kind of work it is and where it came from.

The setting within which most Christians encounter Scripture most of the time is worship. And for many of these Christians, their encounter with Scripture is facilitated if not controlled by their church's use of a lectionary.

As I will discuss, lectionaries are often employed with the best of intentions, and there are several notable advantages to their use. But on the whole, I think, they often lead pastors and congregations to treat the Bible in ways that do not honor what kind of work it is and from whom it came. It leads us to read Scripture in ways that are not in tune with the kind of phenomenon Scripture is, and how the writers of Scripture intended their works to be encountered.

Lectionaries often encourage Christians to read the Bible badly.

The Lectionary: Some Basics

Many Christian communities in America do not make use of a lectionary. I also find that some Christians who belong to communities that use a lectionary are still a bit fuzzy on what a lectionary is and how it guides the reading of Scripture in worship. So, perhaps some words of introduction are in order.

Let's start with the basics. A lectionary is a schedule of assigned Scripture readings for every Sunday, other holy days, and even weekday services, that are intended for edification and proclamation during worship. In some communities, clergy are required to use the assigned lessons for the day, in others it is strongly encouraged and expected, and in still others the assigned lectionary texts function as guides or suggestions.

The lectionaries that are most widely used by Christian communities today in America are the Roman Catholic Lectionary, also referred to as the Lectionary for Mass (LM), and the Revised Common Lectionary (RCL). These two lectionaries are "close cousins," with the RCL, completed in 1992, largely based on the LM. These two lectionaries, as well as those followed by other traditions including Orthodox Churches, intentionally arrange assigned biblical texts in coordination with the church year. The goal of these lectionaries—in conjunction with the church calendar—is to help believers remember and celebrate pivotal events in the story of God's people, especially God's work of salvation in Jesus, and to reflect on what it means to be faithful followers of Christ. More succinctly, their intention is to "allow a community of faith to hear the fullness of the Bible in an orderly manner."[1]

A Brief History of the Use of Lectionaries

Lectionaries have been employed in various forms since the opening centuries of Christianity. But their use by our spiritual ancestors predates Jesus and the church.

During the Babylonian Exile

The use of somewhat systematized readings of Scripture during worship and for the purpose of edification can be traced back to Israelite communities in the aftermath of the Babylonian exile. When the Babylonians invaded Israel and razed Jerusalem in 587 BCE, they destroyed nearly everything that

1. Bower, ed., *Handbook*, 15.

defined Israel as a distinct community: their temple, their monarchy, and their promised land. But as a beleaguered people spread across the Babylonian empire, Israelites in the diaspora somehow managed to congregate in local meeting places to remember and celebrate who and whose they were, and to hope for a better tomorrow. Their sacred traditions, their Scriptures, were the lifeblood of their incredible tenacity and ability to resist assimilation into Babylonian culture. Survivors turned to the Torah, Prophets, and Psalms, and copied, revised, and added onto those traditions, in order to make sense of their tragic past and reconstitute themselves as the people of God.

One result of the dedication with which Israelites engaged their sacred traditions during the Babylonian Exile and the years that followed was a somewhat regular schedule of lessons to be read throughout the year. As summarized by Gail O'Day and Charles D. Hackett,

> The structure of Hebrew Lectionaries seems to have been simple. There were two readings at each synagogue service: reading from the Law (*Torah*) and the Prophets (*Nebiim*) . . . The Torah was read continuously, one book after another. The readings were divided into units so that the readings at each meeting would pick up where the reading at the last had ended. From early on the readings from the Prophets referred to the Diaspora and God's promises for the future were often selected. The readings started with the duty of every Jew to follow the Law. It was through obedience to the Law that individuals grew into their identity as Jews. The readings from the Prophets helped Jews understand their captivity and provided a vision for their restoration in the future.[2]

When some Israelites began to return from the diaspora beginning in the sixth century, they brought with them their practice of meeting in small communities to worship and read Scripture. This practice was eventually denoted by the Greek word, *synagogue*, which literally means "to gather together."

Moving into the Common Era

By the time of Jesus' ministry in the first century CE, the practice of Israelites meeting in synagogues and following a regular schedule of Scripture lessons appears well established. Reading the Torah continuously from beginning to end, with the prophets read selectively to correspond with

2. O'Day and Hackett, *Preaching*, 4.

various seasons or holy days, seems to have been the general rule for synagogue worship. It is important to note, however, that "synagogue practice was far from uniform. Local custom dictated, among other things, the schedule of services and weekly prayers as well as many, if not most, of the specific passages to be read."[3]

Early Christians Reading Scripture

As first-century Israelites, the earliest followers of Jesus continued the practice of worshipping at the Jerusalem Temple and also gathering in synagogues and other local meeting places. After the Temple was destroyed by the Romans in 70 CE and the church began to include more Gentile believers, the practice of meeting in small house churches or public spaces became common. How and when Christians met was likely dictated in part by the level of persecution they were encountering in their particular locale, but in general they celebrated together on Sunday, rather than on the Sabbath, gathering to read Israelite Scriptures, letters from leaders like Paul, and the emerging traditions about Jesus' life and teachings.

Eventually among Christians, Paul's letters and a select group of other epistles, along with early Christian narratives like the Gospels and Acts of the Apostles, came to be regarded as inspired, authoritative testimonies to Jesus and his significance. Christians would eventually adopt the terms "Old Testament" to refer to the Israelite Scriptures, and "New Testament" to refer to the Christian writings on which they conferred the status of sacred Scripture.

We lack the historical evidence needed to reconstruct in detail how Christians in the first three centuries made use of their Scriptures in worship. However, in the mid-second century, Justin Martyr describes as typical Sunday practice that believers gathered to pray, read Scripture, talk about what was read, and then to share a meal of bread and wine. He states that "the memoirs of the apostles or the writings of the prophets are read as long as time permits; then, when the reader has ceased, the president verbally instructs and exhorts them to the imitation of these good things."[4] Some scholars speculate that since we see numerous commentaries on whole biblical books being written by church leaders during this period, that the continuous, community reading of these books was likely common. Yet as with Israelite synagogue worship, "we can reasonably assume that there was

---

3. O'Day and Hackett, *Preaching*, 4.

4 Justin Martyr, *Apologetics*, 65–67; cited in O'Day and Hackett, *Preaching*, 5.

a great deal of variety, both in what was read and how the readings were structured, depending on local custom."[5]

At this point, I just want to pause and draw your attention to two characteristic features of how Israelite believers and early Christians likely read their Scriptures. They read many portions of them continuously, meaning that they worked their way from the beginning of a biblical book to its end. The technical term for this is *lectio continua*. And their reading practices varied due to local needs and customs. We will come back to these two characteristics later.

The Move Toward Greater Uniformity

When Constantine in the fourth century adopted Christianity as a unifying force for his empire, concerted effort was made to regularize Christian theology and liturgy. This eventually included increased focus on the "church year" as a means by which to educate the masses now streaming into the church on the essential touchstones of the Christian story, and to encourage and structure their devotional life. Previously, the early church celebrated Sunday, Easter, and Pentecost. Liturgical life now came to revolve around key events throughout the entire year, providing believers the opportunity "to participate in the founding events of Christianity and, in particular, the events of Christ's life, death, and resurrection."[6] The eventual result is the liturgical calendar that many Christians are familiar with and practice today, though with some degree of variation.

- Advent: the start of the church year, these four weeks are to prepare believers for the advent of Jesus, both as the Lord who will return to fulfill God's kingdom, and as the Christ child who came to live, serve, and die among us.

- Christmas: celebrates the birth of Jesus and the miracle of the incarnation, including Christmas Day and the eleven days following.

- Epiphany: beginning on January 6, commemorates the "manifestation" of Jesus, focuses on Jesus' presentation in the Temple, the visit of the Magi, and Jesus' baptism.

- Lent: beginning with Ash Wednesday, this is a season of reflection, repentance, and fasting. Lasting forty days (not counting Sundays),

5. O'Day and Hackett, *Preaching*, 6.
6. O'Day and Hackett, *Preaching*, 15.

this season remembers Jesus' journey to Jerusalem, arrest, trial, and crucifixion—what is commonly known as the passion of Jesus.

• Easter: the focal point of the church year, rejoicing in the resurrection of Jesus, God's defeat of death, and the salvation of humanity; lasting fifty days, this season concludes with the celebration of Pentecost, marking the bestowal of the Holy Spirit upon believers and empowering them to bear witness to the gospel.

• Season after Pentecost: the time between Trinity Sunday (the Sunday after Pentecost) and Christ the King Sunday (the Sunday prior to Advent), and often referred to as Ordinary Time; during this season the church reflects on what it means to serve our broken world and make the reign of Christ present in our midst.

Once the church year became established, liturgical resources specific to the events and seasons in view were developed, such as prayers, hymns, and even the color of the vestments worn by clergy and other participants. Scripture readings were also keyed to the events and season at hand, and regular schedules developed with designated lessons for much of the church year and all of the major feasts, though these too could be variable in different locales.

Lectionaries Through the Centuries

Within Western Christianity, the Roman Sunday lectionary became the standard for community worship, while the Eastern churches followed their own lectionaries. The Roman Sunday lectionary was a yar-long cycle consisting of two, non-continuous, lessons, usually a selection from the epistles and a Gospel reading, using the same readings every year. In addition to Sunday services, daily services (termed "offices") developed and proliferated which included the reading or singing of psalms. But these offices were not widely practiced, and were often confined to clergy or monasteries. Overall, and compared to the reading practices of pre-Constantinian churches, the Roman Sunday lectionary "radically reduced the amount of scripture exposed to people who only attended Mass."[7]

The Protestant Reformers and the communities they founded, in varying degrees, modified the way in which Scripture was to be engaged. Overall, the reading and preaching of the Bible took on a much more prominent role in the lives of these communities. Lutheran and Anglican

---

7. O'Day and Hackett, *Preaching*, 8.

churches developed modified forms of the Roman lectionary. These included Old Testament passages and additional lessons from the epistles that supported their doctrinal emphases. They also continued to follow the liturgical year. The Reform branch of the Reformation, however, eschewed the lectionary, returning to *lectio continua* as the standard mode for many of the lessons, and also began including Old Testament traditions in their reading and reflection. The importance of the church year also declined among the Reformed communities, as they resisted the constraints of a highly structured liturgical calendar.

The Lectionaries Today: the LM and RCL[8]

The Roman Sunday lectionary was the standard required of Roman Catholic communities up until the unveiling of the new Roman lectionary, the *Ordo Lectionum Missae* (Lectionary for Mass) following Vatican II. The LM introduced three innovations:

1. The cycle of readings shifts from one to three years, allowing many more biblical traditions to be engaged. This also allows for the semi-continuous reading of Matthew, Mark, and Luke, and some portions of the Old Testament.

2. An Old Testament lesson is included every week.

3. A psalm is also included among the weekly readings.

Paralleling this interest in liturgical renewal among Roman Catholics, an ecumenical body of Protestant denominations formed in the mid-1960s and were eventually named the Consultation on Common Texts (CCT). Included among this body's work (which eventually involved Roman Catholics), was ongoing conversation on the use of Scripture in worship, partly in response to the LM. Meanwhile, a number of North American churches produced adaptations of the LM for their own use in the 1970s. This marked a renewed interest in a lectionary cycle for several Protestant bodies.

Then, in 1983, the CCT produced the Common Lectionary, a harmonization and reworking of several of these Protestant adaptations of the LM,

---

8. I am focusing on the LM and RCL for the simple fact that within America they are by far the most commonly used lectionaries. However, many Orthodox communities continue to follow their own lectionaries, and as I noted above, many Christian communities in America do not follow any lectionary. I will have more to say in what follows about a recently developed lectionary, the Narrative Lectionary, that has been embraced by an increasing number of mainline congregations.

and finally the Revised Common Lectionary in 1992. In summary, the RCL is characterized by these features:

1. As with the LM, four biblical passages are featured every Sunday and other holy days: one each from the Old Testament, Psalms, epistles, and gospels.

2. Like the LM, the RCL contains a three-year cycle of readings (referred to as Years A, B, C), with Matthew, Mark, and Luke featured in successive years (in that order). John is integrated into each year.

3. For much of the year, the RCL also encourages congregations to read the Old Testament in light of the New Testament by often pairing what it considers a relevant OT text with the gospel lesson. But it features longer sections of the Old Testament to be read semi-continuously in the season after Pentecost. In doing so, the RCL encourages congregations to read the Old Testament lessons on their own terms, not just as a backdrop to the Gospel readings.

Benefits of the Lectionary

I stated above that the goal of the lectionaries most in use today—in conjunction with the church calendar—is to help believers remember and celebrate pivotal events in the story of God's people, focusing on God's work of salvation in Jesus, and to reflect on what it means to be faithful followers of Christ.

You really can't ask for a better objective than that! And I think that there are several notable advantages to using a lectionary for Sunday worship.[9]

First, committing to a regular schedule of readings that draws widely from the biblical canon prevents pastors and communities from focusing only on a select group of favorite texts. It also encourages communities to engage the Old Testament traditions, which is something that the church throughout its history has not done all that faithfully. In short, lectionaries can reduce our tendency to be overly selective in our reading of Scripture.

---

9. The LM and RCL also include daily lectionaries, and some communities that use these lectionaries encourage members to read through the daily lessons. But in practice, most communities using the lectionary do not actively encourage members to attend to the daily readings, and very few of their members do. For this reason, my discussion of the benefits and disadvantages of the lectionary will focus on the use of the lectionary for weekly worship.

Second, the correspondences between Scripture lessons, liturgy, hymnody, and the church year can facilitate powerful, richly textured, experiential encounters with the pivotal events in the story of God's people and God's work of salvation in Jesus. These elements can work together to draw us into the story of our faith in ways that capture both the head and the heart, and encourage a rhythm to our lives that enacts the patterns of our sacred story. As stated eloquently in the *Handbook for the Common Lectionary*,

> Recalling the events, covenants, and promises in the story of God-with-us enables us to appropriate them for the present moment and be continually transformed by them. These stories across time endlessly rewrite and redirect our past-present-future life.[10]

The corporate nature of this experience can also strengthen the identity, ministry, and witness of Christian communities.

Similarly, church-related publishing houses produce numerous resources coordinated with the lectionary and the church year. These include scholarly commentaries, preaching aids, Sunday school materials, adult study materials, liturgical guides and resources, planning calendars, coffee mugs . . . Okay, maybe not coffee mugs. But all of these resources can help gather an array of voices—prayers, hymns, the Scripture lessons, the sermon or homily, Sunday school activities, adult study groups—speaking to and celebrating a specific element of our sacred story on the same Sunday or holy day. Congregations and parishes that are intentional about coordinating such voices can enhance their calling to be a community gathered around the Word.

Fourth, sharing a common schedule of lessons provides opportunities for conversation between Christians from different churches and denominations about the texts they encounter in worship. Maybe I just have weird friends. But this really does happen, and it is pretty cool when it does.

Gosh. This all sounds great! So what's the problem with using a lectionary?!

Disadvantages and Distortions

Lectionaries are often employed with the best of intentions. To be sure, there are several notable advantages to their use. But as I stated above, they often lead pastors and congregations to treat the Bible in ways that do not honor

---

10. Bower, ed., *Handbook*, 20.

what kind of work it is and where it came from. Here we will consider five features of lectionaries that contribute to their problematic nature.

Prepackaged, Bite-Sized Portions

One of the major shortcomings of the LM and RCL is that they portion out bite-sized segments of Scripture that are relatively short in length, and in my view, often too short. The portioning provided by these lectionaries frequently undermines the literary function of a biblical narrative or epistle text. This is because we simply don't get to read enough of it to really make sense of what its author was getting at, or the role it was meant to play within its literary setting. Or, we only hear part of a story or only one episode when the biblical author intended us to hear the whole story or two or three episodes playing off one another. Lectionaries often unnecessarily limit our purview. They forces our lenses to become microscopes or telescopes, encouraging a circumscribed (monocular) field of view that blurs everything on the periphery.

One often has the impression that the primary criteria for selecting texts is what portion will fit along with three other readings within the setting of worship. While such practical issues are not irrelevant, we need to remember that they were not factors that the biblical authors had in mind when writing these texts! More on this in just a second.

The Old Testament as Backdrop

During nearly all of the church year with the LM, and much of the church year with the RCL, Old Testament lessons are selected thematically with no interest in continuity between texts from one Sunday to the next. With the RCL, this occurs during the first half of the church year, from Advent through Pentecost, when the Old Testament and psalm readings "are chosen for their commensurability with the Gospel reading."[11] Thus, the Old Testament readings are not engaged in a manner that would enable congregants to appreciate their function and setting within their own narratives. They are simply treated as backdrop for the New Testament lesson. This encourages them to be read with little to no interest in their own historical and literary contexts.

11. O'Day and Hackett, *Preaching*, 31.

Semi-, Semi-, Semicontinuous Readings of Biblical Traditions

The RCL and LM do provide "semicontinuous" readings of the Gospels and epistles at times, and the RCL attempts this with the Old Testament lessons in the season after Pentecost. Yet the emphasis needs to be on the very "semicontinuous" nature of these schedules. Some proponents of the RCL fail to acknowledge the discontinuous nature of the "semicontinuous" readings the lectionary provides. Consider this statement from the *Handbook for the Common Lectionary*:

> A close cousin to continuous reading is the method of "semicontinuous reading," which moves through a biblical book, section by section, but skips over passages regarded as less important (e.g., genealogies or lists of kings).[12]

This statement is misleading and deeply troubling. The semicontinuous readings provided by the RCL and LM are actually very *distant* cousins (many times removed!) to the continuous reading common in the early church. If you take a careful look at the RCL and LM lectionary schedules, you will readily see that their semicontinuous readings are often interrupted and frequently skip over major portions of the biblical books they engage. For example, consider these two sequences from the RCL that are regarded as "semicontinuous."

The first sequence focuses on the book of Exodus cycle during the 12th–19th Sundays after Pentecost in Year A.

12th Sunday After Pentecost	Exodus 1:8–2:10
13th Sunday After Pentecost	Exodus 3:1–15
14th Sunday After Pentecost	Exodus 12:1–14
15th Sunday After Pentecost	Exodus 14:19–31
16th Sunday After Pentecost	Exodus 16:2–15
17th Sunday After Pentecost	Exodus 17:1–7
18th Sunday After Pentecost	Exodus 20:1–4, 7-9, 12–20
19th Sunday After Pentecost	Exodus 32:1–14

This sequence does not include any interruptions during which other Old Testament texts are explored. But note how much material is missing and the giant gaps between passages! The exodus story is commonly regarded by both Jewish and Christian theologians as one of the landmark, pivotal moments in all of Scripture. But when the RCL supposedly focuses

12. Bower, ed., *Handbook*, 17.

in on the Israelite's oppression under the Pharaohs and exodus from Egypt (Exod 1:1–15:27), and the crucial events to follow (Exod 16:1–40:38), it only provides a passing glance. By my count, this cycle of readings from Exodus includes 117 verses. The book of Exodus contains 1,213 verses.[13] The RCL's "semicontinuous" reading of Exodus leads us through less than 10 percent of this important narrative.

The second example comes from the RCL's semi-continuous reading of the Gospel of Mark in the season after Pentecost of Year B.

2nd Sunday After Pentecost	Mark 3:20–35
3rd Sunday After Pentecost	Mark 4:26–34
4th Sunday After Pentecost	Mark 4:35–41
5th Sunday After Pentecost	Mark 5:21–43
6th Sunday After Pentecost	Mark 6:1–13
7th Sunday After Pentecost	Mark 6:14–29
8th Sunday After Pentecost	Mark 6:30–34, 53–56
9th Sunday After Pentecost	John 6:1–21
10th Sunday After Pentecost	John 6:24–35
11th Sunday After Pentecost	John 6:35, 41–51
12th Sunday After Pentecost	John 6:51–58
13th Sunday After Pentecost	John 6:56–69
14th Sunday After Pentecost	Mark 7:1–8, 14–15, 21–23
15th Sunday After Pentecost	Mark 7:24–37
16th Sunday After Pentecost	Mark 8:27–38
17th Sunday After Pentecost	Mark 9:30–37
18th Sunday After Pentecost	Mark 9:38–50
19th Sunday After Pentecost	Mark 10:2–16
20th Sunday After Pentecost	Mark 10:17–31
21st Sunday After Pentecost	Mark 10:35–45
22nd Sunday After Pentecost	Mark 10:46–52
23rd Sunday After Pentecost	Mark 12:28–34
24th Sunday After Pentecost	Mark 12:38–44
25th Sunday After Pentecost	Mark 13:1–8

13. https://catholic-resources.org/Bible/OT-Statistics-NAB.htm

As we can readily see, this semicontinuous reading provides a more robust engagement of the Gospel of Mark than occurs with Exodus. But even so, this cycle focused on Mark only engages 232 out of that Gospel's 1,071 total verses.[14] That is just over 20 percent of Mark.[15] There are several other features of this semicontinuous reading that work against engaging the text as it was meant to be encountered. Not only does the cycle frequently skip over passages, most of which are critically important to the flow and development of Mark's narrative, it also starts the cycle towards the end of Mark 3, and stops at the beginning of Mark 13. In doing so, this reading of Mark is devoid of Mark's opening and closing chapters![16]

Also, because the lectionary is a three-year cycle, and features either the Gospels of Mark, Matthew, or Luke in each of those years, John needs to be worked in at various points of the church year. This not only leads to a very disjointed encounter with John's narrative, it also results in interruptions to the cycles featuring the other Gospels. As we see here with Mark, this semicontinuous reading takes a five-week detour into John. These same shortcomings apply to the semicontinuous readings both the LM and RCL provide for the epistle texts. These schedules likewise skip over passages integral to the letters and only engage a small fraction of their material.

A deeply troubling component of the *Handbook for the Revised Common Lectionary*'s description of the semicontinuous reading provided by the RCL is the admission that the lectionary "skips over passages regarded as less important (e.g., genealogies or lists of kings)." But these "less important" (did they actually say that?) passages that are skipped over include volumes of material other than genealogies and lists of kings (which, by the way, often communicate an important theological idea). This statement simply, though sadly, helps me make my point: the lectionary leads believers to think that the biblical passages not featured in the schedule are somehow less important.

Ugh.

14. https://catholic-resources.org/Bible/NT-Statistics-Greek.htm

15. The percentages related to the content of Matthew and Luke are significantly lower, since each of those Gospels are much longer than Mark but covered in almost the same number of Sundays.

16. Similarly, the reading of Matthew in Year A spans Matthew 9–23, and Year C spans Luke 8–23. This is partly, but not wholly, the result of the lectionary and church year featuring Jesus' passion and resurrection during Lent and Easter, and the infancy narratives of Luke and Matthew during Advent, Christmas, and Epiphany.

Misreading Scripture

Bite-sizing Scripture, reading the OT traditions out of context, the not-so-semicontinuous readings of biblical books. Why are these three shortcomings such a big deal?

First, the obvious. One of the objectives of the lectionary is to prevent Christian communities from being overly selective in their use of Scripture. But the lectionary, in reality, actually encourages believers to be selective in their use of Scripture and—even worse—encourages them to ignore or even denigrate portions which they do not read. This is not good.

But also consider this.

Think of your favorite book or movie. Imagine what your experience of that story (fiction or nonfiction) would have been like had you randomly and regularly skipped over pages in the course of your reading, or scenes in the course of your viewing. Would the story have made much sense to you? Sure, you still may have been able to stitch together a rough outline of the main plotlines and characters, but would you be reading the narrative or experiencing the film as its author or screenwriter intended? Just as important, would that story have impacted you in the same way, or even at all?

Most of the Bible is narrative. Most of its works are meant to be read that way—continuously—as a story. The epistles of the New Testament are not narratives, but most are sustained arguments or appeals whose sections build on one another. They are like persuasive essays rooted in specific historical contexts. And they are meant to be read that way—continuously. The earliest Christians knew this, and that is why they often read their Scriptures this way—continuously. We *might* be able to read *some* psalms, proverbs, and segments of the prophets in some degree of isolation from their surrounding literary contexts and still honor their character and intent, but not much else. At least not the way they were intended to be read or heard.

Yet the portioning and scheduling of readings provided by both the RCL and LM work against sustaining narrative or rhetorical continuity from Sunday to Sunday. And incredibly, the framers of the RCL actually encourage reading texts in isolation from one another. In their introduction to the RCL, the Consultation on Common Texts states, "In the opening verses of readings . . . the reader should omit initial conjunctions that refer only to what has preceded."[17] In other words, don't confuse people by letting

---

17. This statement is cited on "Frequently Asked Questions" page of the Vanderbilt University site dedicated to the RCL, under the heading: "What about those scripture verses that open with confusing references, or clearly need prefacing?" https://lectionary.library.vanderbilt.edu/faq2.php.

them know that the text you are reading is inextricably connected to what comes before it!

Exacerbating this problem is the reality of how many congregations commonly make use of the lectionary schedule. Many congregations don't always read every assigned lesson every Sunday. Moreover, denominational resources often focus on a particular lectionary text, encouraging clergy and congregations to toggle back and forth between the OT, epistle, and Gospel lessons for reading and/or preaching, or pastors and priests simply do that on their own. As a result, most congregations and parishes engage the very semicontinuous schedule provided by the lectionary in a very semicontinuous way. The semicontinuous schedule provided by these lectionaries is challenging enough, and then the manner in which that schedule is actually engaged by most communities makes any degree of continuity extremely difficult to maintain.

So, as a result, both the LM and the RCL, along with the preaching/ worship resources aligned with them, encourage an "atomistic" approach to the biblical traditions. That is, the lectionaries encourage clergy and laity to approach biblical texts as if they are self-contained, individual "lessons of faith" that can be faithfully engaged apart from their literary and historical contexts. And so that is what clergy and congregations often do.

And, as we saw in Chapter 1, that is a very bad way to read Scripture. It is kind of like turning Scripture into a quote-of-the-day calendar. It's like channel surfing. It's like the passage read this weird way makes so little sense that the preacher or homilist is simply left to fill the void. Not only does the lectionary limit our access to much of the content of Scripture, in doing so it also short-circuits our ability to read Scripture well.

In prepackaging and processing Scripture into bite-sized, individual portions, these lectionaries facilitate biblical malnourishment. And we wonder why people zone out when Scripture is read in worship, and why biblical illiteracy is so prevalent.

Hang in there. We still have two additional shortcomings of lectionaries to address.

Dicing and Splicing Texts

In the spirit of transparency, I should let you know that this feature of the lectionary is the one I find most troubling. I will do my best to remain calm.

You may have noticed when reviewing the above cycles of readings from Exodus and Mark above, or from your own experience using a lectionary, that it is not uncommon for the lectionary to remove select verses from a scheduled reading. The lectionary will dice and splice texts.

For folks who are sensitive to and appreciate how biblical passages function as theologically charged and artistically composed literature, the lectionary's tendency to dice and splice biblical texts is simply maddening.

Could you imagine doing this to any other form of literary or artistic expression composed by someone else and thinking that was ok? Take Martin Luther King's "Letter from a Birmingham Jail." Let's knock out that paragraph here, another there. Oh, those sentences are not really needed, let's get rid of those too. There we go, that reads much better now, and it will take less time . . . wait a minute, that whole section is really superfluous and overly contentious. There we go . . . delete . . . delete . . . delete. Perfect! Or how about that Mary Oliver poem. I really don't get the redundancy going on there between those lines. Let's tidy that up a bit, shall we? And that one phrase is more than a bit edgy. Cripes, Mary—we can do without that! That Monet! A bit gaudy, don't you think? Let's tone down those colors, and paint over some of those swirly things, and make it look a little more lifelike. Ah, yes. Much better.

Simply criminal behavior. Maybe not a felony but at least a misdemeanor. And simply wrong.

The omission of verses in the passages featured by the lectionary does not receive much attention in resources developed to guide its use. One exception to this is the explanation provided in the second edition of the "General Introduction to the Liturgy" produced by the Sacred Congregation for the Sacraments and Divine Worship of the Roman Catholic Church.

> 77. The omission of verses in readings from Scripture has at times been the tradition of many liturgies, including the Roman liturgy. Admittedly such omissions may not be made lightly, for fear of distorting the meaning of the text or the intent and style of Scripture. Yet on pastoral grounds it was decided to continue the traditional practice in the present Order of Readings, but at the same time to ensure that the essential meaning of the text remained intact. One reason for the decision is that otherwise some texts would have been unduly long. It would also have been necessary to omit completely certain readings of high spiritual value for the faithful because those readings include some verse that is pastorally less useful or that involves truly difficult questions.[18]

18. The liturgical guidelines produced by Rome can be found on numerous sites, but is here taken from http://www.catholicliturgy.com/index.cfm/FuseAction/documentText/Index/2/SubIndex/11/ContentIndex/134/Start/126.

This explanation begins by admitting to the problematic nature of what has become the traditional practice of omitting verses from readings: "for fear of distorting the meaning of the text or the intent and style of Scripture." Amen!

Yet the statement then goes on to summarize its rationale for nevertheless continuing the traditional practice of dicing and splicing on "pastoral grounds." Those pastoral grounds include two main concerns: to prevent readings that are "unduly long." And to maintain use of readings of "high spiritual value" despite the fact that they contain "less useful" or problematic statements within them that could lead to "truly difficult questions." But, the statement explains, all of this can be done while ensuring that the "essential meaning of the text remains intact."

What Does "Essential Meaning" Mean?

The assurance that one can remove from a biblical text some of its content and still retain its "essential meaning" is highly dubious. As short as most passages featured in the lectionary are, a removal of several verses usually constitutes a significant reduction in material. I would argue that in most cases the eliminated material plays a critical role in enacting the intentions of its author. Once you are reading an abridgement of a passage, you can't honestly say that you are reading the actual passage. The "essential meaning" of the original is compromised.

And if a portion of a passage is difficult for us to understand, that is usually a pretty good indication that we are also not comprehending the "essential meaning" of that passage! We are simply covering up the problem without seriously exploring a solution. In this case, "essential meaning" really means what the framers of the lectionary want a passage to mean, or at least what they don't want it to mean. Jesus wouldn't have really said that! God wouldn't have meant (or done) that! So, remove the verses. Eliminate the theological dissonance and the chance that the impressionable faithful might misunderstand or be scandalized by what they hear.

This comes pretty close to censorship (I told you it was criminal). Please consider this as well.

It is of course important for us to do the best we can to discern what a passage "means." But the longer I study Scripture, the more it becomes apparent to me that, as with all profound and powerful literature, its "meaning" is a rather multifaceted phenomenon. Scripture doesn't just "mean," it also compels and transforms. It impacts not just the head, but also the heart.

It does not simply appeal to our reason and cognition (what the Greeks called "logos"), but also our emotion ("pathos" and "ethos").[19]

How Scripture does that, how it engages readers on all of those levels, is through its literary artistry. It is not just *what* Scripture says that makes it a powerful medium for our encounter with God. It is *how* it says it—in ways that capture our imaginations and awaken in us our deepest and truest longings.

For those of us who understand Scripture in this way, and treasure its remarkable ability to capture our heads and hearts, it is especially painful to see biblical texts subjected to such brutish dicing and splicing, as if we should make our encounter with them as convenient and simplistic as possible. The medium of Scripture's profound message on who God is and what it means to be God's people is the way it frames, shapes, or narrates the saving acts of our Creator. Its literary artistry is the lifeblood of its transformative testimonies. When we start scissoring away at those testimonies, much that really matters flutters to the floor. It's like tossing pearls to pigs.

Some Examples

Here are some specific examples from the New Testament Gospels of how the LM and RCL dice and splice passages and the unfortunate implications of that practice. Then, considering the RCL's use of Psalm 139, we will take a more in-depth look at how dicing and splicing texts can lead us to neglect the heart and soul of a biblical text.

One of the most basic literary devices employed by the Gospel writers is called "bracketing," or "enveloping." This means that the Gospel writers intentionally create an ABA pattern with the material that they are presenting, with similar material/ideas (A) sandwiching other material (B). This can occur on a large scale, as when there are very similar elements at the beginning and close of a narrative. For example, scholars have long noted a preponderance of very similar elements in Luke's opening chapters and Luke 24, or the proclamation of Jesus as Emmanuel, "God with us" in Matthew 1:23 and 28:20. The intention of such bracketing in these instances is to emphasize central dimensions of Jesus' identity and saving work (A) as characteristic of his ministry as a whole (B). Scholars typically see this technique as underscoring essential contours of the evangelists' portrayals of Jesus.

On a smaller scale, enveloping often occurs within much shorter sections of the narrative. One common form of such enveloping in the Gospels is to take an account that would normally be relayed all at once, pull it apart,

---

19. See Kuhn, *Heart of Biblical Narrative.*

and insert another action or teaching into that opening. This technique is often employed by the evangelists to draw certain actions or teachings of Jesus into close relationship to one another, to present one episode or action in light of the other. Yet in several instances, the framers of the lectionary dice out the sandwiched material (B), and recombine the enveloping material (A). When they do this, they are clearly circumventing the narrative rhetoric of the evangelists. For example:

First Sunday of Advent (LM): Luke 21:25–28, 34–36

Jesus interrupts his teaching on the return of the Son of Man with the parable of the fig tree.

For some reason, the LM omits this parable from the lesson, while the RCL includes it.

Sixth Sunday after Pentecost (RCL): Matthew 13:1–9, 18–23

Seventh Sunday after Pentecost (RCL): Matthew 13:24–30, 36–43

In both of these lessons, Jesus offers a parable and then an explanation of the parable. But the parable and explanation are separated by other teachings or parables. Here again, the insertion of intervening material was clearly intentional on the part of Matthew. It was essential to his presentation of Jesus' teaching in this section and how he intended it to be engaged by his recipients. But the RCL eliminates the intervening material. The LM does not.

In numerous other instances, the LM and RCL remove material that may not have been inserted as part of the technique of enveloping but is clearly integral to the evangelist's presentation of episodes. One example among many is the handling of Luke 14:1–24 by both the LM and RCL. When engaging this passage, both lectionaries eliminate most of the episode and present the lesson as Luke 14:1, 7–14. This episode integrates a number of themes that are prominent throughout Luke's narrative: Jesus as healer, true Torah righteousness, Jesus' critique of the pursuit of wealth and honor, and Luke's claim that the choices we make on these everyday matters determine whether or not we embrace or reject the arrival of God's kingdom in Jesus. The flow of Luke's account, the occurrence of the teaching in the same temporal setting, and the use of the meal motif to tie it together (vv. 1, 8, 12, 15, 16, 24)—all this indicates that Luke composed 14:1–24 to be encountered as a unit. It is simply not reasonable to assert that we can set aside most of this episode, as do both the LM and RCL, and adequately capture the impact Luke intended it to have on its recipients.

This begs the question of why you wouldn't just go ahead and read all of 14:1–24? Isn't honoring the evangelist's intentions, and the benefits of fully engaging this account, worth an additional ninety seconds of our time?

A More In-depth Illustration: Psalm 139

There are several psalm types represented in the psalter, with the psalms of lament being the most common. A psalm of lament, as we saw back in the Introduction, is one in which the psalmist cries out to God for help while experiencing some situation of distress. These psalms typically contain reasons why God should respond, and often those reasons focus on God's care and love of the psalmist or Israel. They also typically include an expression of trust that God will respond. Psalms of confidence are ones in which the psalmist celebrates his or her trust in God due to God's unrelenting faithfulness and steadfast love. So, as we see, psalms of lament and psalms of confidence and trust have overlapping elements. In light of the reality that the psalter contains numerous examples of combined or hybrid forms, it should not surprise us that its collection of psalms would combine a psalm of confidence paired with a psalm of lament. That is what we have in Psalm 139.

Psalm 139 is an astonishing expression of trust, lament, and call for God to set the psalmist on the right path. It is a profound testimony to what it means to be righteous while facing injustice and oppression. It is, in my view, a masterpiece of biblically grounded, God-centered, authentic faith.

But, if you read the psalm as scheduled by the RCL, you will miss all of that.[20] In every instance in which the psalm occurs in the lectionary, the framers of the RCL don't include four verses of the psalm they apparently find troubling. These four verses are just as important as all the rest.

Please do me a favor. Get out your Bible, or look up Psalm 139 on your phone, and take a few minutes to read through it.

As you see, the bulk of the psalm, its first eighteen verses, contain an eloquent, moving celebration of God's intimate, ever-present care and concern for the psalmist. It's simply beautiful. Yet, as you read on, you also see that the psalmist's celebration of God's all-encompassing presence and care suddenly gives way to an outburst of bitter invective against his enemies, beginning with a call for God's vengeance (vv. 19–22).

---

20. The RCL features the psalm four times in the three-year cycle, listing it as Psalm 139:1–12, 23–24 in Year A and Psalm 139:1–6, 13–18 three times in Year B. The LM does not include Psalm 139 in the Sunday liturgy, though it assigns Psalm 139:1–13, 13–15 for the weekday celebration of the Nativity of St. John the Baptist.

O that you would kill the wicked, O God,
 And that the bloodthirsty would depart from me—
those who speak of you maliciously
 and lift themselves up against you for evil.
Do I not hate those who hate you, O LORD?
 and do I not loathe those who rise up against you?
I hate them with a perfect hatred;
 I count them my enemies.

Whoa. What just happened?

Without warning the psalmist interrupts his eloquent celebration of God's care with a bold demand for God's action that seems to fly in the face of conventional piety and who we are called to be as God's people. He calls on God to respond to the suffering caused by the "wicked" and "blood-thirsty," by annihilating them: "O, that you would kill the wicked, O God!" (v. 19).

To many, these words seem way out of place. They certainly do to the framers of the RCL. But instead of wrestling with the apparent disjunction these verses create, instead of taking the time to engage this psalm deeply and call others to do the same, they simply cut these troubling verses out. No reason to trouble ourselves with the "difficult questions" these verses raise!

But in sidelining these four verses, the RCL rips out the heart and soul of this psalm. What is left is still pretty darn eloquent and profound, but it is not the psalm that the psalmist wrote, that others preserved and passed down, and scores of Jews and Christians have turned to in dark and troubling times. The abridged version pales in comparison to the original. Much is lost.

One of the main purposes of the lament psalms like Psalm 139 (see also Psalms 109 and 137) is to teach believers that even their deepest and darkest thoughts are to be brought before God. And not just brought before God, but *turned over to God*. Notice how Psalm 139 reveals this as the psalmist's motivation. The psalmist opens with the proclamation that he or she is intimately known by God (vv. 1–6). This is followed by the psalmist's celebration of God's unyielding presence and another section which traces God's knowledge of the psalmist to the psalmist's very creation in the womb (vv. 7–18). All of this, all this rejoicing in God's knowledge of and presence with the psalmist, then suddenly leads to the disturbing plea to wipe out the wicked and bloodthirsty. The sudden appearance of this curse is jarring; its focus on vengeance seems completely unrelated to what has just preceded. But reading on, we see that this raw outburst does fit, and fits very well. Note what the psalmist says next, after his call for God's vengeance, to conclude the Psalm (vv. 23–24):

> Search me, O God, and know my heart;
>   test me and know my thoughts.
> See if there is any wicked way within me,
>   and lead me in the way everlasting.

What the psalmist does in Psalm 139 is just what the psalms of lament teach all believers to do: to dare to bring before God their deepest struggles, fears, and even feelings of hatred—to lay them there before God, and then to say, "Okay, God, here it is. I've laid it all before you. Now, search me and know my heart, test me and know my thoughts, see if there is any wickedness in me, and if so, lead *me* in *your* ways." The psalmist knows that he is known by God. The psalmist knows that God is with him and desires abundant life for him. And because of this trust that God is truly by his side in good times and in bad, the psalmist dares to speak even these unsettling words to God. She offers God her darkest thoughts. She gives these thoughts over to God, she *relinquishes* them to God, and asks God to guide her in *God's* ways of justice and mercy.

But without vv. 19–22, we lose all that. We eliminate the elements of lament, anger, and cursing. We misrepresent the form and focus of the psalm. We also short-circuit the psalm's essential logic. Note that without vv. 19–22, vv. 23–24 seem just as out of place, and simply make no sense! In dicing out the verses they find troubling, the framers of the RCL lead congregations to miss elements of the psalm that are certainly integral to its "essential meaning."

And in doing so, in reading the Bible so badly, they also miss an opportunity to discern and bear witness to a critical component of righteousness that is sorely needed in our nation today. Indeed, we are called to name and respond to the injustice and evil perpetrated by others. But as we do this important work, we are also called to bring our anger before and *to* God. We are to ask God to help us discern the evil and injustice that resides within and warps *our own* hearts and thoughts, and instead lead us in the way of faithfulness.

Avoiding "Problem Texts"

A final, troubling feature of the lectionary is its avoidance of whole passages that are deemed problematic or offensive. This practice is pervasive among the framers of the LM and RCL.

That Scripture contains passages which many Jews and Christians find disturbing was noted in chapter 2. As we saw, there are some scary passages in the Bible, in which actions are attributed to characters and to God that may challenge our conceptions of who God is what it means to be God's people. The RCL and LM both steer clear of most of these passages, including:

- God commands genocide (Josh 11:16–20)

- God appeased by human sacrifice (2 Sam 21:1–4)

- God incites David to sin, and David sacrifices others to save himself (2 Sam 24:1–17)

- Elijah slays the prophets of Baal (1 Kgs 18:40)

- God kills Ananias and Sapphira (Acts 5:1–11)

- In addition to these, the RCL does not include the household codes of Ephesians 5:21–33 and Colossians 3:18–4:1, which stress the subservient place of slaves and women.

- Passages revealing disagreements among early Christians are also generally not included by the RCL, such as the controversy over the integration of Gentile believers (Acts 15:1–35), the argument between Peter and Paul over table fellowship (Gal 2:11–14), the argument between Paul and Barnabas over John Mark and their separation (Acts 15:36–41), and the early church's conflict over distribution of resources (Acts 6:1–6). The LM includes portions of Acts 15:1–35 and Acts 6:1–6, but not Acts 15:36–41 or Galatians 2:11–14.

If one of the goals of the LM and RCL is to provide a sanitized encounter with the Bible, then they have been largely successful. But this success comes with a cost. By removing such problem texts from our reading of Scripture, we miss the opportunity to have thoughtful, mature conversations on the character of Scripture. These sanitized encounters with Scripture are also dishonest. When exploring some of these scary or contentious passages in my classes or in adult education settings, I repeatedly hear from students, "I never knew that was in the Bible!" Students are not happy when they realize that their church has hidden these passages from them. They resent it.

Surviving the RCL and LM

As I noted above, the lectionary does offer several advantages. It can guard against some degree of selectivity, it is coordinated with the church year, there are a wealth of liturgical and homiletic resources developed for the common texts, and there is value in having Christian communities from a wide array of traditions gathered around the same readings.

But, on the whole, the lectionary, I think, does much more harm than good. It leads too many communities to read the Bible badly too much of the time.

The reality, however, is that many Christian communities, pastors, and layfolk will continue to use the RCL and LM for decades and even centuries to come. Some won't have a choice. Some that do have a choice will nevertheless discern that eliminating its use will be too disruptive for their particular communities. For pastors, priests, and Bible study leaders in these situations, I offer the following suggestions:

1. Be conscientious of and counteract the tendencies encouraged by lectionaries to treat texts in isolation.

   • Take the time to explain how a particular passage is related to its literary and historical context: be sure that congregants know that the passage is part of a larger whole, and how.

   • Don't follow the lectionary's tendency to read only a short portion of what is clearly a larger passage. Determining the extent of a "passage" can be tricky at times. But remember that truncating what is clearly a narrative episode, an epistolary subunit, psalm, or prophetic oracle often violates and skews the literary and rhetorical integrity of that passage. If in doubt, read more.

2. There is no legitimate reason to dice and splice a biblical passage. It is simply a misrepresentation of that biblical text and undermines its ability to engage both the head and heart of those hearing it. It also leads preachers, bible study leaders, or devotional writers to privilege the verses that have been retained and marginalize those left out. In most cases, splicing and dicing really does lead us to misrepresent the "essential meaning" of a text.

3. Be conscientious of and resist the tendencies of lectionaries to sanitize our encounter with Scripture. While it is natural for communities to gravitate towards certain portions of our shared tradition, and privilege certain texts, there is real value in engaging the "darker" elements of our biblical tradition. It helps us to recognize the struggles of those who composed our sacred traditions, and awakens us to the realization that Scripture may not be best described as the "inerrant word of God." Instead, such passages can help us better appreciate the nature of Scripture as *a gathering of our ancestors' testimonies to God, God's*

steadfast love, and God's salvation, as shaped not only by God's inspira-tion but also by their own limitations and prejudices. Addressing the darker side of the biblical texts can lead us to a more authentic encoun-ter with our tradition and our ancestors in faith. Let's be more honest with our use of Scripture.

4. Take a break from the Lectionary for a portion of the church year, and focus in on an entire epistle, or a major segment of OT narrative (e.g., patriarchal and matriarchal stories in Genesis; the exodus; Elijah/Eli-sha cycle in 1 Kings, etc.), and read it continuously, as was common in the early church. Try a series on the Psalms, or the scary texts of the Bible, or on some other segment of Scripture that may speak anew to the needs of the congregation.

5. Similarly, don't feel so beholden to the lectionary that you are reluctant to set it aside in order to speak thoughtfully and pastorally to a crisis that arises within our nation or your community. The lectionary serves the church, the church does not serve the lectionary.

6. Don't feel the need to read through all of the lectionary texts for an as-signed Sunday. It is better to focus on fewer, or even one, and do it well, than to rifle through all in a cursory fashion. Explore creative mediums for engaging longer texts, such as a dramatic reading or reenactment.

7. If possible, consider the recently developed "Narrative Lectionary." [21] Launched in 2010 by Rolf Jacobson and Craig Koester of Luther Seminary, this lectionary offers a more robust semicontinuous reading of the gospels than the RCL and LM. The NL also features a four-year cycle that leads congregations through the major developments of the biblical story more clearly and effectively than the RCL and LM. Ac-cording to its website, these texts "are arranged in a narrative sequence to help people see Scripture as a story that has coherence and a dy-namic movement." Each year of the cycle follows this pattern:

   a. From September to mid-December the main preaching texts be-gin with the early chapters of Genesis, move through the stories of Israel's early history, the exodus, the kings, prophets, exile, and return.

   b. From Christmas to Easter there is sustained reading of one of the four Gospels.

21. For a helpful overview of the Narrative Lectionary, see the Working Preacher. org site dedicated to the NL: http://www.workingpreacher.org/narrative_faqs.aspx.

   c. From Easter to Pentecost the texts are chosen from Acts and Paul's letters.

   d. During these months of the year, only two texts are selected for each Sunday, with one identified as the primary "preaching" text.

   e. During the summer months congregations are encouraged to feature a sermon series on a biblical book or another topic.

I think the strengths of the NL are its narrative approach to the Old Testament traditions, its more robust reading of the Gospels, and its encouragement for congregations to feature a sermon series in the summer months, during which a more continuous reading of an epistle could be explored. At the same time, the NL is still subject to some of the shortcomings we find with the RCL and LM. Its semicontinuous reading of the Gospels, while more comprehensive, still leaves out much material. Its selections from Acts and the epistles only engage a handful of texts from each of those works. Like the RCL and LM, the NL also unnecessarily shortens texts, and at times (though far less often) will dice and splice them. In summary, I think the NL is still problematic, but less so than the RCL and LM.

Briefly Considering an Alternative

To be sure, any engagement of the Bible, especially during Sunday worship, is necessarily reductionistic. We simply cannot read all of Scripture with undivided attention through the course of our Sunday gatherings. There is also value, I think, in a church year that leads us through and celebrates the landmark events of our faith. But is there an alternative that is better than the options available to us?

Essentials

In my mind, in order for a schedule of readings, a strategy for engaging the Bible, a lectionary, not to do more harm than good, it must

1. offer as much *lecto continua* (continuous reading) or robust semicontinuous reading as possible;

2. enable communities to engage passages of Scripture as they were meant to be; this entails appreciating and safeguarding the literary integrity of biblical passages;

3. still be oriented around the major elements of the church year: Advent, Christmas, Epiphany, Lent, Easter, Pentecost;

4. take a narrative approach the scriptural tradition that celebrates and explores the landmark events of our sacred story;

5. be honest about the true nature of Scripture, including its scary parts;

6. be flexible enough to address the needs and contexts of individual congregations.

Scheduling Scripture

As I see it, the best way to accomplish these essential objectives is to combine two cycles for our reading of Scripture in worship. One of these cycles would direct our reading of the Gospels and be oriented around the celebration of Advent, Christmas, Epiphany, Lent, Easter, and Pentecost. This would be a four-year cycle, with one of the Gospels featured in each of those years (as we currently see in the NL). A seven-year cycle would then guide our encounter of Scripture during the season after Pentecost. This cycle would include the opportunity for much more robust semicontinuous readings of Acts, Old Testament traditions, and continuous readings of some of the epistles. This seven-year cycle would also provide congregations space to explore elements of biblical tradition that are particularly relevant for their times and places. In doing so, this schedule would be less problematic than the current schedules provided by the LM and RCL, and more intentionally reclaim two characteristic features in the way our ancestors in the faith utilized their sacred traditions: continuous reading and flexibility.

To see what this could look like, check out the appendix for a mock-up of these four-year and seven-year cycles.

Reflection and Discussion Questions

1. Do the benefits of lectionaries outweigh their disadvantages? Should churches abandon the use of lectionaries?

2. For Christian communities which do not use a lectionary, what principles should guide their selection and use of Scripture in worship?

3. How do you understand the relationship between the literary artistry and essential meaning of biblical passages?

CHAPTER FIVE

Reading the Bible into Stone and Neglecting the Foundation of True Torah

STONE IS PRETTY IMPORTANT to the Christian tradition. We call God our rock. God inscribes the ten commandments in stone, not once but twice. God presents those commandments to Moses while the latter stands on a very big rock that reaches into the heavens: Mount Sinai (or Mt. Horeb). The Temple walls are made, and remade, of stone upon stone, and are unmade until no stone is left upon another. Jesus' teachings are the solid rock upon which believers must build. Jesus names Simon "Rock" to signal that Peter and his fellow disciples are to be the ones to carry on his ministry of making the kingdom real in their midst. Jesus himself is both the cornerstone and the stumbling block.

That's a lot of stone talk.

This makes good sense. We associate stone with stability and permanence and even the ground beneath our feet. So the biblical writers use it as an image to identify what they find most true about God and what it means to be God's people. It is a very useful and powerful metaphor to express the elemental (pardon the pun) features of our faith and to depict foundational (again, sorry) moments of our sacred story.

But within the biblical tradition, stone can also convey destruction and death. The psalmist calls for the children of those hateful Babylonians to be dashed against the rocks. Violators of the law are to be stoned until they breathe no more, though more often we see stones hailing down onto the righteous. Jeremiah is left to languish in a well. Jesus says that it would be better for those who lead the faithful astray to have been rocketed to watery depths with a millstone bound to their necks before they had the

134

chance. And it was a stone that for the better part of two agonizing days sealed Jesus' tomb.

Within our tradition, stone signals a solid place on which to stand, that which is enduring and true. But stone can also signal when something about us has gone very wrong, when we have neglected, even sought to destroy, what is enduring and true.

For this reason, I think stone is a particularly apt metaphor to use for talking about how we understand and make use of God's Torah, or instruction.

God's Torah is foundational. It is fundamental to how we see ourselves and our responsibilities in relation to God and others. But it has also been easy for us to lose sight of the true nature of God's Torah, and how it is meant to serve as the bedrock of faith. At times, we have turned the living, breathing, dynamic instruction of God into something that is cold, hard, and even deadly.

The Nature of Torah in the Old Testament

The Meanings of "Torah"

The Hebrew word *torah* can have at least three distinct, though related, meanings in relation to sacred tradition. Most literally, it means "law." In this sense the word refers to the legal codes embodied in Israel's Scriptures. Similarly, it later came to refer to a much broader body of legal tradition that developed within Judaism, the Oral Torah, which is now codified in the Mishna and other Rabbinic writings. Israelites also used *torah* to refer to the traditions associated with Moses, the first five books of the Israelite Scriptures or Old Testament, also commonly called the Pentateuch. Hence, the "Law of Moses" indicates Genesis, Exodus, Leviticus, Numbers, and Deuteronomy. These books contain nearly all of the legal tradition within the Old Testament, and so their designation as *torah* seems appropriate to many. However, since these books are actually comprised mostly of narrative, a number of modern scholars have suggested that *torah* is often better translated as "instruction" rather than more narrowly as "law." This translation recognizes that the stories of the Pentateuch, and all the biblical traditions, are meant to be just as instructive as the legal codes. They also provide the narrative context within which the purpose of the legal material is to be understood.

The Purpose and Importance of God's Torah

The translation of *torah* as "instruction," in the minds of many, also helps to capture what is most central about God's Torah: it is meant to be *transformative*. Torah does not simply consist of legal codes that the Israelites are to follow as obedient supplicants. Recall the psalmist's plea that we encountered in the introduction from Psalm 25: "Make me to know your ways, O Lord, teach me your paths!" (v. 4). Torah, embodied in commands and story, song and oracle, is to mold the mind and the heart. It is to shape Israel into a people whose lives reflect the ways and will of the Creator of the universe. It is to teach Israel what it means for them, and all of humanity, to live in right relationship with God, one another, and the rest of creation.

And this, from an Israelite perspective, is the essence of what it means to live. For this reason, numerous traditions within the Israelite Scriptures, or Old Testament, associate Torah with life itself. Among the most eloquent is Psalm 1.[1]

> [1] Happy are those
>   who do not follow the advice of the wicked,
> or take the path that sinners tread,
>   or sit in the seat of scoffers;
> [2] but their delight is in the Torah of the Lord,
>   and on his Torah they meditate day and night.
> [3] They are like trees
>   planted by streams of water,
> which yield their fruit in its season,
>   and their leaves do not wither.
> In all that they do, they prosper.
>
> [4] The wicked are not so,
>   but are like chaff that the wind drives away.
> [5] Therefore the wicked will not stand in the judgement,
>   nor sinners in the congregation of the righteous;
> [6] for the Lord watches over the way of the righteous,
>   but the way of the wicked will perish.

As we discussed in chapter 2, the notion that obedience to God's instruction is elemental to life and prosperity is integral to the Old Testament worldview. Nowhere is this more dramatically relayed in the books of Moses than in Deuteronomy. Here, Israel is on the verge of finally entering the promised land after a forty-year detour through the wilderness. But before

---

1. Translation from the NRSV, though I have taken the liberty of replacing the instances of "law" of v. 2 with "Torah."

they cross over, Moses brings them to a stop. He sits them down and reminds them of the importance of being faithful to God's Torah. He then proceeds to review all of the commandments with them, starting with the Decalogue (Ten Commandments).[2]

Both leading up to and after his lengthy review of God's commands, Moses repeatedly exhorts, even urges, the people to never forget that their prosperity in the land that God is granting them is wholly dependent on their faithfulness to Torah (see 4:1–40; 30:1–20). For example,

> [15]See, I have set before you today life and prosperity, death and adversity. [16]If you obey the commandments of the LORD your God that I am commanding you today, by loving the LORD your God, walking in his ways, and observing his commandments, decrees, and ordinances, then you shall live and become numerous, and the LORD your God will bless you in the land that you are entering to possess. [17]But if your heart turns away and you do not hear, but are led astray to bow down to other gods and serve them, [18]I declare to you today that you shall perish; you shall not live long in the land that you are crossing the Jordan to enter and possess. [19]I call heaven and earth to witness against you today that I have set before you life and death, blessings and curses. Choose life so that you and your descendants may live, [20]loving the LORD your God, obeying him, and holding fast to him; for that means life to you and length of days, so that you may live in the land that the LORD swore to give to your ancestors, to Abraham, to Isaac, and to Jacob. (30:15–20)

From the perspective of the Israelite Scriptures, God's instruction is meant to shape Israel into a people who love, trust, and hold fast to God, walking in God's ways as they together embrace God's gift of abundant provision. In short, Torah is to transform and guide Israel into a people who can truly live. Trust or mistrust in God and God's instruction really is a matter of life or death.

Two Essential Features of Torah in the Old Testament

At the outset of his instruction to the Israelites in Deuteronomy, Moses warns them:

---

2. For this reason, this tradition has been titled "Deuteronomy," for it consists of a second (deutero) giving of the law (nomos).

> You must neither add anything to what I command you nor
> take away anything from it, but keep the commandments of
> the LORD your God with which I am charging you (4:2).

Moses's words here certainly suggest that the entire Torah he received
from God is "written in stone." Since by now he has been carrying those
stone tablets through the wilderness for forty years, we can hardly blame
him. However, as we look more carefully at his enumeration of Torah in
the books ascribed to him and other Old Testament traditions, a more
complex picture emerges. In just a moment, we will examine two characteristic features of Torah as taught by Jesus that stand in tension with this
"all or nothing," or "written in stone" sentiment that Moses here conveys.
Jesus' teachings and actions reveals that there is a core and a periphery to
Torah, and that God's life-giving instruction to us is dynamic and reforming, especially with regard to the peripheral aspects of Torah. But we can
also see these same tendencies already reflected in the Old Testament's
portrayal of God's instruction.

A Core and Periphery

First, both major bodies of legal material in the books of Moses—that granted
at Sinai and embodied in Exodus and Leviticus, and that spoken in the plains
of Moab as recorded in Deuteronomy—suggest a "core and periphery" character to Torah. Both major bodies of legal tradition are prefaced by the Decalogue, the Ten Commandments. This arrangement provides a subtle but clear
indication that these ten commandments embody the essential principles of
God's Torah, of what it means to live in right relationship with:

> *God*
>
> You shall not devote yourselves to other gods (1st command)
>
> You shall not worship idols (2nd command)
>
> You shall not make wrongful use of Yahweh's name (3rd
> command)
>
> You shall honor the Sabbath and keep it holy (4th command)
>
> *One another*
>
> You shall honor the Sabbath and keep it holy (4th command)
>
> Honor your mother and father (5th command)
>
> You shall not murder (6th command)
>
> You shall not commit adultery (7th command)

You shall not steal (8th command)

You shall not bear false witness (9th command)

You shall not covet (10th command)

Creation

You shall honor the Sabbath and keep it holy (4th command)[3]

The rest of the laws that follow, then, are further elaborations of these essential, core commands. These laws govern and guide worship and the maintenance of the sanctuary, relations among Israelites and between Israelites and non-Israelites, and treatment of the land and animals. They detail and address numerous scenarios of how God's people may fail to rightly acknowledge God's sovereignty and holiness, or of how humans may bear false witness, steal, murder, covet, and otherwise neglect one another, or of how humans may fail to be wise stewards of the creation entrusted to their care. The two major bodies of legal tradition include essential commands and then elaboration, a core and then a periphery. This is not to say that the peripheral is unimportant from the perspective of the Old Testament writers. Far from it! But there is a distinction introduced here that later Israelites will draw on to call their fellow Israelites to greater faithfulness to Torah.

Among these are the prophets. To be sure, the failings of Israel that the prophets bemoan are many. But at the center of the prophets' critique of Israel is its betrayal of Yahweh by turning to other gods and its exploitation of its own people. We see this reflected in the historical accounts of Israel's monarchy and their prophetic adversaries, such as in the accounts of David (as we saw in chapter 3), and the infamous kings, Jeroboam and Ahab, among many others. Among their numerous faults, their betrayal of God and their oppression of their own people take center stage.

The writings of the prophets focus on these sins as well. The prophets often utilize poignant and powerful relational metaphors to dramatize Israel's betrayal of Yahweh, portraying Yahweh as the forsaken lover (Jer 2:1–3; Ezek 16:1–22), dishonored parent (e.g., Isa 1:2–3; Hos 11:1–7), and anguished vine-keeper (e.g., Isa 5:1–7; Jer 2:21). The prophets also frequently rail against the Israelites for their exploitation of one another. One common form of this critique is to condemn Israel for fulfilling its obligations to the

3. The fourth commandment regarding Sabbath responsibilities has implications for Israel's relationship with God, one another, and creation. The Sabbath rest is dedicated to God as a day to remember God's work in forming creation (Exodus) or Israel's deliverance from Egypt (Deuteronomy). Moreover, *all* within Israel, including children, slaves, aliens living among them, domesticated animals, and the land on which they dwell, are to take part in this day of rest.

temple and other aspects of cultic worship while neglecting its duty to live rightly with one another. For instance, the eighth-century-BCE prophet, Amos, delivers this scathing rebuke from God:

> [21] I hate, I despise your festivals,
>   and I take no delight in your solemn assemblies.
> [22] Even though you offer me your burnt-offerings and grain-offerings,
>   I will not accept them;
> and the offerings of well-being of your fatted animals
>   I will not look upon.
> [23] Take away from me the noise of your songs;
>   I will not listen to the melody of your harps.
> [24] But let justice roll down like waters,
>   and righteousness like an ever-flowing stream.

The eighth-century-BCE prophet, Micah, similarly castigates the people of Judah for their misplaced piety. In Micah 6, he depicts the Israelite elite responding to the charge of betrayal God has brought against them (6:1–5). Their (sarcastic?) offer to make things right with God (vv. 6–7) and God's response (v. 8) highlight their neglect of what matters most to God.

> [6] "With what shall I come before the LORD,
>   and bow myself before God on high?
> Shall I come before him with burnt-offerings,
>   with calves a year old?
> [7] Will the LORD be pleased with thousands of rams,
>   with tens of thousands of rivers of oil?
> Shall I give my firstborn for my transgression,
>   the fruit of my body for the sin of my soul?"
> [8] He has told you, O mortal, what is good;
>   and what does the LORD require of you
> but to do justice, and to love kindness,
>   and to walk humbly with your God!

It is important to recognize that temple worship was *not* unimportant to these and other prophets who offered very similar critiques. Quite the contrary. But these traditions, along with numerous stories from the Old Testament that do the same, consistently focus on devotion to Yahweh, and love of one another—or justice—as the defining markers of righteousness.[4]

---

4. For other examples of the prophetic critique of temple worship that is not paired with righteousness, and the focus on justice as elemental to God's Torah, see also Isa 1:10–17, Jer 6:16–21, and Mal 2:13–17; 3:1–7.

If love of God and love of others are not characteristic of Israel, nothing else its people do matter.

Dynamic and Reforming

Another feature of Torah that begins to emerge in the Old Testament is that Israel's understanding of God's instruction changes over time. As we compare Moses's initial articulation of God's commands given at Mount Sinai with those he relays as Israel prepares to enter Canaan years later on the plains of Moab, we can see that certain laws have changed.

Exodus 22:21–24	Deuteronomy 24:17–22
Commands not to oppress the resident alien, widow, or orphan.	Also includes instruction about not taking a widow's garment as a pledge and leaving remnants in the field for the alien, widow, and the orphan.

Exodus 23:1	Deuteronomy 19:16–21
Commands not to spread a false report or join hands with the wicked to act as a malicious witness.	Adds instruction on what to do with one who gives a false witness

Exodus 21:2–7	Deuteronomy 15:12–18
Seventh-year release applies only to male slaves, and specifically not to female slaves.	Seventh year release applies also to female slaves.

Exodus 21:2–6; 23:10–11	Deuteronomy 15:1–18	Leviticus 25
Commands that in the seventh year, slaves shall be set free and the land shall lie fallow.	Commands that in the seventh year remission of debts shall be granted and slaves set free.	Commands that in the seventh year, the land shall lie fallow; very detailed instruction on the redemption of ancestral lands in the fiftieth year (Jubilee).

To be sure, these changes are not staggering. But they are enough for us to see that as God's people prepare to enter a new stage of their lives, God's instruction for them undergoes adjustment.[5] As Old Testament scholar Terrence Fretheim explains,

5. To these could be added the several differences in the articulation of the

God's gift of the law is not drawn into a code, but remains integrated with the story of God's gracious activity in the ever-changing history of God's people. Law is always intersecting with life as it is, filled with contingency and change, with complexity and ambiguity . . . This means that new laws will be needed and older laws will need to be recast or set aside.[6]

Fretheim also points out that internal tensions and inconsistencies that we can now see between these laws were not "corrected" by the editors of the Pentateuchal tradition, nor by later editors of biblical traditions.

Rather, old and new remain side by side as a canonical witness to the process of unfolding law. Hence, *development of the law* is just as canonical as individual laws or the body of law as a whole.[7]

This last point is worth repeating. Development of the law, development of God's life-giving instruction to us on what it means to be God's people, is just as canonical, just as *biblical*, as the rest of God's Torah.

The Nature of Torah in the New Testament

The presentation of God's instruction in the Old Testament is at least suggestive if not indicative of two tendencies: to regard some parts of God's instruction as more elemental than others, and to treat God's instruction as dynamic and reforming. Within the New Testament, these elements of God's Torah are brought front and center in Jesus' teachings and the writings of others.

Jesus' Instruction: Dynamic and Reforming

In the Introduction, we considered Matthew 5:17–20 to illustrate the reality that Jesus interpreted Torah very differently than some of his contemporaries.

[17] "Do not think that I have come to abolish the law or the prophets; I have come not to abolish but to fulfil. [18]For truly I tell you, until heaven and earth pass away, not one letter, not one stroke of

---

Decalogue as they are found in Exodus 20:2–17 and Deuteronomy 5:6–21. Regarding these, Enns, (*Inspiration*, 87) states, "God seems perfectly willing to allow his law to be adjusted over time. Perhaps Israel, standing virtually on the brink of the promised land in Deuteronomy, needed to hear the fourth commandment a bit differently."

6. Fretheim, *Pentateuch*, 169.

7. Fretheim, *Pentateuch*, 169. See Brueggemann, *Old Testament*, 583–90.

a letter, will pass from the law until all is accomplished. [19]Therefore, whoever breaks one of the least of these commandments, and teaches others to do the same, will be called least in the kingdom of heaven; but whoever does them and teaches them will be called great in the kingdom of heaven. [20]For I tell you, unless your righteousness exceeds that of the scribes and Pharisees, you will never enter the kingdom of heaven."

Echoing Moses's warning not to add or subtract anything from God's law in Deuteronomy 4, Jesus here announces that he has not come to abolish "the law and the prophets" (referring to the Israelite Scriptures as a whole), but to fulfill them (v. 17). He adds that "not one letter, not one stroke of a letter will pass from the law until all is accomplished" (v. 18).

But, again, if we look carefully at what Jesus goes on to say, we realize that his opening words here are not to be understood as simplistically as they might at first seem. For Jesus immediately goes on to offer his own recasting of several Torah commands marked by the refrain: "You have heard it was said . . . but I tell you . . ." (5:21–48). Some of Jesus' reinterpretations simply amplify the underlying spirit of the particular law in view (e.g., the laws on murder, and adultery [vv. 21-30]).

"You have heard that it was said to those of ancient times, 'You shall not murder'; and 'whoever murders shall be liable to judgment.' But I say to you that if you are angry with a brother or sister, you will be liable to judgment; and if you insult a brother or sister, you will be liable to the council; and if you say, 'You fool,' you will be liable to the hell of fire.

"You have heard that it was said, 'You shall not commit adultery.' But I say to you that everyone who looks at a woman with lust has already committed adultery with her in his heart. If your right eye causes you to sin, tear it out and throw it away; it is better for you to lose one of your members than for your whole body to be thrown into hell. And if your right hand causes you to sin, cut it off and throw it away; it is better for you to lose one of your members than for your whole body to go into hell.

In broadening the purview of these laws to include behaviors and dispositions that might lead up to the physical acts of murder and adultery, Jesus is engaging in a manner of interpreting Torah that would likely not be unique among teachers of his time. The Pharisees are often caricatured by Christians as strict legalists who woodenly clung to every command of Torah. However, the dynamic development of legal tradition we find both in Old Testament traditions and in Rabbinic traditions from as early as the second century CE, strongly suggest that Israelite interpretation of Torah in Jesus' day was also likely quite dynamic and creative in its engagement with Mosaic law. As Walter Brueggemann explains, Jewish interpretive practice as reflected in the Israelite Scriptures and likely in Jesus' day is "(a) intransigently normative and yet enormously open to adaptation; and (b) has an uncompromising sovereign at its center, but with a capacity to attend in delicate ways to the detail of daily existence."[8]

The difference between Jesus and his fellow Israelite interpreters of Torah is not so much a matter of method. Both likely agreed on the fundamental principle and practice of Israelite interpretation that one is to allowed to—even directed to—recast laws so that they can apply to new times and places. This is known as the practice of "binding" and "loosing" Torah. But from the perspective of the Gospel writers, what Jesus and many of his fellow Israelite teachers did not agree on was the extent to which the commands of Torah could be recast, or "loosed."

For when Jesus takes up the Moses's commands on divorce (vv. 31–32; see Deut 24:1–4); oaths (vv. 33–37; see Lev 19:12; Num 30:2; Deut 23:21), compensation/retaliation (vv. 38–42; see Exod 21:24; Lev 24:20), and loving one's neighbor (vv. 43–48; see Lev 19:18; esp. Deut 23:6), he quite radically departs from the original meaning and intent of the laws as articulated by Moses. He essentially sets them aside:

> "It was also said, 'Whoever divorces his wife, let him give her a certificate of divorce.' But I say to you that anyone who divorces his wife, except on the ground of unchastity, causes her to commit adultery; and whoever marries a divorced woman commits adultery.

> "Again, you have heard that it was said to those of ancient times, 'You shall not swear falsely, but carry out the vows you have made to the Lord.' But I say to you, Do not swear at all, either by heaven, for it is the throne of God, or by the earth, for it is his footstool, or by Jerusalem, for it is the city of the great King. And do not swear by your head, for you cannot make one hair white or black. Let your word be 'Yes, Yes' or 'No, No'; anything more than this comes from the evil one.

> "You have heard that it was said, 'An eye for an eye and a tooth for a tooth.' But I say to you, Do not resist an evildoer. But if anyone strikes you on the right cheek, turn the other also; and if anyone wants to sue you and take your coat, give your cloak as well; and if anyone forces you to go one mile, go also the second

8. Brueggemann, *Old Testament*, 595.

mile. Give to everyone who begs from you, and do not refuse anyone who wants to borrow from you.

"You have heard that it was said, 'You shall love your neighbor and hate your enemy.' But I say to you, Love your enemies and pray for those who persecute you, so that you may be children of your Father in heaven; for he makes his sun rise on the evil and on the good, and sends rain on the righteous and on the unrighteous. For if you love those who love you, what reward do you have? Do not even the tax collectors do the same? And if you greet only your brothers and sisters, what more are you doing than others? Do not even the Gentiles do the same? Be perfect, therefore, as your heavenly Father is perfect.

Another example is also instructive. The controversy dialogue of Mark 7:1–23 begins with the Pharisees criticizing Jesus because his disciples were eating with defiled (unwashed) hands (vv. 1–5). Jesus responds by noting the Pharisee's own inconsistency in following Torah (vv. 6–13). Then, in his instruction to the crowd, Jesus teaches that "there is nothing outside a person that by going in can defile, but the things that come out are what defile" (vv. 14–15). When elaborating on this extraordinary teaching with his disciples, Jesus repeats this statement, using gastrointestinal illustrations to drive home the point (vv. 17–19)! Then the Gospel writer drops a bombshell: "Thus he declared all foods clean!" (v. 19).[9] What served for Jesus and many of his fellow Israelites as important, daily reminders of their distinct identity as Yahweh's own and their sense of duty to God's Torah are now set aside. Scores of dietary restrictions rooted in Moses's commands are no longer viewed as relevant to the vocation of God's people (see Lev 11, 17; Deut 14). All foods, Mark makes clear to his recipients, are now clean.

Throughout the Gospels, we see Jesus continually redefining understandings of righteousness that prevailed among at least some of his fellow Israelites.[10] For Jesus, honor gained through legal rectitude pales in comparison to a humble and repentant spirit: e.g., Jesus and the "sinful"

9. So significant is this notice that I do not think it is best framed as a parenthetical comment by Mark (as in the NRSV) but as an interjected, exclamatory comment.

10. Among Jesus' fellow Israelites there were likely competing and quite variable understandings on how to live out Torah. At the same time, cross-cultural anthropological studies of several Mediterranean societies in the centuries preceding the Common Era show that the use of purity and other forms of piety as a means of gaining honor, and for the purpose of social differentiation between and within groups, was common. This is consistent with the Gospels' portrayal of many of Jesus' detractors: they used their piety as a means of elevating their own status and demeaning others (e.g., Matt 23; Luke 20:45–47). For more on this, see Kuhn, *Insights from Cultural Anthropology*, 89–122.

woman in Simon the Pharisee's home (Luke 7:36–50); and the parable of
the Pharisee and Tax Collector (Luke 18:9–14). Compassion and attention to human need prevail above all other requirements of Torah and the
status markers some associate with the Temple: e.g., Jesus healing the man
with the withered hand on the Sabbath (Mark 3:1–6); and the parable of
the Good Samaritan (Luke 10:29–37). Many of Jesus' teachings direct his
followers to identify with the poor, and problematize wealth in a society of
widespread deprivation: e.g., the parable of the Rich Man and Lazarus (Luke
16:19–31); the repentance of Zacchaeus (Luke 19:1–10); and the beatitudes
in Luke 6:20–26. For greed is a reflection in one's trust in wealth, not God, as
the source of blessing, and is thus another form of idolatry: e.g., Jesus' teachings on wealth in the Sermon on the Mount (Matt 6:19–34). Righteousness
is also defined by the Gospel writers as recognizing the presence of God's
reign in Jesus and devoting one's self to Jesus and the kingdom: e.g., Luke
9:21–27, 57–62; Matthew 10:1–15; 28:16–20.

The reason why many (not all!) of Jesus' fellow Israelites, especially
among the elite, found his teachings so troubling, is that Jesus pushed certain conceptions of purity and Torah-keeping to the margins, even those
which are inscribed in the Law of Moses. In their place, Jesus offered the
alternative, radical for many, of fulfilling Torah by following his example
and devoting themselves to what Jesus identified as the core of Torah.

Jesus' Instruction: The Core of Torah

So how then are we to understand Jesus' statement earlier in the Sermon on
the Mount that "until heaven and earth will pass away, not one letter, not
one stroke of a letter, will pass from the law until all is accomplished" (Matt
5:18)? Scholars have struggled to discern Jesus' intention here as presented
by Matthew. On the one hand, like Moses, Jesus seems to be upholding the
sacred and permanent nature of the law in all its detail: not one part of it
is to be displaced. On the other hand, Jesus, as we have seen, so radically
recasts portions of the Mosaic Law that he essentially sets them aside. In
my view, the answer to this conundrum lies in recognizing that for Jesus
the whole of Torah, the whole of God's instruction, is contained in its ir-
reducible core. Already here in his Sermon on the Mount, Jesus reveals the
essence of Torah: "In everything do unto others as you would have them do
to you; for this is the Torah and the Prophets" (7:12). Later, in response to a
legal expert who tries to entrap Jesus by asking, "Teacher, which commandment in the law is the greatest?" Jesus replies:

You shall love the Lord your God with all your heart, with all your soul, and with all your mind. This is the first and greatest commandment. And a second is like it. You shall love your neighbor as yourself. *On these two commandments hang all the law and the prophets.* (Matt 22:34–40)

This, for Jesus, is what constitutes Torah—*all* of it. Note that in both of these passages Jesus makes it clear that he has in view the totality of God's instruction to God's people. Torah, in both its particularity and totality, is right relationship with God and one another: "on these two commandments hang *all the law and the prophets.*" These two commandments are the root and trunk that gives every branch, twig, and leaf of law its meaning and purpose. Thus, if there are any laws which in a new time and place, or as a result of a greater depth of insight into God's will, no longer bear witness to what it means to be rightly related to God and one another (such as most purity codes and dietary restrictions), they are to be pruned away, for they no longer belong. They are no longer Torah. New branches, twigs, and leaves will sprout to take their place.

Following Jesus' Torah

Paul's letters and Acts show early believers taking their lead from Jesus' teachings. The instruction of Paul and others similarly treat God's Torah as dynamic and developing as a result of what God has accomplished and revealed in Jesus, and again on matters that are quite central to Israelite observance of Torah. They also clearly identify the core of Torah, from which all other faithful instruction must emerge.

For example, Paul's Letter to the Galatians along with the Jerusalem conference reported in Acts 15 make it clear that circumcision is no longer required of Gentile converts, despite the command given to Abraham in Genesis 17:9–14 that any male member of his extended household, including any foreigner, was to be circumcised. The only requirements made of the Gentile converts as reported in Acts are to "abstain from things polluted by idols and from fornication and from whatever has been strangled and from blood" (Acts 15:20). Yet Paul seems to overlook even these limited dietary restrictions in his discussion of the "weak" and the "strong" in Romans 14 and in other passages where he is instructing his churches on the matters of food (see also 1 Cor 8:1–13, 10:14–22). Like Jesus, Paul and other early Christians are compelled to set aside commands of Torah they believe are no longer relevant in their time and place.

And like Jesus, Paul considers Jesus' love command—implemented with the guidance of the Spirit—to be first and foremost the sources of God's instruction of what it means to live as God's people (see, e.g., Gal 3–5; Rom 7:1–8:17; 1 Cor 6:12–20; Phil 3:2–11). As Paul states in Romans 8:1–4:

> There is therefore now no condemnation for those who are in Christ Jesus. For the law of the Spirit of life in Christ Jesus has set you free from the law of sin and of death. For God has done what the law, weakened by the flesh, could not do: by sending his own Son in the likeness of sinful flesh, and to deal with sin, he condemned sin in the flesh, so that the just requirement of the law might be fulfilled in us, who walk not according to the flesh but according to the Spirit.

Then in Romans 13:8–10, Paul speaks to this "just requirement of the law" which the ongoing ministries of Jesus and the Spirit enable believers to fulfill. He exhorts the church:

> Owe no one anything, except to love one another; for the one who loves another has fulfilled the law. The commandments, "You shall not commit adultery; You shall not murder; You shall not steal; You shall not covet"; and any other commandment, are summed up in this word, "Love your neighbor as yourself." Love does no wrong to a neighbor; therefore, love is the fulfilling of the law.

In Galatians, we see Paul embroiled in a full-blown crisis. Other Christians have come into this church community he founded and began teaching the Galatian faithful that the Gentiles converts among them must be circumcised and follow other commands of Torah in order for them to be forgiven by God. In response, and with great angst, Paul exhorts the Galatian church to reject those demanding that Gentile converts be circumcised. Paul beseeches them to set aside these commands of the law and to live by the guidance of the Spirit. He then states in Galatians 5:5–6:

> For through the Spirit, by faith, we eagerly wait for the hope of righteousness. For in Christ Jesus neither circumcision or nor uncircumcision counts for anything; the only thing that matters is faith working through love.

Later, he adds in 5:13–14:

> For you were called to freedom, brothers and sisters; only do not use your freedom as an opportunity for self-indulgence, but through love become slaves to one another. For the whole law

is summed up in a single commandment, "You shall love your neighbor as yourself."

Paul's focus on the Spirit and Jesus' love command did not mean for Paul a dismissal of Torah. Far from it. As with Jesus, for Paul it meant some Torah commands God previously spoke through Moses need to be recast or even set aside so that the core purpose of God's law might now be more fully realized among God's people.

Core and Change—God's Plan for Torah and Us

What we see suggested in the Old Testament's presentation of Torah, and especially among the prophets, is clearly on display in the New Testament. There is a core to Torah: love God, and love others. And how the specifics of Torah are to be lived out in our times and places—these can flex and change.

Change Can Be Good

In fact, they *must* flex and change in order for the fundamental purpose of Torah to actually matter, to actually be lived out, in new times and places. So here is an important truth we must understand as we talk about and try to be faithful to these two features of Torah. It is *not* the case that the core of Torah is really all that matters, and the peripheral codes and instructions are simply expendable. Rather, it is *through the peripheral* that the fundamental purpose of Torah is to be lived out and make a difference in the lives of real communities. The peripheral is also—even just as—important! But the peripheral—this essential feature of Torah—is the part of Torah that is *changeable* because it is responsive to

- the needs and opportunities of the moment,
- and the developing insight of God's people as guided by the Spirit.

Jesus' and Paul's recasting of God's instruction are dramatic examples of what Fretheim calls "a canonical witness to the process of unfolding law," the developmental nature of God's Torah.

Part of the Plan

Now taking a step back and expanding our gaze, we can see that within Scripture's narrative revealing the history of the relationship between God and

God's people—climaxing in the life, death, and resurrection of Jesus—how humanity is to live out its calling as God's people develops throughout. Set within the biblical story, this ongoing development of Torah is thus presented as part of God's unfolding plan to bring humanity back into right relationship with God, one another, and creation. In other words, God accomplishes God's saving purpose, God helps us make the kingdom real in our times and places, through such continuing and reforming instruction on what it means to live out the core of God's Torah in our times and places.

We Should Expect as Much

I think that most Christians, once they sat down and thought it through, would find the notion of God's instruction as dynamic and reforming pretty uncontroversial. After all, as Christians, our sense of ethics, conduct, church membership, and worship is heavily dependent upon this very notion. Not many of us refuse to trim our sideburns (Lev 19:27), abstain from eating pork and shellfish (Lev 11, 17), offer animal sacrifices, forbid the wearing of clothes with two different types of fabric (Lev 19:19), or entertain the idea of selling our children into slavery, at least not seriously (Exod 21:7–11). Not many of us require circumcision for church membership or continue to observe the Sabbath or celebrate Passover, at least not in the traditional sense. For us, how Jesus, Paul, and the other writers of the New Testament reshaped our understanding of Torah has become normative.

Many Christians, I think, would also find uncontroversial the notion that Jesus continues to instruct and guide believers. Jesus' promise of ongoing instruction through the ministry of the Holy Spirit is firmly rooted in the New Testament. During his poignant farewell speech to his disciples in John's gospel, Jesus tells his disciples that he has not finished revealing to them everything they need to know, for time and their lack of maturity have not allowed it. Yet after him will come the Spirit who will "guide you into all the truth" (John 14:15–17, 25–26; 16:13–14). As we saw above, Paul assures his fellow believers that the Spirit will help them discern God's will their times and places. Accordingly, trust in the "illumination by the Spirit" holds a central place across Christian theological tradition.

Our Calling to Bind and Loose Torah

I mentioned in the introduction that interpretation is an essential part of the vocation of God's people. In chapter 2 we reviewed Matthew 16:13–20, in which Jesus passes on to his disciples the duty of "binding and loosing"

Torah. That is, he assigns to them the long-established interpretive practice of discerning when and how Torah is to be bound to present circumstances and situations, or when it is to be loosed from them. Set within its surrounding context, Jesus' commission to Peter and the other disciples here establishes that when his followers interpret Torah guided by Jesus' instruction and example, they do so with the authority of heaven.

Guided by Jesus' Teaching and Example

But already in the very next passage we learn that Peter is not an infallible interpreter of the times or God's will (16:21–23). Jesus discloses to his disciples that he must go to Jerusalem and be arrested and killed by the elders, chief priests, and scribes. Peter rejects this: "God forbid it, Lord!" Shockingly, immediately following the dramatic moment when Jesus names Simon "Rock," upon which Jesus will build his church, "and the gates of Hades will not prevail against it" (v. 18), Jesus renames Peter "Satan" and scolds him for becoming a "stumbling block" (v. 23). You have to feel at least a little sorry for Simon here. But Jesus' scathing rebuke makes it clear to Peter that faithful interpretation is only possible when Peter, and the rest of us, have our minds not on human things, but divine things. Faithful interpretation is only possible when we are guided by the example and ongoing instruction of the one who gives his life for us and the kingdom of God.

As we have already seen, from the perspective of the Gospel writers, Jesus' instruction represents the fullest manifestation of what God desires for humanity. Jesus' authority as the teacher of God's Torah outstrips that of Moses, as Jesus radically recasts or even sets aside commandments of old. It is by following Jesus' commands that true righteousness is found, a righteousness that exceeds that of the Scribes and Pharisees (Matt 5:19–20) and that which provides a foundation for life and living that will not fail (Matt 7:24–29). John also presents Jesus as the fullest disclosure of the will and ways of the Father, in both his actions and words (see, e.g., John 8:21–30, 17:14). Likewise, Paul refers to Jesus as the "fulfillment of the law" (Rom 10:4) and (as we saw above) cites Jesus' love command as the essential requirement of Torah.

In the Nitty Gritty of our Daily Lives

Because of the importance of Jesus' instruction, it might surprise readers of Scripture to find that much of Jesus' teaching takes place in rather pedestrian and sequestered settings. To be sure, Jesus is presented by the Gospel writers as doing a lot of "preaching" in front of large crowds or in the temple precincts. However, most of his instruction takes place in private conversation with his disciples and even his adversaries. The ways of the kingdom are shared with those who walk with Jesus from town to town on the dusty back roads of Galilee or Judah, or sit at table with Jesus in the homes of folk as diverse as Pharisees, tax collectors, common laborers, and widows. It is in these intimate settings that Jesus does much of his teaching about the kingdom of God. Moreover, Jesus' words are often initiated in response to the questioning, searching, even accusations of Jesus' conversation partners, such as we find in many of the "controversy dialogues" involving Jesus and other Israelite teachers. In short, Jesus' instruction was deeply incarnate in the real lives of real people.

Not only does much of Jesus' teaching take place in the context of intimate or contentious conversation, the form of Jesus' teaching as presented by the Gospel writers further calls his followers to consider how the arrival of God's kingdom is to reshape their grasp of the world. Jesus teaches mostly in parables! Jesus is a storyteller, offering radical, parabolic vignettes that challenge his listeners to grasp the mind-blowing ways the kingdom of God is to intersect and transform their lives. As Rachel Held Evans reflects,

> The good news is as epic as it gets, with universal theological implications, and yet the Bible tells it [in parables] from the perspective of fishermen and farmers, pregnant ladies and squirming kids. This story about the nature of God and God's relationship with humanity smells like mud and manger hay and tastes like salt and wine. It is concerned, not simply with questions of eternity, but with paying taxes and filling bellies and addressing a woman's chronic menstrual complications. It is the biggest story and smallest story all at once.[11]

With Holy Imagination

The point of Jesus' instruction, it seems to me, is to get his followers to start thinking—to start imagining how they might shape their lives in ways that reflect the reality of God's reign. He wanted to begin cultivating in them *the disposition of discernment*. That was, after all, the work he said his Spirit would continue to inspire within them (John 14:26; 16:12–15). He did not want his followers simply to parrot theological maxims back and forth, or quibble over details of the law, but to reflect creatively with one another, as he did with

11. Evans, *Inspired*, 150.

them, what it means to welcome the saving rule of God into their lives. Jesus was after wisdom, not rule keeping. When the disciples longed for easy answers, he told them stories. When they clung to long-held dichotomies, he challenged their concretized simplicity. When they thought they had the kingdom figured out, Jesus sought to awaken their imaginations.

As I mentioned above, Jesus' mode of instruction is *very* Jewish. His fellow Israelite teachers had long valued the place of both law (*halakah*) and story (*haggada*) in their sacred tradition, and the interplay between them, in helping them to discern God's will and ways. But more so than many of his contemporaries, we see Jesus willing to loose major elements of *halakah* in order to fashion a people who would have, as Jeremiah foretold, God's Torah written upon their hearts (Jer 31:33). It was the core of Torah—love of God and neighbor—that must be remembered and replicated in the messy, smelly, difficult, day-to-day lives of his followers in order for Jeremiah's words to come true, and in order for God's kingdom to be present among and through them (see John 15:1–17). And in order for that to truly happen, his followers needed to relearn to how to read their tradition and their times, together, with holy imagination.

This poses very important implications for us who dare to take on this vocation of binding and loosing God's instruction with holy imagination. We are called to see, understand, and discern God's Torah as Jesus teaches us to see, understand, and discern it. Like Peter, sometimes we do this well. When we do, we strengthen the church's transforming ministry and the powers of darkness are impotent against it. And like Peter, sometimes we do not do this well. We set our minds on human things, become stumbling blocks to those who might otherwise open their hearts to God's grace, and let Satan through the doors.

Binding and Loosing Badly

Sadly, the church's history is peppered with examples in which it has acted more like Satan than Jesus. In these moments, Christians have used Scripture to validate acts of violence and oppression against others. In short, members of the church have bound passages, often in very distorted and twisted ways, to situations and circumstances in order to canonize their own privilege, prejudice, and power. They have also loosed—or simply ignored—those passages testifying to Christ's sense of justice, and calling them to love all as they love themselves.

Weaponizing the Bible for Power and Privilege

Here are some examples.

For millennia, the church has cited distorted readings of the Gospels and other biblical traditions to encourage the subjugation, murder, and genocide of Jewish people. Christians have been both active participants in these atrocities and passive bystanders. Tragically, anti-Semitism continues to be alive and unwell among too many American Christians today.

Various church bodies partnered with European and later American powers to colonize, exploit, and subjugate indigenous peoples, appealing to the conquest narratives of Joshua (Manifest Destiny), and even (as we saw) the story of the Magi.[12]

Many American Christians in both the North and the South pointed to the New Testament's affirmation of slavery to validate this barbaric practice and to argue against abolition.[13] White supremacists continue to draw from biblical texts to justify their ongoing denigration of African Americans, Jews, and others.[14]

Many American Christians have supported and actively campaigned for the death penalty, despite the lack of evidence that it deters violent crime, and the mountain of evidence that its application is racially biased.[15] As their Scriptural basis, supporters cite commands calling for the capital punishment of murderers and other violators of the law, including "an eye for an eye, and a tooth for a tooth" (see Exod 21:23–25). In doing so, they completely ignore what Jesus had to say about this command in his Sermon on the Mount (Matt 5:38–42).

In the next chapter, we will discuss in more detail what strike me as two additional examples of using Scripture to maintain unjust patterns of power and privilege. Christians have drawn from the patriarchal tendencies of both the Old and New Testaments, including specific New Testament passages, to support oppression of women and ongoing dismissal of women's gifts for leadership within the church and society. Christians have also drawn from Old and New Testament prohibitions against same-gender sexual relationships to oppress homosexual persons and dismiss their gifts for leadership in the church.

These examples reveal how we have often read Scripture through distorted lenses and with rock-hard hearts, how we have even weaponized Scripture while completely ignoring its fundamental core. Still, as

12. See Scott, "Dimensions of Manifest Destiny."

13. We will discuss the affirmation of slavery found in several New Testament texts in the next chapter.

14. See, e.g., Southern Poverty Law Center, "Hate in God's Name;" Anti-Defamation League; "Christian Identity."

15. Death Penalty Information Center, "Race."

disheartening as these examples are, it is also important to point out that Christians have also railed against these injustices committed in the name of Christianity, and not just in retrospect, but often while they were being committed. Compelled by Jesus' command to love God and one another, they bound and loosed Torah through a very different set of lenses and with very different hearts.

Reading without Holy Imagination

Throughout our history, and certainly in America today, we often treat Scripture and even Jesus' teachings more as a rule book than as a guide to imaginative discernment focused on the core of Torah. Christian Smith, in *The Bible Made Impossible*, identifies ten assumptions or beliefs that characterize the "biblicism" so common to American Protestantism. Among them, three are particularly relevant to our conversation here:

> *Total Representation*: the Bible represents the totality of God's communication to and will for humanity, both in containing all that God has to say to humans and in being the exclusive mode of God's true communication.

> *Complete Coverage*: The divine will about all of the issues relevant to Christian belief and life are contained in the Bible.

> *Universal Applicability*: What the biblical authors taught God's people at any point in history remains universally valid for all Christians at every other time, unless specifically revoked by subsequent scriptural teaching.[16]

Each of these beliefs about the Bible contribute to the tendency of many American Christians to concretize God's instruction. These Christians regard Torah as fixed and complete, written in stone in ancient times and yet somehow containing all of the "universally applicable" instruction we need to live faithfully as Christ's disciples today.

Handbooking the Bible

This leads to still another tendency that Smith identifies, which he calls the "Handbook Model."

> The Bible teaches doctrine and morals with every affirmation that it makes, so that together those affirmations comprise something like a handbook or textbook for Christian belief and

16. Smith, *Bible Made Impossible*, 4–5.

living, a compendium of divine and therefore inerrant teachings on a full array of subjects—including science, economics, health, politics, and romance.[17]

If you are not familiar with this tendency, here is a quick and easy way for you to see it on display for yourself. Simply type "what the Bible says about _____" into your favorite online search engine, fill in the blank, and away you go. Smith is not exaggerating when he says that Christians find inerrant teachings on a "full array" of subjects in the Bible. My search yielded critical biblical insights on pets, video games, airplanes, aliens, cremation, and tattoos.[18] While it is certainly good and appropriate for Christians to look to Scripture for guidance, this tendency to "handbook" the Bible is problematic on several counts.

For example, let's say that you wanted to find out what the Bible has to say about dating. You turn to your trusty online search engine, type in the magic words, and you come up with only about 124,000,000 results to comb through. By the time you carefully read through all of those entries, of course, enough years will have gone by that dating may no longer be an option or of interest to you. Maybe that is part of the strategy.

But if you do push on determined to find out what the Bible has to say about dating, you will find a wide array of "biblical" views on the topic. Here we are back to the reality of "pervasive interpretive pluralism" that we discussed in chapter 2. The biblical laws on dating, while "universally applicable," are unfortunately rather difficult to figure out. This *might* have something to do with the fact that the Bible doesn't actually address the modern practice of dating in any direct way.

Among the diverse treatments of the issue you will find, some simply string together an assortment of verses that they judge somehow connected to dating. Often, there is little to no explanation accompanying the verses and the reader is left to figure out how the verses listed offer biblically sound guidance on courtship.[19]

Others take the opposite approach, providing a lot of explanation with biblical texts provided in parentheses. But in these cases, it is often not

17. Smith, *Bible Made Impossible*, 5.

18. See, e.g., https://www.gotquestions.org/Bible-pets.html; https://www.christianpost.com/trends/what-does-the-bible-say-about-video-games.html; https://www.openbible.info/topics/airplanes; https://www.biblestudytools.com/topical-verses/bible-verses-about-aliens/; https://www.focusonthefamily.com/family-qa/cremation-a-biblical-perspective/; https://www.biblestudytools.com/topical-verses/what-does-the-bible-say-about-tattoos/. Smith (7–10) also details how this handbook approach dominates the evangelical book-publishing market, listing over fifty titles as examples.

19. See, e.g. Bible Study Tools, "Dating Bible Verses;" Open Bible, "Dating;" Bible Info, "Dating."

clear how the biblical texts cited support many of the claims being made.[20] Moreover, very little to no attempt is made to understand those passages within their own literary or cultural contexts. The writers simply assume the "universal applicability" of the verses they cherry pick from Scripture. Such "proof-texting" is another instance of the "I don't interpret the Bible, I just read it" approach we discussed in the introduction, and the dismissal of our ancestors' testimony in chapter 1.

Still other resources acknowledge that the Bible doesn't directly speak to the modern phenomenon of dating, and they instead appeal to broader principles related to human coupling, marriage, self-control, and living rightly with God and one another. Some of these discussions, in my view, offer much more nuanced and thoughtful reflections on the topic (even though they still tend to take biblical passages out of context and fail to realize that the Bible doesn't offer a single model for marriage).[21] Nevertheless, should we be calling the results of even these more nuanced and sophisticated treatments "the biblical view of dating"? For when we use simplistic language such as "the biblical view of dating," we are implying that the Bible provides clear "rules" that are to guide dating relationships. But this simply is not the case. Rather, these resources are *inferring* what might be sound practices for dating based on an array of passages that speak to other forms of human relatedness. Yet such inference, as the evidence clearly shows, does not lead to self-evident conclusions. Different Christians identify different biblical principles to guide their reflection, and even those that share similar sets of principles will offer different views on how those are to be applied to Christians' quest for the love of their life.

The language of "the biblical view of _____," and this tendency to handbook the Bible, obscures the reality that the Bible doesn't directly speak to many of the realities that we face in our times and places. It also obscures the reality that the perspectives and tendencies—"the reading glasses"—we bring to the Bible often have more to do with what we get out of the Bible than with what the Bible actually says.[22] "The biblical view of _____" does not identify the self-evident revelation of God if only we would just open our Bibles and start reading. It signals our attempts to claim the Bible's authority for what think or assume the Bible teaches. That distinction is important.

The tendency to handbook the Bible also does not foster the holy imagination Jesus was seeking to cultivate in his followers. The notion that

---

20. See, e.g., 412Teens.org, "What does the Bible Say about Dating or Courting?"

21. See, e.g., McLeroy, "What Does the Bible Say About Dating?"

22. Strangely, some treatments of dating openly acknowledge the highly inferential nature of their reflection and yet at the same time still insist on claiming the views on dating they offer are purely "biblical"! See, e.g., Croft, "Biblical Dating."

it is only between the covers of our Bibles that we can encounter God speaking to all the needs and questions we have does not align with what Jesus taught us about Torah. Rather, Jesus' words and actions model for us the practice of *discernment*: bringing the center of Torah, the testimonies of our ancestors, and the Spirit into dynamic and reforming conversation with the realities of our lives and the people we are called to serve.

Indeed, the sacred testimonies our ancestors preserved in Scripture, are to be an integral part of that conversation and discernment! For this reason, our calling to bind and loose God's instruction should never, like many of the attempts to handbook the Bible, abandon the witness of our ancestors and their own noble efforts to discern God's will in their own times and places—not through neglect, not through ignorance of our ancestors' struggles and hopes, not by proof-texting their words into what we want them to say. Rather, to read the Bible *biblically*, we must enact the patterns of engaging sacred tradition that our ancestors and Jesus himself taught us: dynamic, heartfelt, humble reflection with one another on what it means to live out the core of Torah—to love God and one another—in our times and places.

Only then will we avoid our anxious tendencies to entomb God's word in stone and break off pieces to hurl at others. Only then will Christ's Torah be for us the living rock upon which we are to stand.

Reflection and Discussion Questions

1. When it comes to God's instruction, what would you identify as core, and what would you identify as peripheral?

2. Can you think of instances in which your understanding of what it means to live faithfully have changed? What led you to change your mind?

3. If it is true that God's instruction to us is dynamic and reforming, what difficulties or challenges might that create for Christian communities? What challenges might it create for you?

4. What are some examples of how Christians weaponize Scripture today?

CHAPTER SIX

Reading Culture as Bible and Ignoring the Spirit

ABOUT A DECADE AGO, I had the honor of leading a five-day crash course on the Gospels for a group of Haitian church leaders, including male pastors and several female laity. The pace was slow-going, as I suspected it would be. I was not proficient in their native Creole, so the students and I spoke to one another through an interpreter. My preferred classroom technology is a piece of chalk and a blackboard, so I did not mind the lack of a projector or interactive smart board. But the chalk board in that classroom was lumpy and pitted, the chalk kept flaking and breaking, and I struggled to create diagrams that resembled what I intended. And the questions! Some were about the Gospels and the specific topics before us, but many were about other matters related to the Bible and faith that the students were eager to know.

Including the first question—on the first day, after I offered just a few introductory comments—by a male clergy:

"Dr. Kuhn, do you think that women should be pastors? What does the Bible say?"

I had been told by the missionary couple hosting us that this was a hot issue among the Haitian churches that formed the school and seminary where I was teaching. Women in these communities were the backbone of their churches, among the most educated, and often the leaders in outreach ministry to their fellow Haitians. Some of these gifted and dedicated women had been agitating to be recognized as ordained pastors. Many of the male clergy were resisting.

Still, the question took me by surprise. Only thirty minutes into our four days together, in the middle of my overview of the Gospels' historical setting, this off-topic, bombshell of a query! I looked around. The rest of the class was eagerly awaiting my response.

This was probably not my finest pedagogical moment. But my task-oriented inclinations would not be so easily waylaid! I assured the class that at some point during the week, I would share my thoughts on the topic, but now the task at hand was to focus on the Gospels.

My time with those students was an intense, deeply enriching experience. Their eagerness to learn was humbling and inspiring. As the days slipped by, I simply forgot about that first question on the first day of class and my assurance that I would offer my perspective. But the students had not. Later that week, as we were wrapping up our final session together, *several* hands suddenly shot up in the air.

"Dr. Kuhn! Does the Bible say that women can be pastors? Tell us what you think! You promised you would answer us!" The rest of the class nodded. They were waiting for this moment.

I only had myself to blame for being caught off-guard. I reclaimed my professorial composure, cleared my throat, and replied, "This is not an easy question to answer. We would need another five days together to examine what the Bible has to say about the matter. Some passages would seem to support the idea that women can and should serve as pastors, and some would seem to prohibit it."

Dead silence. Downcast and sidelong glances. Despite the impeccable politeness the students showed me all week, and were attempting to show still now, their frustration and disappointment with my response was obvious. As a respectable biblical scholar with no time to address the issue adequately, this was certainly the most responsible answer I could give! But they were hoping for much more. They wanted to know! And I was putting them off again.

I wracked my brain for anything I could offer that might be useful. Nothing. Then, the answer simply came, more from my heart than my head.

"But, I can tell you this. My wife is a pastor. And she is a very good pastor."

The room erupted. Women jumped out from behind their desks, dancing and singing. Male clergy cradled their heads in their hands and moaned. Many simply laughed, reveling in the scene. Some began speaking in tongues.

I was astounded. Several of these students had wakened in the predawn darkness and walked for hours through sections of Port au Prince that were virtual war zones at that time to get to class each morning. They did this to attend a course on the Gospels. Yet the course literally began and ended with the question foremost on many of their minds.

And the answer I gave that led the room to erupt had little to do with my "expertise" as a biblical scholar. It was simply my testimony as a husband and church member.

This moment underscored for me two important realizations that many other experiences have affirmed. First, topics related to gender and sexuality are of incredible importance to people of faith. Sex, in both senses of the word, really matters to us. Second, when it comes to our deliberation on such topics, testimony borne out of personal experience is often the most powerful and transformative.

So, chances are, this chapter—which continues the discussion of the previous chapter on binding and loosing Torah as it addresses the role of women within the Christian community and homosexuality—is going to be of interest to you. We will also see that people's thinking on these issues often has just as much to do with their hearts as their heads.

Competing Cultural Contexts

In the introduction, and throughout the preceding chapters, I have emphasized the crucial role that context plays in the interpretation of just about anything. When it comes to interpreting the Bible in particular, it is important that we take into consideration the historical/cultural and literary contexts of the passages we engage. It is also important that we be mindful of the contexts we ourselves bring to our reading of the Bible—including our own cultural and personal biases. As we saw, these three sets of contexts comprise the worlds behind the text, of the text, and in front of the text. Reading glasses that are attentive to these contexts are much better equipped to help us makes sense of biblical passages than those that are not.

One of the indisputable realities of the biblical writings is that all of them have been composed within cultural contexts in which male superiority and heterosexuality were the norm. It is also indisputable that throughout most of their existence the biblical writings have been heard and interpreted within cultural contexts in which male superiority and heterosexuality were the norm. Thus, we would expect that both the biblical writings and our interpretation of them would reflect these cultural biases.

Indeed they do.

The Worlds Behind and of the Text

The biblical world is a man's world. Men rule. Men are the movers and shakers of the pivotal events of salvation history. It is their voices that we

(almost) always hear. As the authors of 1 Corinthians 14:33–36 and 1 Timothy 2:8–15 among others say, women are to be subordinate and silent! Even
God is portrayed as male (most of the time).

It is also pretty darn clear that heterosexual coupling is the norm in the
biblical writings, even if such coupling takes on a variety of forms, despite
what some defenders of "traditional" marriage like to claim. There are also
several clear prohibitions against same-gender sexual relations in both the
Old and New Testaments (see, e.g., Lev 18:22, 24; 1 Cor 6:9–10; 1 Tim 1:10;
Rom 1:26–27). Some have argued that the New Testament prohibitions
against same-gender sexual relations are actually referring to the specific
practice of pederasty (adult males using male minors for sexual gratifica-
tion) or male prostitution, the only forms of same-gender sexual relations
common in the first century. But such readings ignore the basic grammar
and logic of these passages, especially Romans 1:26–27. They also overlook
significant evidence indicating that consensual, same-gender relationships
were not uncommon in the first century.[1]

In short, the biblical world is pretty much a straight man's world. And
for the better part of two thousand years, our cultures and interpretive traditions reinforced the normative, and privileged, position of straight men.
They have been the movers and shakers of daily life and the pivotal events of
Western society. It is their voices that speak to us from the pages of history.
They have also been the ones whose interpretation of Scripture really mattered, at least to most of us.

The Worlds in Front of the Text

But recently, many American Christians are encountering the biblical writings through sets of reading glasses that no longer assume that patriarchy
and heterosexuality are normative—that they *must* or even *should* govern
human relationships. This has led to two major points of dispute among
American Christians today: the role of women in the church, and the ap-
propriateness of same-gender coupling.

To draw again from terminology I utilized back in chapter 3, American
society in the last seventy-five years or so has birthed "social movements"
that in varying degrees have led many Americans to rethink the normative
status of patriarchy and heterosexuality, and even the binary character of
sexuality and gender. In response, "counter movements" have developed to
reassert traditional notions of male privilege, human sexuality, and marriage.
For the most part, these counter movements have been led by moderate

1. See Kuhn, "Natural and Unnatural Relations."

and conservative Christians, including evangelicals, Roman Catholics, and Orthodox. Though the revolutionary understandings of sexuality and gender roles have gained much ground over the last several decades among Americans, we are still very much living in the tension created by these social movements and their corresponding counter movements.

A Clash of Cultures and Lenses

Competing claims about the Bible and culture are at the heart of the debates over the place of women in the church and homosexuality. Advocates for the full recognition of women's gifts for leadership and service in the church, including their ordination as pastors or priests, argue that the patriarchy reflected and seemingly endorsed by biblical writings is a consequence of their cultural context. Advocates for the acceptance and normalization of same-gender coupling argue similarly. They point out that the biblical authors had no knowledge of sexual orientation and the reality that it exists along a continuum. Rather, the views of the biblical authors on same-gender coupling simply reflect understandings of human nature common at the time. In sum, the normalization of patriarchy and heterosexuality (to the exclusion of homosexuality) in the Bible reflects the culturally bound perspectives and biases of the biblical writers, not the universally binding will of God. It is more descriptive than prescriptive. Thus, we are free to discern God guiding us in new directions on these matters.

Advocates for maintaining traditional limits on the roles of women in the church and even society, and traditional notions of human sexuality, argue the opposite. They insist that the Bible's normalization of patriarchy and heterosexuality is not simply due to the cultural baggage of the biblical writers. Rather, the perspectives expressed on these matters within the Bible truly reflect God's will for humanity for all time, for the Bible is the Word of God. To think and to act otherwise, many traditionalists would argue, is to choose the misguided values of our modern cultural context over the truth of God.

I have already tipped my hand in the preceding chapter on where I come out on these two issues. I believe that God's instruction to us is dynamic and reforming, and that we are called to embrace the heart of Torah as taught by Jesus—to love God and love one another—as guided by the Spirit. I think we can move to a different understanding of certain matters than expressed by our ancestors in the faith, including those bearing witness in the New Testament, though we must always do this carefully, respectfully, prayerfully, and in community with other believers. I also believe that

God is calling—has been calling—Christians to do just that with regard to the role of women in ministry and same-gender coupling. In the pages to follow, I will explain why. But before we get to these specific topics, we first need to put some groundwork in place.

Admitting and Embracing the Slippery Slope

I can understand that many readers will likely respond to the above paragraph (and likewise, the preceding chapter) with serious concerns. Sure, God's instruction is dynamic and reforming to the degree that many of the commands of the Old Testament are to be "loosed," or set aside. But the notion that the Holy Spirit can lead us to understandings of faithful living that conflict with the writers of the New Testament? This introduces a degree of ambiguity into what it means to live as God's people that many will find troubling and confusing. It also seems to place us squarely on the proverbial "slippery slope." If it is okay for women to serve as pastors, and homosexuality is no longer sinful, then what else?

Well, a number of things really, such as women not wearing head coverings in worship or having short hair (1 Cor 11:5–6), men having long hair (1 Cor 11:14), and neglecting to greet one another with a holy kiss (Rom 16:16; 1 Cor 16:20; 2 Cor 13:12; 1 Thess 5:26). There are *many* things believers are commanded to do in Scripture, including several from the New Testament, that we no longer regard as relevant for us, and I think rightly so.

As I stressed in the preceding chapter, Scripture itself often reworks and reprioritizes elements of God's instruction, even to the point that some commands and prohibitions are essentially set aside. The upshot of this is that *Scripture itself places us on the slippery slope by its own example.* And in varying degrees, all Christians follow the Bible's lead. Note that Jesus, Paul, and the other writers of the New Testament never tell us to set aside *all* of the purity codes, or many of the other (sometimes downright obscure) commands contained in biblical books such as Leviticus and Numbers. Yet most Christians regard most of these instructions as non-binding, as well as others from the New Testament that we have just noted. How did this slippage in legal rectitude come about? Not in a moment of instantaneous clarity, but through years of debate, prayer, and discernment among Christians.

The issue is not whether we are on the slippery slope. All of us are! After all, as Christ's disciples, we are called to bind and loose Torah! And if something as sacred as Torah is to be subject to our thoughtful, prayerful discernment and *adjustment*, then all the more so our culture.

The Example of Slavery

This issue of slavery led to much debate and division among Christians around the world, including American Christians in the eighteenth and nineteenth centuries. This example is particularly relevant for us to consider here, since it is a clear example of later Christians coming to understand an incredibly weighty issue directly related to the life of faith *very* differently than the writers of Scripture, including the New Testament. And rightly so. But it wasn't easy.

What the New Testament Really Says about Slavery

Some scholars argue that the New Testament writers do not affirm slavery, but merely tolerate it as an unavoidable part of the social fabric of the ancient world. I believe this perspective is well intentioned, but not a valid interpretation. The New Testament household codes addressing the slave-master relationship reflect an attitude towards slavery that goes well beyond resigned toleration (see Eph 6:5–9; Col 3:22–4:1; 1 Tim 6:1–2). Consider, for example Ephesians 6:5–9:

> [5]Slaves, obey your earthly masters with fear and trembling, in singleness of heart, as you obey Christ; [6]not only while being watched, and in order to please them, but as slaves of Christ, doing the will of God from the heart. [7] Render service with enthusiasm, as to the Lord and not to men and women, [8] knowing that whatever good we do, we will receive the same again from the Lord, whether we are slaves or free. [9]And, masters, do the same to them. Stop threatening them, for you know that both of you have the same Master in heaven, and with him there is no partiality.

To be sure, the writer of this and other New Testament texts addressing slavery offer instructions intended to safeguard the integrity of both slaveholders and slaves. Yet at the very same time, the writer urges that the slave-master relationship be maintained with an extraordinary degree of devotion on the part of the slave, beyond what would otherwise be typical: "obey your earthly masters with fear and trembling, in singleness of heart, as you obey Christ" (v. 5). In fact, a Christian slave's service of his or her earthly master is considered as part of his or her service and devotion to Christ and to God (vv. 5–6). The author believes that in God's *future* kingdom the distinction between master and slave will ultimately vanish (v. 9). Yet remarkably, the hope in God's eternal blessing is cited as *motivation for the proper exercise*

of the practice of slavery by both master and slave, *not* the cessation of it (vv.
8–9). To underscore this point further, consider also 1 Tim 6:1–2.

> Let all who are under the yoke of slavery regard their masters as
> worthy of all honor, so that the name of God and the teaching
> may not be blasphemed. Those who have believing masters must
> not be disrespectful to them on the ground that they are members
> of the church; rather they must serve them all the more, since
> those who benefit by their service are believers and beloved.

Here too slaves are admonished to maintain loyal and submissive service
their masters as part of their faithful witness to God. The tone and content of these two passages addressing slavery is simply not that of resigned
toleration.

A number of scholars have also pointed to Paul's letter to Philemon as
an example of the New Testament writings challenging the practice of slavery.
But in requesting the release of the slave, Onesimus, Paul is doing nothing to
challenge slavery as a social institution. Paul clearly recognizes that Philemon
has a claim on Onesimus (vv. 8–10, vv. 18–20). Moreover, in the ancient Mediterranean, the release of slaves was not uncommon, but could occur in several
ways, including the adoption of a slave by another and payment for his or her
freedom. Note Paul's description of his relationship with the slave in v. 10: "I
am now appealing to you for my child, Onesimus, whose father I have become
during my imprisonment." Paul then goes on to say that any outstanding debt
resulting from Onesimus's release should be charged to Paul's account, while
slyly adding, "I say nothing about your owing me even your own self" (v. 19).
Paul is simply requesting the release of a particular slave who has become
dear to him, and does so in a manner that follows the customs governing the
practice of slavery in his time.

We will consider one more text, and in light of our American experience of slavery, this one is particularly difficult to read: 1 Peter 2:18–21.
It appears in a section of 1 Peter that is encouraging believers to live as
servants of God and to be accountable to worldly authority. Here the author
exhorts slaves to bear their unjust suffering at the hands of abusive masters
knowing that when they do, they have God's approval and follow in the
example of Jesus:

> [18] Slaves, accept the authority of your masters with all defer-
> ence, not only those who are kind and gentle but also those who
> are harsh. [19]For it is to your credit if, being aware of God, you
> endure pain while suffering unjustly. [20]If you endure when you
> are beaten for doing wrong, where is the credit in that? But if
> you endure when you do right and suffer for it, you have God's

approval. [21]For to this you have been called, because Christ also suffered for you, leaving you an example, so that you should follow in his steps.

In sum, the writers of the New Testament fastidiously maintain the institution of slavery—including abusive forms of it—as consistent with the Christian life.

The Clear-Cut but Unfaithful Biblical Case for Slavery

For this reason, many centuries later American Christian opponents to emancipation found a solid, biblical case already laid out for them when it came to defending the practice of slavery. Richard Furman, prominent Baptist pastor and leader, presented an essay to Governor John Wilson of South Carolina in 1823 entitled, "Exposition of the Views of the Baptists, Relative to the Coloured Population In the United States."[2] Citing the relevant passages from the New Testament epistles, Furman points out that

> In things purely spiritual, slaves appear to have enjoyed equal privileges; but their relationship, as masters and slaves, was not dissolved. Their respective duties are strictly enjoined. The masters are not required to emancipate their slaves; but to give them the things that are just and equal, forbearing threatening; and to remember, they also have a master in Heaven.

Based on these passages, Furman presents what seems to him and many others the inevitable, obvious, and biblically sound conclusion:

> Had the holding of slaves been a moral evil, it cannot be supposed, that the inspired Apostles, who feared not the faces of men, and were ready to lay down their lives in the cause of their God, would have tolerated it, for a moment, in the Christian Church. If they had done so on a principle of accommodation, in cases where the masters remained heathen, to avoid offences and civil commotion; yet, surely, where both master and servant were Christian, as in the case before us, they would have enforced the law of Christ, and required, that the master should liberate his slave in the first instance. But, instead of this, they let the relationship remain untouched, as being lawful and right, and insist on the relative duties.

2. Furman, "Exposition."

Historian Mark Noll reports that this and other biblically rooted defenses of slavery were widely held among Christians throughout the Western world, "put forward by Catholics and Protestants, both Europeans and North Americans."[3]

The Less Clear-Cut but Faithful Biblical Case for Abolition

Noll also points out that those Christians advocating for the abolition of human bondage lacked equally clear-cut biblical statements to support their cause. In the face of the rather straightforward New Testament affirmations of slavery, the anti-slavery advocates needed to appeal instead to the "general principles of the Bible," that is, "justice and righteousness."[4] Noll reports that a pivotal moment in shifting public sentiment on slavery was the publication of Harriet Beecher Stowe's *Uncle Tom's Cabin* (1852). According to Noll, the book "provided one of the era's most powerful examples of the abolitionist appeal to the general spirit of the Bible." This narrative led readers into a poignant encounter with the dehumanizing evils of slavery, deftly inviting empathy for characters shackled to bondage and abuse. In juxtaposition to these dark realities, readers witnessed in the voices and actions of its characters—both white and black—Jesus' command to love. In the end, many were moved to recognize that slavery and much that goes along with it undeniably violates the will of God and the teachings of Christ.

> The significance of Stowe's *Uncle Tom's Cabin* for the biblical debate over slavery lay in the novel's emotive power. More effectively than [anti-slavery] debaters like Jonathon Blanchard or Francis Wayland, Stowe exemplified—rather than just announced—the persuasive force of what she regarded as the Bible's overarching general message.[5]

Such inspired testimony—that of slaves, their advocates, and that of the Spirit—led many Christians to see through the "biblically sound," self-serving defense of our slave-holding, justice-denying culture, and instead to follow Jesus.

But many supporters of slavery just weren't buying it, and some responded with startling vehemence. For example, at the height of the debate and on the cusp of war in 1861, Presbyterian Henry Van Dyke countered, "When the Abolitionist tells me that slaveholding is sin, in the simplicity of

3. Noll, *Civil War*, 34.
4. Noll, *Civil War*, 41.
5. Noll, *Civil War*, 44.

my faith in the Holy Scriptures, I point him to this sacred record, and tell him, in all candor, as my text does, that his teaching blasphemes the name of God and His doctrine."[6]

Binding, Loosing, and Loving as Jesus Did:
Some Guiding Principles

As I stressed in the preceding chapter, Jesus' command to love God and to love our neighbors is the core of Torah. Every other command is peripheral and subject to change and even dismissal if it no longer advances Torah's purpose. This applies not only to Christian tradition, but also to elements of our culture that demean and dehumanize. No matter how long-standing, no matter how central to our sense of community and identity, or to prevailing patterns of power or resource distribution, if elements of our culture do not lead us to love God and others as we should, they are simply, as Paul would say, "rubbish" (Phil 3:2–11). Also recall, again, Paul's description of our essential calling in Romans 12:1–2: "do not conform any longer to the patterns of this world, but be transformed by the renewing of your minds . . ."

On the one hand, Jesus' dual love command may strike us as wonderfully straightforward. What could be easier than just loving God and others? On the other hand, things get pretty messy and complicated when we try to live out this command in the nitty gritty of our times and places. For this reason, it is easy to see why throughout the centuries Christians have invested much energy in composing lists of "do's and don'ts." We like things to be clear and concrete! We want to know the answers, in black and white! This is understandable.

But it has also been the case that when we compose our lists stipulating how Christians should live, we often end up privileging and even authorizing cultural norms and prevailing patterns of power, as if they are fundamental to our faith. We treat culture as our Bible. Sometimes, as we saw with slavery, that is a really bad thing.

Still, isn't there more we can say about Jesus' commands to love God and love one another that may provide us with some guidance on how we can use them to assess the lists of rules and commands we inevitably create? I think there is. While not providing us with all of the specifics we might want, the Gospels show us at least four characteristic ways Jesus himself put the core of Torah into action.

---

6. Van Dyke, *Abolitionism,* 7, cited in Noll, *Civil War,* 19.

Championing Repentance and Humility

Throughout the Gospels, Jesus stresses that repentance and humility are essential to welcoming, and being part of, the kingdom of God. The notion that humans in general and God's people in particular often need to repent, to literally "turn around"—to recognize that they are heading in the wrong direction and make a major course correction—is elemental to biblical tradition and Jesus' teaching as presented by the gospel writers (e.g., Mark 1:14–14). Also, as we saw in chapter 1, ancient Roman and Israelite society was highly stratified. It was also a society in which the pursuit and bestowal of honor shaped the social interactions of many within each class. As cultural anthropologists would say, Mediterranean culture was *agonistic*, meaning that it was characterized by the constant *struggle* of people to maintain or gain honor, and often at the expense of someone else. In sharp contrast to this cultural norm, Jesus repeatedly champions humility and meekness before God and others, in contrast to honor-seeking behavior, as true to the cadences of the kingdom.

Transgressing Boundaries

In his commentary on Mark's gospel, Don Juel labels Mark 1:40–3:6 as "Transgressor of the Boundaries."[7] It is an apt title for this section of Mark, for in it we see Jesus crossing all sorts of law-inscribed lines to share the truth about the kingdom of God and to make its blessings real among those to whom he ministered. But this would also be an apt descriptor for all of Jesus' ministry as depicted by each of the Gospel writers. Very simply, Jesus violates boundaries, even long-standing legal and cultural ones. He brings down walls that have been erected around people and communities, and redraws the map of what it truly means to be part of the kingdom of God.

Honoring the Integrity of All

Many of the boundaries that Jesus transgresses and redraws are those that demean and divide people. Jesus' embrace and empowerment of the marginalized, his popularity around "sinners and tax collectors," his elevation of a Canaanite woman as having "great faith" (Matt 15:21–28) and depiction of a Samaritan (Luke 10:24–37) as a heroic keeper of Torah, his healing of the Gerasene demoniac (Mark 5:1–20), and repartee with an adulterous

7. Juel, *Mark*, 43–57.

divorcee of Samaria (John 4:1–30), are a few of many instances in which Jesus values and honors the integrity of those that his society has characteristically marginalized or shunned. Jesus regarded his followers as brothers, sisters, and friends, and in doing so shared with them the honor that was due to him as God's beloved Son (see John 15:12–17).

Issuing God's Call to Serve

One of the ways Jesus honored the integrity of others was not only to identify them as children of God and welcome them into God's reign, but also to call them to follow him in serving and loving others (see John 13:31–35). All of them are worthy of this vocation, including females, who follow Jesus as disciples (Luke 8:1–3), who sit at Jesus' feet (Luke 10:38–42), who are the first humans to announce his arrival and significance (Luke 1:46–56), and proclaim his resurrection to others (Luke 24:8–11; John 20:11–18).

Illustration: Jesus, Simon the Pharisee, and the "Sinful" Woman (Luke 7:36–50)

The encounter Luke records in Simon the Pharisees' home is a useful one, I think, for seeing these characteristic features of how Jesus lived out his understanding of Torah in action.

> [36] One of the Pharisees asked Jesus to eat with him, and he went into the Pharisee's house and took his place at the table. [37] And a woman in the city, who was a sinner, having learned that he was eating in the Pharisee's house, brought an alabaster jar of ointment. [38] She stood behind him at his feet, weeping, and began to bathe his feet with her tears and to dry them with her hair. Then she continued kissing his feet and anointing them with the ointment. [39] Now when the Pharisee who had invited him saw it, he said to himself, "If this man were a prophet, he would have known who and what kind of woman this is who is touching him—that she is a sinner." [40] Jesus spoke up and said to him, "Simon, I have something to say to you." "Teacher," he replied, "speak." [41] "A certain creditor had two debtors; one owed five hundred denarii, and the other fifty. [42] When they could not pay, he canceled the debts for both of them. Now which of them will love him more?" [43] Simon answered, "I suppose the one for whom he canceled the greater debt." And Jesus said to him, "You have judged rightly." [44] Then turning towards the woman, he

said to Simon, "Do you see this woman? I entered your house; you gave me no water for my feet, but she has bathed my feet with her tears and dried them with her hair. [45] You gave me no kiss, but from the time I came in she has not stopped kissing my feet. [46] You did not anoint my head with oil, but she has anointed my feet with ointment. [47] Therefore, I tell you, her sins, which were many, have been forgiven; hence she has shown great love. But the one to whom little is forgiven, loves little." [48] Then he said to her, "Your sins are forgiven." [49] But those who were at the table with him began to say among themselves, "Who is this who even forgives sins?" [50] And he said to the woman, "Your faith has saved you; go in peace."

The Surrounding Literary Context: Jesus, the Healer of All Sorts

Before considering how this encounter illustrates Jesus' practice of Torah, we do well to examine briefly how Luke frames the scene. Following his "sermon on the plain" in 6:20–49—which includes a shorter version of some of the same material in Matthew's Sermon on the Mount (Matthew 5–7)— we see Jesus engaged in or talking about his healing ministry. Throughout the Gospel, Jesus offers healing to those across the social spectrum, but most often the marginalized. In this section of Luke, recipients include the slave of a Roman centurion (7:1–10) and a widow's son whom Jesus returns to life (7:11–17). Later, when questioned by John's disciples on whether Jesus is really the messiah John expected, Jesus replies,

> Go and tell John what you have seen and heard: the blind receive their sight, the lame walk, the lepers are cleansed, the deaf hear, the dead are raised, the poor have good news brought to them (7:22).

After John's disciples depart, Jesus turns to the crowds and criticizes those who rejected John's ministry, including Pharisees (vv. 24–32). He then adds, referring to himself,

> The Son of Man has come eating and drinking, and you say: "Look, a glutton and a drunkard, a friend of tax collectors and sinners!" Nevertheless, wisdom is vindicated by her children.

Thus, the literary context in which this story is set underscores the powerful and pervasive healing ministry of Jesus, especially on behalf of the marginalized. It also emphasizes the elite's rejection of God's purposes for themselves by rejecting John, Jesus, and the wisdom of God they reveal.

Jesus' encounter with Simon the Pharisee, a "sinful" woman, and the invited guests in Simon's home in 7:36–50 continues Luke's focus on these themes. The "healing" Jesus here offers the nameless woman may be of a different sort, but as Jesus calls her to go in "peace" (v. 50), he announces her restoration to wholeness. She is among the "sinners" that gravitate to Jesus, the "poor who have good news brought to them." Simon, meanwhile, is among those who reject Jesus as the Son of Man sent by God and fail to understand the nature of true righteousness.

The Setting and Scandalous Trespass

Jesus is invited to eat with Simon the Pharisee in his home. This setting conveys an atmosphere of very high decorum in which purity observance surrounding meal-times was a prominent concern. The Pharisaic attention to purity emerges repeatedly in the surrounding narrative (5:27–32; 6:1–11; 11:37–40) and was likely well known to Luke's recipients. Meal settings were not only attentive to the social status of those involved, but scrupulous Israelites in Jesus' day refused to share table with Gentiles and other sinners due to the danger of "cross-contamination." Think of Easter brunch with your fastidious grandmother, or a dinner party at Downton Abbey, and then turn up the decorum meter another several notches.

In setting the scene this way, with his repeated mention of "Pharisees"/"Pharisee's house" in the opening verses (vv. 36–37), Luke accentuates the scandalous nature of an uninvited guest's trespass. A "woman in the city, who was a sinner" enters a domain forbidden to all like her (v. 37). Even more disturbing, this trespasser and transgressor of decency begins fawning over Jesus. Here the narrative slows, as Luke encourages us to attend to each of the woman's acts of humble yet indecorous devotion: standing behind Jesus at his feet and weeping, she engages in the continuous activity (Greek geeks: note the imperfect tense) of bathing his feet with her tears, drying them with her hair, kissing his feet, and anointing them with costly perfume (vv. 37–38).

Simon is Scandalized

Although we do not know why the woman is regarded as "sinful" by her community, her very presence and even more so her intimate actions in the context of a dinner gathering would be seen by most in this culture as simply indecent. Luke's casting of the setting and its characters indicates this woman of ill repute—at least from the perspective of Simon and his other guests (and perhaps many of Luke's recipients!)—"comes into this scene like an alien, communicable disease."[8] No wonder Simon the Pharisee is beside himself with disgust that Jesus allows a woman such as this to touch him, and doubts Jesus' prophetic insight: "If this man were a prophet, he would have known who and what kind of woman this is who is touching him— that she is a sinner!" (v. 39).

Jesus' Response: "Do you see this woman?"

"Simon," Jesus replies, "I have something to say to you." And in what follows, we see Jesus' practice of Torah poignantly unveiled.

Jesus begins his lesson to Simon with a parable. There are two debtors who owe their creditor vastly different sums, one five hundred denarii, and the other fifty. When neither can pay, the creditor cancels the sums of both. Now who will love the creditor more?

The answer is obvious, of course, and Simon gets it. The one with the greater debt. "You have judged rightly," Jesus affirms. But as Jesus' instruction unfolds, he is going to ask Simon to see what is not at all apparent to him.

"Then turning to the woman, Jesus said to Simon, 'Do you see this woman?'" Again, another statement of the obvious. But here too, what is obvious on the surface is meant to point Simon to a more complicated, underlying reality that Jesus wants him to comprehend. Simon doesn't really see the woman, at least not as he should. Simon sees her as a manifestation of much of what he loathes. To him, this woman is a scandal, an embodied rejection of Torah, and to make matters worse she has invaded his home!

Yet the norms of purity and decency as Simon and many of their fellow Israelites define them are not Jesus' norms. Jesus transgresses these boundaries separating pure and impure and establishes other markers of true Torah-keeping in their place. Simon sees this woman as a contagion. Jesus tells Simon he should see her as she truly is: as a fellow human being, and also as a paragon of righteousness.

Jesus points out to Simon that he has neglected to provide Jesus the service of hospitality due to an honored guest. But the woman has not (vv. 44–46). Jesus' celebration of the woman's acts of devotion recalls—and radically reframes—the very same acts that were the source of Simon's disgust. In bathing his feet with her tears, and drying them with her hair, in kissing and anointing Jesus, the woman reveals her faith and righteousness. She humbly acknowledges that she has turned from God and hurt

8. Green, *Luke*, 307.

others. She offers gratitude for the love and forgiveness she has received (v. 47). Her actions bear witness to her trust in Jesus as the manifestation of God's saving reign (v. 50).

Here, as in so many other Gospel stories, we see Jesus transgressing boundaries, championing repentance and humility, and honoring the integrity of those society demeans and marginalizes. But what about that other element of Torah-keeping so characteristic of Jesus' ministry, issuing God's call for others to serve? Jesus says to the woman, "go in peace," knowing that her trust in God's forgiveness and mercy open the way for her to enter into God's realm. Set within the context of Luke's narrative, we could certainly infer that if the woman truly embraces Jesus' invitation for wholeness, she will join others in working to advance God's kingdom in their midst. Perhaps she is among the female disciples Luke speaks about in the very next passage (8:1–3).[9]

But Jesus' call to serve God and live Torah rightly in this passage is not so much directed at the woman. She has already taken the steps that Jesus emphasizes as a critical markers of true righteousness: repentance, humility, and devotion to Jesus. Her "great love," in response to her many sins being forgiven (v. 47), affirms that she is already finding her way into God's kingdom. Jesus' call to serve God and live Torah in this scene, rather, is directed at Simon. It culminates in the very next phrase Jesus utters in vs. 47, to conclude his lesson to the Pharisee: "But the one to whom little is forgiven, loves little."

These ominous words certainly apply to Simon. But note their irony! They lead us to realize here at the passage's end that Simon loves little not because he has so little for which to be forgiven. On the contrary. He loves Jesus (and God) little because he fails to recognize his own substantial need for forgiveness. But the irony cuts even deeper than this. Simon is also "one to whom little is forgiven" *because* he loves little.

Jesus tries to help Simon see the woman through her acts of love and devotion: not to revile her as a contagion, but to truly see her as one who acknowledges her brokenness and yet becomes a model of true piety, to see her as one he should honor and emulate. In doing so, Jesus also tries to help Simon see his own impurity. Simon, simply yet tragically, neglects the core of Torah. He is unaware that the Torah he was using to guide his relations with God and others could only lead to his separation from God and others. Jesus here attempts to show Simon and his fellow Pharisees that the righteousness is first and foremost love for all others. Simon was surely

---

9. Though there is no reason to conclude, as some church tradition maintains, that the "sinful" woman in this passage is Mary Magdalene.

taught and surely believes, "You shall be holy, for I the LORD your God am holy" (Lev 19:2). For Jesus, this means above all else, "Be merciful, just as your Father is merciful" (Luke 6:36).

Jesus transgresses boundaries, champions repentance and humility, honors the integrity of those society demeans and marginalizes, and issues God's call to serve as Jesus' disciples. This is how we see him live out the central requirements of Torah: to love God and all others. Let's now consider how these same principles of living out Torah might be applied to our culture's normalization of patriarchy and heterosexuality.

The Prevalence and Character of Patriarchy

In his text *The Gendered Society*, Michael Kimmel reports, "Virtually every society of which we have knowledge claims some differentiation between women and men, and virtually every society exhibits patterns of gendered inequality and male domination."[10] Kimmel and other anthropologists point out that while gender inequality exists in varying forms and degrees, male domination is elemental to human society, at least as we homo sapiens have formed it over the last several thousand years. Anthropologists offer competing theories on when, how, and why patriarchy has become so pervasive within human communities. But the reality of patriarchy is not in dispute. Almost without exception, we have constructed systems that invest select males, including male heads of kinship (family) groupings, with greater political and economic control, and elevated social status.

Yet the political, economic, and social forms of male privilege we create are really the "tip of the iceberg" when it comes to patriarchy. These systems are manifestations of a culture, a worldview, which values males above females, and what it identifies as masculine characteristics above female characteristics. For the last several millennia of our existence, we have idealized males and the attributes we often assign to masculinity: power, aggression, sexual domination, reason, control. We have also idealized females and many of the attributes assigned to femininity. But many of these attributes are regarded as having lesser value (care for children, compassion) than masculine characteristics; some are seen as outright dangerous and in need of control (emotional, irrational, alluring/seductive). And the most cherished of female attributes is submission.[11] Gerda Lerner explains that a "founding metaphor" of our Western philosophical tradition is the belief that "women are incomplete and damaged human beings of an

---

10. Kimmel, *Gendered Society*, 65.
11. Johnson, *Gender Knot*, 84–88.

entirely different order than men."[12] Most of us today would find such a view extreme, even bizarre. But it was standard among the philosophical and religious thinkers who played a critical role in justifying and perpetuating the patriarchal culture Western civilization has embraced for millennia. Jewish and Christian thinkers are among them.

Unquestionably, over the last century, many societies worldwide have striven for and achieved reduced levels of gender inequality, including the United States.[13] The Women, Peace and Insecurity Index, measuring women's inclusion in society, physical and economic security, and exposure to discrimination, shows significant gains for women even within countries that remain among the worst.[14] Patriarchy's grasp of human society has slipped. Yet it still remains powerful and pervasive, including within the United States. The US lags behind many other nations in two categories: women elected to national legislatures, and community safety, including domestic violence.[15] American women still fall behind their male counterparts in pay for equal work, despite legislation designed to prevent it. Women also continue to be severely underrepresented in positions of leadership in business, medicine, law, academia, and social service agencies.[16]

Including in the church. In fact, in many American Churches, women are told that their gender disqualifies them from serving in leadership positions, and as pastors or priests.

Reading Scripture Through a Lens of Male Privilege

Much like the opponents to abolition in the eighteenth and nineteenth centuries, those seeking to defend patriarchal attitudes and limits on the role of women within the church have biblical passages at the ready to support their views.

12. Lerner, *Creation of Patriarchy,* 199–211.

13. The entire November 11, 2019 issue of *National Geographic,* titled "Women: a Century of Change," provides a wealth of valuable data and personal testimonies on the status of women worldwide.

14. See Berman-Vaporis et al., "Peril, Progress, Prosperity."

15. National Coalition Against Domestic Violence, "Statistics." See Tracy, "Patriarchy and Domestic Violence."

16. Warner et al., "Women's Leadership Gap;" National Association of Social Workers, "Role of Female Leadership."

Women are to be Silent

Two that figure prominently in such arguments are from the Pauline epistles. First Timothy 2:8–15 appears in an epistle attributed to Paul but which
most scholars believe was written in Paul's name well after Paul died.[17] The
epistle focuses on matters of church worship and order, while noting some
of the pernicious false teachings and mispractices that are threatening communities like that of Timothy's. One of the disorderly activities the writer
identifies here in 1 Timothy 2, it appears, is that women have assumed positions of leadership in some of the churches and are speaking with authority
during gatherings of the community.

> [8] I desire, then, that in every place the men should pray, lift-
> ing up holy hands without anger or argument; [9] also that the
> women should dress themselves modestly and decently in suit-
> able clothing, not with their hair braided, or with gold, pearls,
> or expensive clothes, [10] but with good works, as is proper for
> women who profess reverence for God. [11] Let a woman learn in
> silence with full submission. [12] I permit no woman to teach or to
> have authority over a man; she is to keep silent. [13] For Adam was
> formed first, then Eve; [14] and Adam was not deceived, but the
> woman was deceived and became a transgressor. [15] Yet she will
> be saved through childbearing, provided they continue in faith
> and love and holiness, with modesty.

We also find a very similar perspective expressed in 1 Corinthians
14:33b–36, a passage near the end of a long section addressing several issues
related to community worship (1 Cor 11:2–14:40).

> [33b] As in all the churches of the saints, [34] women should be silent
> in the churches. For they are not permitted to speak, but should
> be subordinate, as the law also says. [35] If there is anything they
> desire to know, let them ask their husbands at home. For it is
> shameful for a woman to speak in church. [36] Or did the word of
> God originate with you? Or are you the only ones it has reached?

Many Christian communities, Protestant, Roman Catholic, and Orthodox, that deny women ordination as pastors and priests turn to these

17. First Timothy along with 2 Timothy and Titus together comprise what are often
called the "Pastoral Epistles," because they provide Timothy and Titus with instruction
on how to best guide their communities. For several reasons, including style of writing, theological emphases, and the issues addressed, most Pauline scholars judge these
epistles to be letters written well after Paul's death, as if to say, "If Paul were alive today,
this is what he would tells us about . . ." This practice, called honorable pseudepigraphy,
was rather common in antiquity.

texts to justify their positions. We can see why. The passages place severe limits on the authority women may hold within Christian communities. They are to be subordinate (1 Tim 2:11; 1 Cor 14:34). They are not to teach or have authority over a man (1 Tim 1:12a).

However, most groups that cite these passages to justify their refusal to ordain women at the same time minimize other aspects of these passages, including their prohibition against women speaking in worship for any reason (1 Tim 2:12b; 1 Cor 14:35). I think there are at least two reasons for this. First, female prophets exist in Israelite and early Christian communities, and 1 Corinthians 11:5 indicates that female prophets are speaking in early Christian worship settings. Paul offers guidelines for this practice, but he clearly affirms it. This contradicts what is said in 1 Corinthians 14 and 1 Timothy 2. Second, a prohibition against women speaking in worship for any reason would be severely offensive to many women and men in Roman Catholic and conservative Protestant communities today. The impracticality of the command forces these communities to interpret these texts in ways that reframe or simply ignore their rather straightforward prohibitions against any form of female speech in worship. This is an instance of the "world in front of the text" strong-arming the interpretation of the text.

Let's take a look at how "The Declaration on the Question of Admission of Women to the Ministerial Priesthood," the last definitive statement affirming the Church's position on the ordination of women composed by the Vatican's Sacred Congregation for the Doctrine of the Faith (1975), handles this contradiction:

> Paul in no way opposes the right, which he elsewhere recognises as possessed by women, to prophesy in the assembly (1 Cor 11:15[sic 1 Cor 11:5]); the prohibition solely concerns the official function of teaching in the Christian assembly.[18]

The Declaration is at least to be commended for attempting to address the contradiction. Statements published by other church bodies simply gloss over it.[19] The rationale here is that the form of "speaking" the biblical writers identify as problematic only refers to the utterances of women who are seeking to claim "the official function of teaching in the Christian assembly." This interpretation, however, is problematic on several fronts. That there was

18. Sacred Congregation for the Doctrine of the Faith, "Declaration."

19. See, e.g., the statements published by the Missouri Synod Lutheran Church, under the tab "The Ordination of Women to the Ministerial Office," (https://www.lcms.org/about/beliefs), and the Southern Baptist Convention "Resolution on Ordination and the Role of Women in Ministry (http://www.sbc.net/resolutions/1088/resolution-on-ordination-and-the-role-of-women-in-ministry).

a recognized and regulated, "official function of teaching" practiced in the early church at this point is far from likely. First Corinthians 11–14 itself suggests the opposite: Paul is attempting to provide some semblance of order to a worship scene that was quite chaotic and within which many voices were participating. It is also hard to figure that prophecy would not be regarded as part of the church's teaching ministry, in light of its regular occurrence within early Christian worship and Paul's esteem for early Christian prophets, whom he regards as second only to apostles (see 1 Cor 12:28).

But even more problematic, both passages clearly have in mind forms of speaking other than "official teaching." The writer of 1 Timothy 2 states, "Let a woman learn in silence with full submission" (v. 11). This includes illicit teaching, but also any form of speaking. A blanket gag order for women is even more obvious in 1 Corinthians 14, in which the writer states, "If there is anything they desire to know, let them ask their husbands at home. For it is shameful for a woman to speak in church" (v. 35). The clear sense here is that women were not even to ask questions during gatherings of believers![20]

Creation Demands It

Another dimension of 1 Timothy 2 that is sometimes cited to support denying women ordination is its claim that women assuming authority over men violates the order of creation and disregards women's culpability in introducing sin into the world.

> [13] For Adam was formed first, then Eve; [14] and Adam was not deceived, but the woman was deceived and became a transgressor. [15] Yet she will be saved through childbearing, provided they continue in faith and love and holiness, with modesty.

---

20. More recently, the Pontifical Biblical Commission, in *The Inspiration of Sacred Scripture*, offers more nuanced readings of 1 Timothy 2 and 1 Corinthians 14. In part three of the work, entitled, "The Interpretation of the Word of God and its Challenges" (see 152–54), it acknowledges the problematic nature of the justification 1 Timothy 2 provides on why women should remain silent: woman was second in the order of creation and the first to sin. The Commission also views the commands to silence in both texts as relative to the culture of that time, and not necessarily binding on Christian communities today. The Commission even suggests that the prohibition against women teaching with authority was culturally relative. However, it does not elaborate on the implications of this view. Moreover, the Commission points out in the foreword (xiv) that "the present document of the Biblical Commission does not constitute an official declaration of the Church's Magisterium on this topic."

Such appeals fail to appreciate the very distorted, and just plain misogynistic, reading of Genesis 2–3 provided by the writer of 1 Timothy 2.

In fact, when you look carefully at Genesis 2, and resist the urge to automatically read it through a patriarchal lens as Christian tradition has most often done, it soon becomes apparent how extremely countercultural this story was for its time. Really.

> [18] Then the LORD God said, 'It is not good that the man should be alone; I will make him a helper as his partner.' [19]So out of the ground the LORD God formed every animal of the field and every bird of the air, and brought them to the man to see what he would call them; and whatever the man called each living creature, that was its name. [20]The man gave names to all cattle, and to the birds of the air, and to every animal of the field; but for the man there was not found a helper as his partner.

> [21]So the LORD God caused a deep sleep to fall upon the man, and he slept; then he took one of his ribs and closed up its place with flesh. [22]And the rib that the LORD God had taken from the man he made into a woman and brought her to the man. [23]Then the man said,

> "This at last is bone of my bones
>   and flesh of my flesh;
> this one shall be called Woman,
>   for out of Man this one was taken."

> [24]Therefore a man leaves his father and his mother and clings to his wife, and they become one flesh. [25]And the man and his wife were both naked, and were not ashamed.

Note that the structure, character speech, and repetition in the account of the woman's creation (vv. 21–25) emphasize the *sameness* of the man's and woman's respective natures and the complementary character of their identity and calling, *not* the subservience of woman to man. The substance of the first human used to create the second—the rib—is taken from its side. After the second human is created, the first human declares "This *at last* [unlike the others] is bone of my bones and flesh of my flesh" (v. 23), and then the narrator states "and they become one flesh" (v. 24). To be sure, when we hear the woman described as "helper" (vv. 18, 20), it is easy for us to assume her inferior or secondary status to the man, because in *our* cultural context a "helper" is often a subordinate. But this is simply not how the word (*ezer*) functions in ancient Israelite culture, as evidenced by how it is most often used in the Old Testament: in reference to *God* as deliverer and provider! Here in this story it identifies the woman as one who can provide assistance for the man that he is not able to provide for himself (see vv. 18, 20).

As for Adam being "first," that too does not appear to be of interest to the writer of Genesis 2. In fact, Adam's act of naming himself as "man" and his partner as "woman" (v. 23b) indicates the biblical writer's recognition that gender becomes part of the human experience only when the woman is created. Moreover, the subservience of woman to man enters into creation not here as part of the natural order God intended, but only later as a consequence of humanity's sin against God and one another (see 3:16).

Women are to Blame and Only Good for Making Babies

There are two other features of 1 Timothy that are no longer commonly cited by Christian communities to support their marginalization of women. They are just too extreme. But these features are still important for us to address in order to unmask the prejudices underlying the writer's prohibitions against women. The author of 1 Timothy 2 claims that the first sin of humankind is the responsibility of woman alone. But this is difficult to reconcile with Genesis 3. The narrative implies that Adam was with the woman during her twisted (pardon the pun) conversation with the serpent and readily accepted the forbidden fruit from her hand (3:6). Note too that Adam's excuse in v. 12 can hardly be seen as credible, since he blames both the woman *and* God for his transgression: "The woman who you gave to be with me..." (v. 12). I also think it very unlikely that Paul would concur with the writer of 1 Timothy 2 on the origin of human sin. In Romans, Paul emphasizes that sin came into the world through Adam, who Paul views as representative of humanity in general (see Rom 5:12–21).

Finally, the author of 1 Timothy 2:8–15 concludes his diatribe against women by reinvigorating an age-old, patriarchal, and oppressive trope: what is most essential to a woman's worth—and, amazingly, even her ability to be saved!—is her calling to bear children (v. 15). I very much doubt that Paul would share this view. In fact, I think he would be livid that such words were penned in his name. He would consider them a "perversion of the gospel of Christ" (Gal 1:7), and might even tell the writer of this passage to go castrate himself (see Gal 5:12).

All the Apostles are Men

Still another argument offered by some ecclesial bodies denying ordination to women is that Jesus only appointed male apostles. Certainly, if Jesus had wanted women to be ordained, he would have selected at least some women to serve as apostles.

Admittedly, I can see why this argument would be compelling for many. Jesus had female disciples, so why did he not call a female apostle? If Jesus had wanted women to be ordained, then why not welcome them into the office that serves as the paradigm for ordained ministry in Christ's church? This argument is particularly convincing in traditions that argue for unbroken apostolic succession from the original apostles to the teaching and sacramental authority of the church today, including the authority to ordain.

The problem with this argument is that we don't see the writers of the New Testament treating the "office" of apostle as a paradigm for an office of ordained ministry, or even as a precedent for who is allowed to teach and proclaim the gospel and who is not.

To be sure, Jesus did call apostles to be a distinct group within the larger body of his disciples (e.g., Luke 6:12–16), and this group continued to exist for a time within the early church (Acts 1:12–26; 1 Cor 12:28). In Acts, Luke traces the ministry of the apostles in the church's first months and years. Luke shows them serving a critical role in proclaiming the good news of what God has done in Jesus and establishing the church within Jerusalem and Judea. But as Luke's narrative unfolds, and the gospel spreads beyond Judea, it becomes clear that the preaching and teaching ministry of the church also extends beyond the apostles to include others as well. And this occurs without the apostles' sanction or authority. Theirs is not an "official office" that gets passed down to others through some sort of "ordination" they mediate.

We should expect as much based on how Luke portrays the proclamation of the good news in his gospel. Already in its opening chapters, we hear God's revelation in the voices of Elizabeth, Mary, Zechariah, Anna, and Simeon. Jesus sends home the Gerasene from whom he cast out a demon to "declare how much God has done for you" (8:39). Luke pairs and follows the sending out of the twelve (Luke 9) with the sending out of the seventy (Luke 10), the latter receiving the same commission and authority as the former. After the seventy return, and share their experiences with Jesus, Jesus exclaims,

> "I thank you, Father, Lord of heaven and earth, because you
> have hidden these things from the wise and the intelligent and

have revealed them to infants; yes, Father, for such was your gracious will. All things have been handed over to me by my Father;
and no one knows who the Son is except the Father, or who the
Father is except the Son and anyone to whom the Son chooses
to reveal him." (10:21–22)

Returning to Acts, the proclamation of the good news by others beyond the apostolic circle begins among those the apostles do indeed commission. But these soon-to-be evangelists are not commissioned by the
apostles to "serve the word," but to wait tables, a task that apparently did not
befit the apostles!

> [1] Now during those days, when the disciples were increasing in
> number, the Hellenists complained against the Hebrews because
> their widows were being neglected in the daily distribution of
> food. [2] And the twelve called together the whole community of the
> disciples and said, *"It is not right that we should neglect the word
> of God in order to wait at tables.* [3] *Therefore, friends, select from
> among yourselves seven men of good standing, full of the Spirit and
> of wisdom, whom we may appoint to this task,* [4] *while we, for our
> part, will devote ourselves to prayer and to serving the word."* [5] What
> they said pleased the whole community, and they chose Stephen,
> a man full of faith and the Holy Spirit, together with Philip, Pro-
> chorus, Nicanor, Timon, Parmenas, and Nicolaus, a proselyte
> of Antioch. [6] They had these men stand before the apostles, who
> prayed and laid their hands on them. (Acts 6:1–6)

But at least two of these commissioned table-waiters soon become heroic champions of the word of God themselves: Stephen (see 6:8–8:1) and
Philip (8:4–8, 26–40; 21:8). Moreover, Jesus himself commissions a former
enemy of the way, Saul (Paul), to bring Jesus' name "before Gentiles, kings,
and before the people of Israel" (9:15). While Paul takes on the title of "apostle," Luke and Paul himself make it clear that Paul received his commission
directly from Jesus, not the twelve (see Gal 1:1–2:14). Then halfway through
Acts, we see the focus of the narrative turn from the apostles to Paul and
a host of others, including Barnabas, some nameless "men of Cyprus and
Cyrene," Agabus, Silas, Timothy, Aquila, Priscilla (a woman!), and Apollos.
After Acts 15, the apostles disappear from the narrative. From this point on,
those who Luke presents as fulfilling Jesus' commission at the start of Acts—
to spread the gospel throughout Jerusalem, Judea, Samaria, and to the ends
of the earth (1:8)—are outside the apostolic circle.

Simply put, the twelve are not regarded by Luke as a group with an exclusive office to proclaim the good news, and one that they must authorize

in others in order for their testimony to be valid. That concept is simply foreign to Luke's understanding of faithful witness. Rather, faithful testimony,
in the mind of Luke, is commissioned by Jesus and empowered by the Spirit.
For this reason, as he presents a myriad of witnesses to Jesus and "the word,"
Luke states over and over again:

> "And Elizabeth was filled with the Holy Spirit and exclaimed with a
> loud cry . . ." (Luke 1:41–42).

> "Then his father Zechariah was filled with the Holy Spirit and spoke
> this prophecy . . ." (1:67).

> "Guided by the Spirit, Simeon came into the temple . . ." (2:27).

> "Jesus, full of the Holy Spirit, returned from the Jordan . . ." (4:1).

> "Then Jesus, filled with the power of the Holy Spirit, returned to Gali-
> lee . . ." (4:14).

> "Stay here in the city until you have been clothed with power from on
> high" (24:49).

> "But you will receive power when the Holy Spirit has come upon you,
> and you will be my witnesses in Jerusalem, in all Judea and Samaria
> and to the ends of the earth" (Acts 1:8).

> "All of them were filled with the Holy Spirit and began to speak . . ."
> (2:4).

> "And they were all filled with the Holy Spirit and spoke the word of
> God with boldness . . ." (4:31).

> "seven men of good standing, full of the Spirit and wisdom . . ." (6:3).

> "But they could not withstand the wisdom and Spirit with which he
> [Stephen] spoke . . ." (6:10).

> "When they came up out of the water, the Spirit of the Lord snatched
> Philip away . . ." (8:39).

> "so that you [Paul] may regain your sight and be filled with the Holy
> Spirit . . ." (9:17).

> "While Peter was speaking, the Holy Spirit fell upon all who heard the
> word . . ." (10:44).

> "for he [Baranabas] was a good man, full of the Holy Spirit and of faith
> . . ." (11:24).

"Agabus stood up and predicted by the Spirit that there would be a famine . . ." (11:28).

"So, being sent out by the Holy Spirit, they [Paul and Barnabas] went down to Seleucia . . ." (13:4).

"But Saul, also known as Paul, filled with the Holy Spirit, look intently at him and said . . ." (13:9).

"[Paul, Silas and Timothy] having been forbidden to speak the word in Asia . . ." (16:6).

"the Holy Spirit came upon them [Ephesian converts], and they spoke in tongues and prophesied . . ." (18:6).

"And now, as a captive to the Spirit I [Paul] am on my way to Jerusalem . . ." (20:22).

Luke cannot make it more clear. It is the Holy Spirit, unmediated by tradition or office, that empowers and authorizes the teaching ministry of the early church. Similarly, no New Testament document understands apostolic succession or ordination as a necessary requirement for faithful teaching within the church. This is a later, post-biblical development first documented in what is commonly titled the *First Letter of Clement*, the date for which ranges from the end of the first well into the second century CE.

Challenging Patriarchy: Social Movement and Countermovement in Early Christianity

Please go back and reread 1 Timothy 2:8–15 and 1 Corinthians 14:33–36. Note the vehemence both passages convey, and the universal character of the condemnation implied by their prohibitions. Recall the strong misogynistic tone of 1 Timothy 2, with its emphasis on the subordinate and sinful nature of women. What has gotten under the skin of these writers?

The most likely explanation is that in some early churches women were speaking and teaching in worship, and doing so with authority that was granted to them by their communities. Other New Testament texts, including letters Paul wrote, affirm this was indeed the case! Women like Anna (Luke 2:36–38) and Philip's daughters (Acts 21:9) and others (1 Cor 11:5) actively prophesied (see also Acts 2:17–18!). Women like Priscilla (Acts 18:26; Rom 16:3), or Euodia and Syntyche (Phil 4:2–3), taught or evangelized as Paul's "co-workers." Women like Phoebe served in positions of leadership (Rom 16:1–2). Paul even regards a woman and fellow prisoner, Junia, as "prominent among the apostles" (Rom 16:7). And these are only the women we know about! This practice among early Christian communities, of recognizing and valuing the testimony and leadership of women, transgresses the gender roles typical of the Mediterranean's patriarchal culture in which maleness was the ideal and femaleness was often denigrated.

> In the Greco-Roman World, masculinity was defined in relation to its ostensible antithesis: namely femininity. To be a "manly" man was *not* to be a woman, and in order to maintain that manliness, men had to avoid traits that were typically associated with women. Men, or at least "true" men, were characterized as being dominant, active, and self-controlled, whereas women were characterized as being subordinate, passive, and excessive, especially in terms of displaying emotion, loving luxury, and being overly concerned with their appearance. With these polarities of dominant/subordinate, active/passive, and self-controlled/excessive, the underlying assumption is that "man" is both the social superior and the unspoken norm . . . Indeed, the overarching man/woman polarity evident in ancient texts is construed in hierarchal terms, with "man" at the top and "woman" at the bottom of this vertical axis of power.[21]

Likely inspired by Jesus' inclusion of female disciples, the recognition of women's gifts for teaching and leadership within the early church is one of several features marking early Christian communities as countercultural social movements.

However, as 1 Timothy 2 and 1 Corinthians 14 clearly indicate, not all within these early Christian communities were comfortable with the eschewal of social convention when it came to women. They launched a countermovement to put women back in their place and, as witnessed in 1 Timothy 2, they appealed to their prejudicial views of women as excessively emotional, loving luxury, and being overly concerned with appearance to justify the prohibitions levelled against them.

Did Paul himself change his mind on the place of women in the community? This is possible. But as noted earlier, most scholars understand 1 Timothy to be written in Paul's name well after his death, and it seems very unlikely that Paul would blame women as the cause of human sin and so

---

21. Wilson, *Unmanly Men*, 40–41. Wilson's text offers a helpful and well-researched account of the virulent patriarchy common to both Roman and Jewish culture in Jesus' day. She also details how Jesus, Paul, and other male characters in Luke's narrative engage in practices and experience humiliations that would lead them to be seen as emasculated or "unmanly" according to the norms of their context. In doing so, Wilson argues, Luke presents Jesus as redefining true masculinity as suffering on behalf of others.

radically change his views on how believers are saved. How then are we to make sense of 1 Corinthians 14:34–35, within a letter Paul almost certainly wrote? These verses migrate to different locations in several early manuscripts of 1 Corinthians. Coupled with the reality that they express a perspective on women that is difficult to reconcile with Paul's commendation of female prophets, teachers, and deacons elsewhere in his letters (including 1 Corinthians), the transient nature of vv. 34–35 suggests that Paul did not compose them, but they were added later to his letter as part of the countermovement against the emergence of female leaders in the early church. These verses are likely a forgery.

Patriarchy and Torah Today

History shows us that within the early church, the countermovement wins out. Patriarchy returns as a fundamental principle guiding the shape and practice of Christianity.

And it still does for many. But think about this. Christians today still deny women the opportunity to accept a call into ordained ministry simply because they are, well, women.

Doesn't that just strike you as weird, and not a little sad or perhaps, understandably, quite infuriating? Especially when you realize that this age-old "tradition" is informed by a host of assumptions about women and their worth relative to men, and rooted in a cultural worldview that has developed in large part to justify male privilege and power? What proponents of even "soft patriarchy" and other defenders of "men and women are equal but just have different roles" struggle to address today are that the roles reserved for men—both inside and outside the church—are the ones at the top of the ecclesial, social, and economic hierarchies we have created. That is a rather strange conception of equality.

Proponents of patriarchy within the church have passages like 1 Corinthians 14 and 1 Timothy 2 locked and loaded. But again, note the vehemence and misogyny of these instructions. As we have seen, these passages are so extreme that most patriarchal Christians today do all they can to tone them down, misrepresenting what the passages really have to say so that they can still use the parts that support their perspective. They want to claim these passages as the Word of God, universally true for all times, but either ignore or cloak their true character. This reading strategy betrays two realities: these proponents of patriarchy are reading Scripture badly, and these are passages not worthy of Christ's Torah for us today.

As we saw above, Jesus called women as disciples. The only woman we ever see Jesus effectively (but compassionately) "shush" is Martha. She was attempting to deny her sister, Mary, a seat among the disciples listening to Jesus' teaching. Jesus tells Martha to mind *Mary's* place, for the calling Mary has chosen "will not be taken away from her" (Luke 10:38–42). Jesus didn't tell women to be quiet. If he had, it would have taken the other disciples a lot longer to figure out that he was raised from the dead (see Matt 28:10). And, I really can't imagine a more significant element of "official Christian teaching" than Jesus' resurrection.

So why didn't Jesus call female apostles? My best guess is that he knew his followers were not ready for it. And even though his extremely countercultural calling and treatment of female disciples inspired some communities within the early church to regard women as valuable partners in ministry and invest them with authority, early Christian history and even our scriptural tradition indicates that Jesus was right—just like we were not yet ready to recognize the evil that slavery surely is. Jesus left us with more work to do, with more binding and loosing to figure out, with the Spirit pulling us, sometimes kicking and screaming, towards a fuller understanding of what it means to love others as we should.

Reconsidering Homosexuality

Like proponents for the abolition of slavery, and the full inclusion of women in the life and ministry of the early church, those advocating the same for couples in same-sex relationships also face an arsenal of biblical passages arrayed against them.[22] As noted earlier, some have tried to dismiss the plain-sense meaning of passages such as Romans 1:26–27 and 1 Corinthians 6:9 by arguing that these passages really only have pederasty or male prostitution in view. Yet this reasoning fails in the face of Romans 1:26–27, which implies consensual sexual relations between males and also clearly references female homosexuality. It also rests on an inaccurate understanding of New Testament's historical context, as it overlooks the prevalence of consensual sexual relations between males in the Roman world. In addition to these prohibitions, Scripture nowhere endorses same-gender, homoerotic relationships.

However, as we read through the biblical traditions, we find that Scripture does provide us with a rather clear conception of God's intentions for

22. For a representative view of a conservative American Christian position on homosexuality, see the position paper of the Southern Baptist Convention, Mohler, Jr., "Homosexuality and the Bible."

human coupling: intimate relationship, mutual edification, rearing and instruction of children, protection, security, hospitality, etc. Scripture also unveils features of human relatedness that lead to blessing: interdependence, mutuality, respect, intimacy, loyalty. If there are homosexual relationships that exhibit those features of blessed, human relatedness, and largely fulfill God's intentions for human coupling, shouldn't that give us pause when denouncing the sexual intimacy that is also an important part of, and even a resource for, the blessing those couples share with one another?

The Bible may not endorse homosexuality per se, but it does say a lot about the kind of relatedness that leads us more deeply into God's intentions for humanity. Looking back through our history as God's people, it also teaches us to be careful about identifying certain persons and lifestyles as intractably opposed to the will of God, especially when the standards for doing so reside on the periphery of our faith and may be transcended by later God-given insight and instruction. Remember Ezra and Nehemiah's concerns about the purity of Israelite marriage when Israelites began to take non-Israelite wives (see chapter 2). Remember the drastic, exclusive, unwelcoming yet Torah-approved steps they took to restore the proper order of that institution: divorce and abandonment of their foreign wives and children. Remember Isaiah's radical proclamation (in response to Ezra's policies) that God's house is big enough for those foreigners, and that they too will participate fully and faithfully in God's restored community. Remember the early church debating and eventually setting aside the requirements of circumcision and dietary codes, despite the laws of Moses, so that Gentiles could freely become part of that community. Remember Christians appealing to the epistles to justify the horror of slavery, and others appealing to Jesus' love command and the biblical call to justice to bear witness to the more faithful way. Reflecting on this chapter of our history, Rachel Held Evans offers insight useful for the church in any age:

> I think it's important to remind ourselves now and then that we've been wrong before, and that sometimes it's not about the number of proof texts we can line up or about the most simplistic reading of the text, but rather some deep, intrinsic sense of right and wrong, some movement of the Spirit, that points us toward truth and to a better understanding of what Scripture really says.[23]

Guided by the Spirit, many believers have come to discern Jesus leading them to a deeper, intrinsic sense of right and wrong, pointing them to a better understanding of Scripture and what it means to be God's people.

23. Evans, "Is Abolition 'Biblical'?"

In seeking to live out Torah as Jesus did, many are now fully and rightfully welcoming LGBTQIA+ persons as fellow sisters and brothers in Christ.

The Ongoing Witness of Scripture and Spirit

The ongoing witness of the Spirit—as Jesus, Paul, and other New Testament witnesses tell us—is the critical element in faithfully discerning and living out Christ's Torah in our times and places. This certainly does not mean that we have progressed beyond the instruction offered Scripture, as though we have outgrown it. Far from it! As I have stressed throughout this chapter and the previous chapters, the instructions guiding behavior given in both testaments, when viewed within their contexts and especially through the lens of Jesus' own instruction, are the starting point for discerning how we are to live as Christ's disciples. We must honor the testimonies of our ancestors.

But the instructions codified in Scripture are not the end point of our deliberation on what it means to live as God's people, nor should they be. These instructions are themselves rooted in specific historical contexts, and many of their elements are shaped more by human culture and limited human knowledge than by the core of God's Torah. We also must remember that Jesus hoped to cultivate in his followers the gift of thoughtful, imaginative, Spirit-led discernment. He was after disciples who had Torah written on their hearts, not disciples who would try to reduce biblical instruction into tidy lists of do's and don'ts. For Jesus—the living Word—continues to come to us and again say, "You have heard it was said . . . but I tell you . . ." and so calls us to discover more deeply what it means to live out the essence of his Torah.

This is hardly an easy or straightforward calling, this charge to bind and loose Torah, to live out the command to love God and one another with all that we have in all that we do. Repentance and humility, transgressing boundaries that divide and demean, honoring the integrity of others, issuing God's call to serve and love others—these essential elements of righteousness don't always come easy for us. But Christ-inspired Torah-keeping *necessitates* that we recognize our allegiance to code and culture can often be more about our limited perspectives and insecurities than about God's will. It *necessitates* that we open our hearts to the testimony of the Spirit, a testimony that leads us to see and honor in others what can only come from God. And once we encounter such testimony, once we are confronted with the God-given integrity and giftedness of those that our culture has taught us to demean, subjugate, and dehumanize, our tidy lists suddenly seem so petty, cruel, and small-hearted.

"Dr. Kuhn, should woman be pastors? What does the Bible say?"

Looking back, I wonder why I hesitated and initially struggled to reply to this question posed by my Haitian students and friends. The answer that really mattered, the interpretation that was really directed by the Spirit, was obvious.

Reflection and Discussion Questions

1. Are there instructions in Scripture that you don't think should guide the lives of Christians today? Why do you think they are no longer applicable?

2. How has the patriarchal character of our culture impacted you, and your views on the role of women in society and the church?

3. In what other ways do you see our culture influencing the behavior of Christians today?

4. What do you think about the notion that Christians are to "bind and loose" as guided by Scripture *and* the Spirit? How is that supposed to work?

Reading the Bible Well

"I don't interpret the Bible! I just read it!"

I INTRODUCED YOU TO this table-pounding yet well-meaning gentleman in the introduction. He did not want his reading of Scripture unnecessarily complicated by some over-eager college professor fresh out of graduate school! I can appreciate where he was coming from. His way of reading Scripture worked just fine, and he had been doing it for years. In the end, perhaps the most important thing is that he was reading his Bible, in conversation with others, and his faith was nurtured by that spiritual discipline. We could use more folks like him in the church.

But as I also stressed in the introduction, any act of discerning meaning is an act of interpretation. The interpretation of Scripture is an unavoidable necessity. We never "just read" Scripture, or anything for that matter. I also stressed that how we go about interpreting Scripture is in large measure shaped by a conglomeration of preconceived notions, experiences, settings, and dispositions that we bring with us to the Bible. We each encounter Scripture through our own personalized set of "reading glasses" that are in varying degrees similar and dissimilar to those worn by fellow Christians. We each bring to Scripture our own "world in front of the text."

The chapters following the introduction have highlighted some of the reading tendencies of North American Christians that I believe distort the testimony God inspired our ancestors in the faith to provide in Scripture. We sometimes read the Bible badly. The reading glasses we don are not always properly calibrated to receive from Scripture what God wants us to get out of it. We sometimes end up reading the Bible "against the grain," or at cross purposes with, its witness to Jesus and the kingdom of God. We have even used Scripture to dehumanize and abuse others.

This tendency, of course, is certainly not unique to North American Christians. Scripture itself reveals that misunderstanding God's word and will was common among God's people, including Jesus' earliest followers. This is one more reason why humility and repentance have always been so important for us. They pave the way for us to receive the Spirit and take hold of God's transforming grace. They enable us to recognize our need to adjust our lenses in order to understand God's word and live out God's will more fully.

This short conclusion gathers up insights from the preceding chapters, and adds a few more, on what I think it means to read the Bible well.

Seeing Scripture Clearly

Essential to a useful lens, or hermeneutic (remember that word?), for reading Scripture well is that it is true to the Bible's own nature and purpose as sacred testimony. Here are four characteristics of Scripture that a well-rounded set of reading glasses will allow us to see, and appreciate.

The Human Nature of Scripture

Throughout the preceding pages, I have cautioned against the perspective that the Bible is the "inerrant Word of God." This understanding of Scripture fails to appreciate that the Bible is a God-inspired yet also very human work. As a gathering of testimonies to God and God's will for humanity, the Bible is subject to many of the same limitations that characterize other human writings. Collectively, these writings contain contradictions of fact, cultural biases and assumptions, and even contrasting perspectives on what God is like and what it means to be God's people.

The Real-life Testimonies of Real People in Real Times and Places

At the same time, the very human character, the messiness of these writings, reflects their sacred, inspired genius. As I bemoaned in chapter 2, a lens that treats the Bible as inerrant and infallible fails to acknowledge what appears so obvious to many others. That is, the biblical writers interacted dynamically and creatively with their sacred traditions—even the ones they thought came from God. They claimed the right and the responsibility to celebrate certain dimensions of their encounters with God and to focus on those aspects of God's will for them that were most relevant to their circumstances and struggles. God gave our ancestors the space and freedom they needed to wrestle with, reflect upon, and make sense of their experiences of God and the testimonies of their predecessors in their own times and places. God grants us that same freedom as well. Even if that means we will not do it perfectly.

The miracle of Scripture is not that God so controlled the humans who composed it that it inerrantly entombs the voice of God alone. The miracle of Scripture is that it is one more instance of God allowing God's word to become incarnate in our varied hearts and minds and voices. The Bible is a wondrous embodiment of God's invitation for us and our communities of faith to celebrate, struggle with, and be transformed by our encounter with Emmanuel, God with us.

Dynamic and Reforming

Relatedly, when we step back and cast a broad gaze across the expanse of biblical tradition, it becomes clear that God's instruction to Gods' people has been dynamic and reforming. As our ancestors in the faith engaged in the struggle to discern God's will for them, they were often led to make adjustments to how God's Torah was to be lived out in their particular settings. We see this reflected in the major bodies of legal tradition within the Old Testament. We also find that Jesus' teaching marks a radical recasting of Torah and prevailing understandings of righteousness, but always around an enduring, nonnegotiable center: loving God and neighbor. Our scriptural tradition bears witness to the reality that there is both a core and periphery to Torah, and what is peripheral is subject to adjustment as we discern what it means to loose and bind God's instruction in our times and places.

Unity in Many Voices

Despite the wide variety of settings and concerns these writings reflect, and the multitude of voices they present, the biblical writings—remarkably and I would say miraculously—also present a largely unified account of the relationship between God and God's people, God's character, and God's will for humanity. This is one of those elements of Scripture in which God's guiding hand is most apparent. Amidst its diversity, the Bible proclaims a coherent story (see Appendix Two).

This element of Scripture can be seen in several of its features, but most readily in the "summaries" interspersed throughout the biblical tradition: passages in which the author, or a character within the story, pauses to review events that have either already taken place or are yet to come, or both. Often, these biblical summaries cast wide their purview over major segments of the history between God and God's people. When within a narrative, summaries often occur at key moments in the life of Israel and function not unlike a soliloquy in a play: the action in the narrative stops and a character steps forth to offer an explanation of how the critical moment at hand is to be understood in relation to the larger story of God's dealings with humanity and Israel (e.g., God's call to Moses: Exod 3:1–22; Moses' call for Israel to remember and trust in God: Deut 1:1–3:29, Josh 24:2–13; predictions of unrelenting disobedience and destruction: Lev 26:1–46, Deut 28:1–68; the Davidic covenant and building of the Temple: 2 Sam 7:1–29, 1 Kgs 8:22–53; God's salvation of humankind in Jesus: Acts 2:14–36; 7:2–50). When occurring in non-narrative material, such as in the Psalms or prophetic traditions, the summaries likewise serve the function of uniting the moment at hand with the overarching story of God's relationship with Israel (e.g., Jer 7:1–8:3, Pss 78, 105, 136). The summaries also consistently emphasize certain dimensions of God's character and will, indicating these as features basic to the biblical portrait of God.[1]

I am going to ask you to pull out your Bibles one last time and turn to Nehemiah 9. Set within Judah during the Persian period, the book of Nehemiah tells of the struggles and perseverance of the Israelites as they rebuild the walls of Jerusalem, an important step in making the city secure and defensible. It also tells of Israel's rededication to God and God's Torah. On a day of national confession, Ezra stands to offer a sermon that provides the most expansive summary of the biblical story within the Old Testament. Beginning with creation, Ezra traces their history through Abram and Exodus, Mount Sinai and the Golden Calf affair, the wilderness wanderings and conquest of Canaan, leading finally to monarchy, destruction, and their present moment in exile. The conclusion to Ezra's historical review recalls a confession of God's character that emerges in the aftermath of the Golden Calf affair (see Exod 34:6) and from that time on resonates throughout the Old Testament: "Nevertheless, in your great mercies you did not make an end of them or forsake them, for you are a gracious and merciful God" (Neh 9:31).

This summary unifies the entire record of Israel's history up to that point within a coherent story that dovetails with the other summaries we encounter throughout the Old Testament and others appearing in the New Testament. Rehearsing the pivotal moments spanning from creation to exile, it also testifies to elemental aspects of God's character and will: God is

---

1. For a more detailed account of biblical summaries and other features of the Bible which presume or proclaim an overarching story of the relationship between God and creation, see Kuhn, *Having Words*, chapter 6.

Creator, Covenant Maker, Savior, Instructor. God calls for Israel's trust and obedience, and yet responds to Israel's propensity towards faithlessness and injustice not only with discipline but forbearance, for God is above all else merciful and gracious, slow to anger and abounding with steadfast love and faithfulness.

Attending to these four characteristics of Scripture enable us to see it for what it truly is. While defenders of inerrancy claim that this doctrine is necessary for ensuring the truthfulness of the church's teachings, it not only distorts the nature of Scripture but also makes it much more difficult for those who embrace it to discern a biblically informed faith. Inerrancy leads us to overlook much of what is so wondrous, miraculous, and truly edifying about the Bible. It also prevents us from reading Scripture as it was meant to be read: as a dynamic, messy, sometimes conflicting gathering of inspired testimonies held together by a coherent, overarching witness to God's character, God's love for humanity, and our calling to be God's people.

Honoring our Ancestors, and Reading with Self-Awareness

The world behind the text. The world of the text. The world in front of the text.

Context is (almost) everything. Without thoughtful regard for context, we are at risk of simply hearing in Scripture an echo of our own voices, and seeing in Scripture a reflection of our own conceptions of God and faith. For those who read Scripture with the primary goal of self-affirmation and justifying the status quo, disregarding context is quite advantageous. Like putty, the passages of Scripture can simply be worked into the shape desired by those "reading" it. Yet for those committed to Paul's call to "not conform any longer to the patterns of this world but be transformed by the renewing of your minds," a "context-less" reading of Scripture just won't do.

To honor the testimony of our ancestors preserved in the Bible to who God is and what it means to be God's people, we need to know something about their times and places, struggles and yearnings, hopes and dreams. We need to know something about how the calling they were discerning from God led them to turn away from and challenge the embodiments of sin and injustice prevalent in their midst. We also need to engage carefully the writings they produced, taking seriously their giftedness as writers, and the literary and rhetorical artistry that is the vehicle for the testimonies they composed.

To honor the testimony that the Spirit is seeking to speak among us today as we reflect on the testimonies of our ancestors, we also need to be

self-aware. We need to be mindful of how our individual and collective histories and experiences, and how our own times, places, and cultures might
condition the way we encounter what Jesus is still trying to teach us. We also
need to be aware of the tendencies of our species: to view life as an agonistic,
zero-sum game, to construct systems of male domination characterized by
the grossly inequal distribution of resources, to invest a select group of elite
with the power to create and preserve our political, social, and religious insti-
tutions. We need to be aware of our human tendency to interpret our sacred,
liberating traditions guided more by fear and hatred than trust and love.

Following Torah as Jesus Teaches Us

The understanding of Torah I have argued for in the preceding pages is un-
abashedly *christological*. That is, it makes sense of Torah guided by what I
understand to be Jesus' characterization and treatment of Torah. I argue that
Jesus' interpretive tendencies should be the standard by which we assess our
own interpretive tendencies and traditions.

The most critical element in Jesus' regard for and use of Torah is
that it is defined by its center: to love God and love neighbor. As a result,
anything—no matter how well established within our sacred traditions or
our cultures—that does not honor the center of Torah is simply no longer
Torah for us. It is to be set aside. Just as importantly, all of the rules, policies, and traditions we continue to develop as we seek to live out God's instruction today are provisional. They mark (we trust) our best attempts to
be faithful to God's instruction in our times and places. But we must also
be humble enough to recognize that we may screw it up, and at times quite
badly (as we did with slavery), or may simply not yet be mature enough
to grasp the fullness of what it means to love God and others (as we have
regarding women in ministry and homosexuality). Jesus is still teaching
us, and we need to keep listening.

Faithful Discernment, Trusting Discernment

For as we also saw in the preceding pages, Jesus is not after followers who
create neat and tidy lists of do's and don'ts, even if he understands our need
to do so. Rather, what really matters, what is truly transformative, what
more so than anything else opens the way for the kingdom to be present in
our midst, is a heart that remains open to Jesus' instruction.

Most often, English translations of the Bible render the Greek noun,
pistis, as "faith," and the verb *pisteuo*, as "believe." But I don't think these

translations best capture how these terms are most often used by Jesus and the New Testament writers. In our cultural context, we often associate "faith" and "believe" with one's cognitive assent to statements of propositional truth. From there, it is a short skip and a hop to thinking "faith" as a commitment to a certain set of doctrines, and salvation as dependent upon one's commitment to a particular formulation of dogma. Church history, sadly, is filled with examples of this kind of thinking. It has energized schism, excommunication, execution, and genocide.

Instead of "faith" and "believe," I think the underlying Greek terms would be better translated as "trust," as both noun and verb. Trust still includes a cognitive dimension; it still implies a commitment to a certain conception of God and what it means to be God's people. But I think it better captures the volitional and relational dimensions of heart and will that are so apparent when Jesus calls others to "follow me," or when Paul speaks of "offering our bodies as living sacrifices, holy and pleasing to God." It also helpfully signals that trust in the form of courage is essential to faithful discipleship and discernment, both in Jesus' day and ours.

Courage is essential, because following Jesus then and now is so countercultural, sometimes even counter-*ecclesial*. The same tendencies towards injustice, self-preservation, scarcity, privilege, and discrimination that have characterized our human past and infiltrated the church continue to challenge American Christians today. As followers of Jesus, we are called to discern God's Torah with an unwavering commitment to humility and repentance, transgressing boundaries that divide and demean, honoring the integrity of others, and issuing God's call to serve and love others. We are called to bold, prophetic witness, that decries injustice, and somehow does so from a center of lovingkindness for all, even for the perpetuators of those injustices (Matt 5:44–47; 1 Cor 13). We are to defend the essentials of our faith, while resisting the urge to construct and defend complex edifices of dogmatic purity, understanding that above all else *mercy* defines God's holiness, and our likeness to God (Matt 5:48).

Trust, our eschewal of the fear that so often haunts our past and present, is essential to our place within, and our embodiment of, the kingdom of God. Trust enables us to proclaim and celebrate the enduring truth that the word God desires most to speak to us and others is grace.

APPENDIX ONE

The Whole Bible Lectionary (WBL)

WHAT FOLLOWS IS A lectionary designed to engage the biblical traditions in more depth than the current lectionaries most commonly used by American Christians, and Christians around the world. Its goal is to help communities of faith deeply encounter the testimony of their spiritual ancestors as they discern what it means to bear witness to Jesus and God's reign in their own times and places.

Like the present lectionaries, the WBL revolves around major seasons of the church year: Advent, Christmas, Epiphany, Lent, Easter, and Pentecost. But it contains several features that diverge significantly from the Lectionary for Mass (LFM), Revised Common Lectionary (RCL), and Narrative Lectionary (NL), while sharing several similarities with the NL.

1. Like the NL, the WBL abandons the three-year cycle and reads extensively from all the Gospels in a four-year cycle, from Advent through Pentecost. This corrects the marginalization of John by both the LFM and RCL, and facilitates a more robust, semicontinuous reading of the Gospels.

2. Unlike the NL, however, the WBL uses most of the Sundays of Advent and Easter to engage additional teachings of Jesus in Matthew, Luke, and John. With Mark, it uses the apocalyptic discourse of Mark 13 during Advent while featuring James during the season of Easter. This enables the WBL to cover substantially more material from the Gospels than the NL.

3. Unlike any other lectionary, the WBL uses a seven-year rotation for the "Post-Pentecost Cycle." This enables users of the lectionary to encounter many more biblical traditions than the LFM and RCL, and in some

instances in more depth than the NL. Due to its importance, an Old Testament Story sequence, capturing the landmark events of the first testament, is scheduled in years 1 and 4 of the Post-Pentecost cycle.

4. The WBL features only one reading each Sunday. Users are encouraged to supplement that reading with either a psalm or another biblical tradition that provides helpful background information for the lesson in view. For instance, while reading through the prophetic traditions, worship leaders may find it useful to include lessons from the historical books that address the same period in Israel's history (e.g., supplementing Isaiah 56 with a reading from Ezra 9–10). Or, when reading through the New Testament traditions, worship leaders may read Old Testament lessons that are clearly in view by the New Testament authors (e.g., supplementing Mark 1:1–15 with Isa 40:1–11).

5. The WBL often provides longer readings to ensure the literary integrity of each selection, and it *never* splices and dices individual passages.

6. Users of the WBL are encouraged to treat its reading schedule as a guide, and to diverge from it when pressing matters or concerns in the lives of their congregations could be better addressed by other biblical traditions.

Finally, an important qualification. The following schedules reflect my attempt to provide as balanced and thorough an engagement with the biblical traditions as allowed by its four- and seven-year cycles. However, any lectionary schedule for the church should be developed in consultation with others. Thus, I present these schedules to illustrate the possibilities of this alternative format and strategy, and not as a lectionary ready for congregational use.

Four-Year Advent–Pentecost Cycle[1]

Year 1: Matthew

First Sunday of Advent	24:1–28	The End of This Age
Second Sunday of Advent	24:29–44	The Advent of the Son of Man
Third Sunday of Advent	25:31–46	Sheep and Goats

---

1. For the sake of simplicity, I am assuming the maximum number of Sundays possible from Advent through Pentecost to map out the four-year cycle. Slight adjustments would need to be made occasionally to account for the variability in the number of Sundays of the Epiphany season.

Fourth Sunday of Advent	1:1–25	Immanuel Arrives
Nativity of the Lord	Luke 2:1–20	The True Lord and Savior is Born
First Sunday after Christmas Day	2:1–18	The Magi's Faith, Herod's Rage
First Sunday after the Epiphany	2:19–3:17	John Testifies and Jesus is Anointed
Second Sunday after the Epiphany	4:1–17	Satan Tempts Jesus
Third Sunday after the Epiphany	10:1–25	Jesus Sends Out the Twelve
Fourth Sunday after the Epiphany	10:26–42	Bold and Courageous Witness
Fifth Sunday after the Epiphany	11:20–29	Revelation to Infants
Sixth Sunday after the Epiphany	12:1–21	The Servant of God
Seventh Sunday after the Epiphany	14:1–36	John is Killed, Jesus Feeds and Heals
Transfiguration Sunday	16:24–17:13	Humiliation and Transfiguration
Ash Wednesday	18:1–14	True Greatness
First Sunday in Lent	18:15–35	Forgiveness
Second Sunday in Lent	20:1–16	Laborers in the Vineyard
Third Sunday in Lent	20:17–34	True Service and Sight
Fourth Sunday in Lent	21:18–32	The Time to Believe is Now
Fifth Sunday in Lent	22:34–40	The Greatest Commandment
Palm Sunday	21:1–17	Jesus Ransacks the Temple
Maundy Thursday	26:17–30	Passover
Good Friday	26:31–27:66	Passion
Easter Sunday	28:1–20	Resurrection
Second Sunday of Easter	5:1–16	Sermon on the Mount
Third Sunday of Easter	5:17–33	Sermon on the Mount
Fourth Sunday of Easter	5:34–48	Sermon on the Mount
Fifth Sunday of Easter	6:1–18	Sermon on the Mount
Sixth Sunday of Easter	6:19–34	Sermon on the Mount
Seventh Sunday of Easter	7:1–12; 24–29	Sermon on the Mount
Day of Pentecost	Acts 2:1–36	The Good News Erupts

Year 2: Mark

First Sunday of Advent	13:1–13	The Temple Shall Fall
Second Sunday of Advent	13:14–27	The End of the Age
Third Sunday of Advent	13:28–37	The Advent of the Son of Man
Fourth Sunday of Advent	Isaiah 11:1–9	The Righteous King Arrives
Nativity of the Lord	Luke 2:1–20	The True Lord and Savior is Born
First Sunday after Christmas Day	Isaiah 42:1–20	God Lifts Up God's Servant
First Sunday after the Epiphany	1:1–15	The Beginning of the Good News
Second Sunday after the Epiphany	1:14–45	Jesus Calls and Heals
Third Sunday after the Epiphany	2:1–28	Jesus Breaks Boundaries
Fourth Sunday after the Epiphany	4:1–34	Jesus Teaches in Parables
Fifth Sunday after the Epiphany	5:1–20	Jesus Crosses Over and Saves
Sixth Sunday after the Epiphany	5:21–43	Jesus Restores Life
Seventh Sunday after the Epiphany	7:1–23	What Truly Defiles
Transfiguration Sunday	8:27–9:8	Humiliation and Transfiguration
Ash Wednesday	9:30–37	True Greatness
First Sunday in Lent	9:14–29	Jesus Casts Out an Evil Spirit
Second Sunday in Lent	10:17–31	The Grieving Rich Man
Third Sunday in Lent	10:32–52	True Service and Sight
Fourth Sunday in Lent	11:1–25	Jesus Ransacks the Temple
Fifth Sunday in Lent	12:28–44	The Greatest Commandment
Palm Sunday	14:3–11	Anointing and Betrayal
Maundy Thursday	14:12–31	Passover
Good Friday	14:32–15:47	Passion
Easter Sunday	15:42–16:8	Resurrection
Second Sunday of Easter	James 1:1–18	Faithful Endurance
Third Sunday of Easter	James 1:19–2:13	Be Doers of the Word
Fourth Sunday of Easter	James 2:14–26	Faith Without Works is Dead
Fifth Sunday of Easter	James 3:1–18	Taming the Tongue
Sixth Sunday of Easter	James 4:1–17	Faithful Living

Seventh Sunday of Easter	James 5:1–20	Patience and Prayer of the Righteous
Day of Pentecost	Acts 2:1–36	The Good News Erupts

Year 3: Luke

First Sunday of Advent	1:1–25	The Birth of John Foretold
Second Sunday of Advent	1:26–38	The Birth of Jesus Foretold
Third Sunday of Advent	1:39–56	Mary Announces God's Deliverance
Fourth Sunday of Advent	1:57–80	The Prophet of the Most High is Born
Nativity of the Lord	2:1–20	The True Lord and Savior is Born
First Sunday after Christmas Day	2:21–52	Simeon and Anna Prophesy
First Sunday after the Epiphany	3:1–22	The Ministry of John the Baptist
Second Sunday after the Epiphany	3:23–4:13	Satan Tempts Jesus, Son of Adam
Third Sunday after the Epiphany	4:14–30	Jesus Rejected at Nazareth
Fourth Sunday after the Epiphany	5:1–16	Jesus Calls and Heals
Fifth Sunday after the Epiphany	7:1–17	Jesus Heals Outsiders
Sixth Sunday after the Epiphany	7:18–35	The Messengers of John
Seventh Sunday after the Epiphany	7:36–50	A Righteous Woman
Transfiguration Sunday	9:18–36	Humiliation and Transfiguration
Ash Wednesday	9:43b–62	True Greatness
First Sunday in Lent	10:1–24	Jesus Sends Out the Seventy
Second Sunday in Lent	10:25–42	Parable of the Good Samaritan
Third Sunday in Lent	14:7–33	Parable of the Great Banquet
Fourth Sunday in Lent	15:11–32	Parable of the Two Sons
Fifth Sunday in Lent	16:14–31	Parable of the Rich Man and Lazarus
Palm Sunday	19:28–48	Jesus Ransacks the Temple
Maundy Thursday	22:1–38	Passover
Good Friday	22:39–23:56	Passion
Easter Sunday	24:1–12	Resurrection

Second Sunday of Easter	24:13–49	Jesus Appears to His Disciples
Third Sunday of Easter	6:12–26	Sermon on the Plain
Fourth Sunday of Easter	6:27–36	Sermon on the Plain
Fifth Sunday of Easter	6:37–49	Sermon on the Plain
Sixth Sunday of Easter	20:1–19	Teaching in the Temple
Seventh Sunday of Easter	20:20–40	Teaching in the Temple
Day of Pentecost	Acts 2:1–36	The Good News Erupts

Year 4: John

First Sunday of Advent	16:16–24	Sorrow Will Turn into Joy
Second Sunday of Advent	17:1–26	Jesus Prays for His Disciples
Third Sunday of Advent	Ezekiel 37:1–14	Dry Bones Shall Live
Fourth Sunday of Advent	John 1:1–18	The Word Comes into the World
Nativity of the Lord	Luke 2:1–20	The True Lord and Savior is Born
First Sunday after Christmas Day	1:19–42	The Lamb of God
First Sunday after the Epiphany	2:1–12	Wine Turned into Water
Second Sunday after the Epiphany	3:1–21	Nicodemus Comes to Jesus by Night
Third Sunday after the Epiphany	4:1–42	Jesus and the Samaritan Woman
Fourth Sunday after the Epiphany	6:22–40	Jesus, the Bread of Life
Fifth Sunday after the Epiphany	6:60–71	Many Disciples Leave Jesus
Sixth Sunday after the Epiphany	8:1–20	Jesus Testifies on Behalf of the Father
Seventh Sunday after the Epiphany	9:1–41	Jesus Heals a Blind Man
Transfiguration Sunday	10:1–21	Jesus the Good Shepherd
Ash Wednesday	10:22–42	Jesus Rejected by His Own
First Sunday in Lent	11:1–44	Jesus Raises Lazarus
Second Sunday in Lent	12:1–11	Mary Anoints Jesus
Third Sunday in Lent	12:27–50	Jesus Speaks About His Death
Fourth Sunday in Lent	13:1–17	Jesus Washes His Disciples' Feet
Fifth Sunday in Lent	13:21–38	Betrayal and Love
Palm Sunday	12:12–26	Jesus Enters Jerusalem

Maundy Thursday	18:1–27	The Betrayal and Arrest of Jesus
Good Friday	18:18–19:42	Passion
Easter Sunday	20:1–18	Resurrection
Second Sunday of Easter	20:19–31	Jesus Appears to the Disciples
Third Sunday of Easter	21:1–19	Jesus and Peter
Fourth Sunday of Easter	14:1–14	Jesus the Way to the Father
Fifth Sunday of Easter	14:15–31	Jesus Promises the Holy Spirit
Sixth Sunday of Easter	15:1–17	Love One Another
Seventh Sunday of Easter	15:18–16:15	Testify Boldly
Day of Pentecost	Acts 2:1–36	The Good News Erupts

Seven-Year Post-Pentecost Cycle[2]

Year 1

Acts of the Apostles (13 weeks)

3:1–4:22	Peter Heals and Testifies, the Elite Resist
4:32–5:16	All Things in Common
6:1–8:3	Stephen: Martyr of the Word
8:4–40	Philip Testifies to the Suffering Servant
9:1–22	Saul's Heart and Eyes are Opened
10:1–48	God's Revelation to Peter and Cornelius
12:1–25	The Way Under Siege
14:1–28	The Ministry of Paul and Barnabas
15:1–21	Controversy in Community
17:1–34	Paul the Persistent Preacher
25:1–27	Paul at Trial
26:1–32	Paul Testifies to the Elite
28:11–30	Paul Bears Witness to the End

---

2. Again for the sake of simplicity, I am using the average of twenty-five Sundays in the seasons after Pentecost over a seven-year span.

The Old Testament Story (12 weeks)

Genesis 1:1–2:4a	Creation of a Blessed World
Genesis 2:4b–25	Relationships Central to the Created Order
Genesis 3:1–24; 6:5–22	Sin, Alienation, and Disorder
Genesis 9:1–17; 15:1–6	New Beginnings: God's Plan for Israel and Humanity
Exodus 1:8–2:24	The Heroes of Israel's Salvation
Exodus 3:1–22	God Calls Moses and Reveals God's Self
Exodus 19:1–6; 20:1–21	Covenant and Commandments
Exodus 32:1–14; 34:1–9	God as Merciful and Gracious
Joshua 24:1–28	Israel Settles in the Promised Land
2 Samuel 7:1–17	God Makes a Covenant with David and His House
1 Kings 8:1–53	Solomon Dedicates the Temple and Foreshadows Destruction
Nehemiah 9:1–37	In Exile: Remembrance and Hope

Year 2

Romans (9 weeks)

1:1–15	Paul Greets the Roman Church
1:16–25; 3:9–20	The Depravity of Humanity
3:21–31	God's Gift of Forgiveness Through Jesus
5:1–21	Christ Dies for Us
6:1–23	A Choice Between Life and Death
7:1–25	Our Struggle with the Law
8:1–17	Life in the Spirit
8:18–39	God's Love in Christ
12:1–20; 13:8–10	Serving God by Loving One Another

Genesis (9 weeks)

12:1–20	God's Covenant with Abram
18:1–15	A Son Promised to Abraham and Sarah
18:16–33	Abraham Bargains with God

22:1–19	God's Command to Sacrifice Isaac
32:22–32	God Wrestles with Jacob
37:1–36	Joseph is Betrayed by his Brothers
38:1–30	Judah and Tamar
41:1–57	Joseph Interprets Pharaoh's Dream
47:1–26	Joseph Saves Egypt and His Family

Exodus (7 weeks)

4:1–31	Moses Resists God's Call
5:1–23	Pharaoh Resists God's Command
6:28–7:25	The Plagues Begin
10:21–11:10	Darkness and Final Warning
12:21–51	Death of the Firstborn
13:17–14:31	Crossing of the Red Sea
16:1–36	Manna in the Wilderness

Year 3

Hebrews (6 weeks)

1:1–4; 2:5–18	Jesus: Pioneer of our Salvation
4:12–5:10	Hold Fast to Your Trust in Jesus
8:1–13	Jesus the High Priest: Mediator of a New Covenant
10:19–39	The Call to Persevere
11:1–39	By Faith
12:1–12	The Endurance of the Faithful

Deuteronomy (4 weeks)

1:1–5; 4:1–40	Moses Calls for Trust and Obedience
6:1–25	Hear, O Israel
15:1–18	Instructions for the Sabbath Year
30:1–20	Choose Life!

Amos (4 weeks)

1:1–2; 2:4–16	God Issues Judgement Against Judah and Israel
4:1–13	God is Coming!
5:1–24	God's Call for Justice
9:1–15	Destruction and Restoration

Isaiah (11 weeks)

5:1–30	God Laments Israel's Betrayal and Injustice
6:1–13	The Call of Isaiah
11:1–12:6	New Life After Destruction
36:1–22	Sennacherib Threatens Jerusalem
37:1–38	God Delivers Jerusalem
40:1–11	Comfort, O Comfort My People
45:1–19	Cyrus Sets the Exiles Free
52:13–53:12	The Suffering Servant
55:1–13	God's Provision and Providence
56:1–8	All Are Welcome in God's House
59:1–19	Prayer of Petition

Year 4

Galatians (6 weeks)

1:1–24	Paul is Astonished
2:1–14	Paul's Conflict with Peter
2:15–3:9	The Heart of the Gospel
3:19–4:7	The Place of the Law
5:2–15	The Service Christ Demands: Love
5:16–6:18	Live by the Spirit

Philippians (4 weeks)

1:1–26	Paul's Witness to Christ
2:1–18	Living Like Jesus
3:1–4:1	Striving for Salvation
4:2–9	Final Exhortations

Jonah (3 weeks)

1:1–2:9	Jonah Flees From God
3:1–10	The Ninevites Repent
4:1–11	Jonah's Anger

The Old Testament Story (12 weeks)

Genesis 1:1–2:4a	Creation of a Blessed World
Genesis 2:4b–25	Relationships Central to the Created Order
Genesis 3:1–24; 6:5–22	Sin, Alienation, and Disorder
Genesis 9:1–17; 15:1–6	New Beginnings: God's Plan for Israel and Humanity
Exodus 1:8–2:24	The Heroes of Israel's Salvation
Exodus 3:1–22	God Calls Moses and Reveals God's Self
Exodus 19:1–6; 20:1–21	Covenant and Commandments
Exodus 32:1–14; 34:1–9	God as Merciful and Gracious
Joshua 24:1–28	Israel Settles in the Promised Land
2 Samuel 7:1–17	God Makes a Covenant with David and His House
1 Kings 8:1–53	Solomon Dedicates the Temple and Foreshadows Destruction
Nehemiah 9:1–37	In Exile: Remembrance and Hope

Year 5

1 Corinthians (8 weeks)

1:1–25	Spiritual Gifts and Unity in Christ
3:1–23	Call for Unity
5:1–13; 6:12–20	Sexual Immorality
10:1–11:1	Shun Idols, Glorify God
11:17–34	The Lord's Supper Rightly Observed
12:1–21	The Gifts of the Spirit
13:1–13	The Greatest Gift: Love
15:1–26	Resurrection

Joshua (5 weeks)

1:1–18	Preparations for Invasion
2:1–24	Rahab the Faithful
6:1–27	The Fall of Jericho
7:1–26	The Sin of Achan
10:1–15; 11:16–20	The Conquest of Canaan

Ruth (3 weeks)

1:1–22	Ruth Pledges Herself to Naomi and God
2:1–3:18	Ruth and Boaz the Redeemer
4:1–22	A Son is Born

1–2 Samuel (9 weeks)

1 Samuel 8:1–22	Israel Requests a King
10:17–11:14	Saul Becomes King
13:1–15	Saul's Untrusting Sacrifice
16:1–23	David and Saul

17:1–58	David and Goliath
24:1–22	David Spares Saul's Life
2 Samuel 5:1–6:23	David Established as King
2 Samuel 11:1–12:15	David: Adulterer and Murderer
2 Samuel 24:1–17	David's Tragic Census

Year 6

Ephesians (5 weeks)

1:1–23	Blessings in Christ Jesus
2:11–22	The Household of God
3:14–4:24	Becoming New Selves
5:21–6:9	First-century Codes for Christian Households
6:10–20	The Armor of God

Revelation (8 weeks)

1:1–20	John's Vision of the Son of Man
3:14–22	Jesus' Message to Laodicea
4:1–5:14	The Scroll and the Lamb
12:1–17	The Woman and the Dragon
13:1–18	The Beasts of Hell
18:1–24	The Fall of Babylon
20:1–15	The Final Defeat of Satan
21:1–22:7	The New Jerusalem

Jeremiah (7 weeks)

1:1–19	The Call of Jeremiah
7:1–28	Jeremiah Proclaims God's Judgement
21:1–10	Israel Shall Fall to Babylon
26:1–24	Jeremiah Prophesies in the Temple

28:1–17	Jeremiah is Opposed by Hananiah
34:8–22	The Treachery of Israel's Elite
31:1–14; 31–34	Jeremiah Announces Restoration

Proverbs (5 weeks)

1:1–32	Heeding the Call of Wisdom
2:1–15	The Blessing of Wisdom
8:22–36	Lady Wisdom
15:1–33	Some Sayings of Solomon
23:1–12	Some Sayings of the Wise

Year 7

Colossians (4 weeks)

1:1–14	Paul Greets the Colossians
1:15–29	The Supremacy of Christ
2:6–23	Life in Christ
3:1–17	Holy Living

First Letter of John (3 weeks)

1:1–2:6	Walk in the Light
2:7–17	Love the Father
4:1–21	God is Love

1–2 Kings (14 weeks)

1 Kings 3:1–28	Solomon's Prayer
1 Kings 4:20–34	Solomon's Prosperity and Wisdom
1 Kings 11:1–13	Solomon's Betrayal and the Nation Divides

1 Kings 12:20–33	Jeroboam's Sin and Condemnation
1 Kings 16:29–17:24	Ahab, Jezebel, and Elijah
1 Kings 18:1–46	God Triumphs over the Priests of Baal
1 Kings 19:1–21	Elijah's Doubt and Restoration
1 Kings 21:1–29	Naboth's Vineyard
2 Kings 4:1–37	Elisha's Miracles
2 Kings 5:1–19	Elisha Heals Naaman
2 Kings 18:13–37	Sennacherib Threatens Jerusalem
2 Kings 19:1–37	God Protects Judah
2 Kings 22:1–22	Josiah Repents, Destruction Announced
2 Kings 24:1–25:21	The Fall of Judah and Exile

Esther (4 weeks)

1:1–2:23	Esther Becomes Queen
3:1–5:14	Haman Plots Revenge Against Mordecai and His People
6:1–8:17	Haman's Downfall and Mordecai's Rise
9:1–10:3	The Israelites Prevail Over Their Enemies

The Biblical Story in Summary

THE FOLLOWING IS A summary of the biblical story that traces through the landmark events of the Old and New Testaments. These events and the elements of God's character to which they bear witness are often the focus of summaries that we encounter throughout Scripture. They are also frequently referenced by the biblical writers in other texts.[1]

Part 1: God Creates a World of Blessing and Gives Humanity a Calling

God speaks into being a wonderful creation, teeming with life and provision. As part of this creation, humanity is given special capabilities and responsibilities as those created in God's image (Gen 1:1–2:4a). The "meaning of life" for humanity is to live in right relationship with God, one another, and creation, and in doing so to participate in and steward the blessing God intends for all creatures (Gen 2:4b–25). With God, this is to be a relationship of intimacy, trust, and dependence. With one another, humanity is to pursue relationships of intimacy, interdependence, respect, and mutuality. With creation, humanity is to care for the natural world so that it continues to be a place of beauty, diversity, and abundant blessing for all of God's creatures. In the very early stages of the biblical story, we see God, humanity, and creation together participating in the wondrous blessing of God's new world.

1. For a more detailed account and description of the biblical story, see Kuhn, *Having Words with God*, chapters 6–7. See also Bartholomew and Goheen, *The Drama of Scripture*.

Part 2: Lack of Trust, Messed up Relationships, and Destruction

Humanity's relationship with God was to be characterized by humanity's intimacy with God, trust in God, and dependence on God. But the serpent slithers his way into the garden of Eden and puts before the woman and Adam a most enticing temptation: "Go ahead, eat the fruit! You won't die! God just wants to keep you stupid. God is hiding things from you!" (Gen 3). Then the serpent's final words fan the embers of temptation into a flame. "Eat it! And you will know everything God knows. In fact, you will be *like* God." The woman takes the fruit and eats. Adam, standing idly by, follows suit, and suddenly creation begins to warp awry. The relationships which are the foundation of the created order start to unravel. Adam and the woman (later named Eve) fail to trust in God, and the intimacy between God and humanity suffers a terrible blow. The intimacy between Adam and his wife likewise deteriorates, and now Adam shall rule over his wife. Enmity shall characterize the encounters between the serpent and the children of Adam, signifying the fear and distrust that mars the relationships between humanity and other creatures. As a result of these now warped relationships, creation becomes a far less abundant place than God intended. Humanity is cast out of the garden. The gift of procreation will be accompanied by excruciating pain. Adam will toil over the land, and his labor will produce mostly thistles and thorns. The tree of life is barred against their trespass, and to dust humanity shall return. For humanity, death—not life!—will have the final word.

In the narrative that follows, humanity continues to fall fast and hard. Already in the next chapter, Cain, in a fit of jealousy, murders his brother Abel. Lamech kills another and boasts. By chapter 6, humanity has become almost irredeemably corrupted. Here we encounter some of the most tragic and heart-wrenching verses in all of Scripture. Things have gotten so bad, and humanity has gone so wrong: "The LORD saw that the wickedness of humankind was great in the earth, and that every inclination of the thoughts of their hearts was only evil continually." And God "was sorry that he had made humankind on the earth, and it grieved him to his heart. So the LORD said, 'I will blot out from the earth the human beings I have created—people together with the animals and creeping things and birds of the air, for I am sorry that I have made them'" (Gen 6:5–7). These opening chapters introduce us to a fundamental truth of the biblical story: when humanity fails to trust in God as the source of blessing, and instead trusts in something else, they begin to tread a path that leads to disobedience, alienation from God, one another, and creation, and finally destruction. So essential are these right relationships to the ordering of creation! They are the threads that hold the finely woven tapestry of creation together. When they disintegrate, creation itself unravels. And at this point in the story, God is about to wash the world into dissolution. God is going to unmake the terrible mistake God made.

Part 3: God Preserves the Relationship and Seeks To Restore Humanity

Fortunately, there are other fundamental truths at work in the biblical story, and one that is most central to this story is the truth of God's mercy and steadfast love. Yes, God was to bring destruction upon the earth in the form of a flood. "But Noah found favor in the sight of the LORD" (Gen 6:8). For the sake of one righteous man, God spares humanity, and what was supposed to be a story of calamitous judgment becomes—in the span of a single verse!—a story of deliverance and a new beginning. God knows that humanity will still struggle to be faithful, but God now resolves to stick it out with creation no matter what the future holds (Gen 8:20–22; 9:1–17).

Indeed, humanity continues in its sinful ways. Shortly after the land is repopulated, humanity once again seeks to "make a name for itself" and elevate itself to the realm of the divine, as it builds the tower at Babel (Gen 11:1–9). God scatters humanity abroad on the earth, confusing its language. But God does not leave humanity to its own misguided tendencies. God now embarks on a new plan to reconnect with humanity and bring all of creation back to a state of abundant blessing. He chooses one man and woman, Abraham and Sarah, from whom he is going to birth a nation that will be God's people, Israel (Gen 12:1–3; 15:1–6). They are to be a people who learn God's ways and partake in God's blessing. They will reveal to the rest of the world the abundant life that comes from living rightly with God, one another, and creation. This is, in short, what the rest of the biblical story is about. This is its main "plot-line": God's struggle, through a people that will be God's own, to teach humanity God's ways, to call them back to right relationship, and to bring them back to the blessing God intended for them from the very beginning.

Part 4: God and Israel, a Rocky Relationship

The rest of the Old Testament focuses on the history of the relationship between God and God's people, Israel. God's promise to Abraham—to make him into a great nation, to protect him, and give him an abundant land in which to dwell—is passed on from generation to generation. We see God's promise to bless and protect Abraham's descendants repeatedly put to the test, and each time God is faithful. Most notably, God delivers Abraham's descendants from a severe famine by bringing them into the land of Egypt (the story of Joseph: Gen 37–50). Many years later, after the Egyptians had begun to enslave Abraham's descendants, God delivers them from Egypt (Exod 1–15). Now, God continues the task of teaching them what it means to live rightly with God, one another, and creation. On Sinai, God makes another covenant with Israel: if they trust God and walk in God's ways, then they shall be not only God's treasured possession, but also a nation set apart to be a "kingdom of priests" to the other nations of the world (Exod 19:1–6). God then gives them God's law, beginning with the Ten Commandments (Exod 20:1–21). These instructions, if they follow them, will lead the Israelites into the kinds of relationships with God, one another, and creation that will be for them a source of blessing. In following these commands, Israel will also bear witness to God and God's ways, and thus become a source of blessing for all the nations of the earth.

Yet the relationship between God and God's people is a rocky one. Repeatedly, Israel fails to trust in God and walk in God's ways. In turn, God corrects God's wayward children. Still, the faithlessness of God's people continues. They are quick to turn to other gods. They set aside and even forget God's commands, and fail to trust in God's provision (Exod 32:1–14). God's ongoing discipline yet forgiveness of Israel reveals God's character as merciful and gracious, abounding in steadfast love and faithfulness (Exod 34:6). In the end, God fulfills God's promise to bring them into the promised land.

Once settled in the land, Israel continues to be blessed by God's protection and guidance. God appoints prophets to confront and teach them, and leaders to rescue them from their enemies, including eventually a king. God enters into a covenant promising David God's blessing and an eternal dynasty for David and his descendants (2 Sam 7:1–17). The Temple is built and God's presence dwells among them (1 Kgs 6–8). Under Solomon, David's son and the wisest of all kings, God brings Israel into a period of tremendous prosperity (1 Kgs 10). Indeed, at this point in the story Israel is now poised to fulfill its calling to be a source of instruction and blessing for the nations of the world.

But as meteoric as is Israel's rise, so too is its fall, and within a generation Israel becomes a divided nation and a shell of what was under Solomon's early rule. Throughout this part of Israel's story there are several examples of faithful prophets, judges, and kings. There are moments when the people as a whole dedicate themselves to God. But such moments are short-lived. Most in Israel spurn God's ways. They (including Solomon!) seek out other gods (1 Kgs 11). Their leaders oppress the people, victimize the poor, and idolize power and wealth (Mic 2:1–3:12). God repeatedly sends prophets to rebuke them. Sometimes, the leaders and people listen to the prophets and repent, for a time. But in the end, over the centuries to follow, Israel returns to its infidelity and finds itself on a path leading to destruction. First the northern kingdom, Israel, and then the southern kingdom Judah, are destroyed by invading armies, and the survivors are carried off into exile. Nearly all that has defined Israel as a people and nation is now gone: land, temple, king (2 Kgs 25; Neh 9:1–37).

Part 5: God's Promise for a New Beginning, and Waiting . . .

By now, we have come to know this God as a God of new beginnings. So even though destruction comes to God's people as a result of their unrelenting faithlessness, it does not surprise us that from the tattered remains of their relationship, God once again beckons Israel to start anew by returning to God and God's ways. God promises to restore Israel as a people (Isa 40:1–11). Through the words of the prophets, God describes to them a future, glorious kingdom, a time of unparalleled intimacy with God that will be matched by their unparalleled faithfulness (Jer 31:31–37). It is with this promised hope in view, and God's people waiting for its fulfillment, that the Old Testament ends.

Part 6: The Promise Fulfilled in Jesus, the Messiah

Central to the New Testament story is the claim that God's promised restoration of Israel is accomplished in the life, death, resurrection, and ongoing ministry of Jesus Christ (Messiah). Jesus inaugurates the long-awaited kingdom of God, performing wondrous acts of healing in order to demonstrate the kingdom's arrival and its power over the forces of destruction and death. Jesus also teaches what it means to become part of God's kingdom. Yet as he does so, Jesus upends established notions of piety and faithfulness. Jesus redefines for his fellow Israelites and others what it means to live rightly with God and one another. Jesus upholds the central purpose of God's Torah, but he sets aside many of the previous commandments in order to help believers understand more fully what it means to love God and one another. Jesus also challenges his society's fixation on honor and power, setting aside social conventions that marginalize people and railing against the elite for hoarding their wealth while many struggle to survive. Jesus so devotes himself to God and the kingdom that he continues to heal, teach, and challenge even though he knows it will eventually lead to his rejection and death. In an astounding and unimaginable act of grace, God accepts Jesus' death on the cross—at the hands of humanity—as that final sacrifice that once and for all proclaims the depth of God's mercy and forgiveness for humanity. Sacrifice is no longer needed in the temple. God's pardon and welcome is now freely given to all—Israelites and Gentile alike—who open their hearts to receiving it and embrace the arrival of the kingdom in Jesus. Jesus' resurrection announces the good news that death is not the end of the relationship between God and humanity. Like Jesus, all people can now be raised to life to live eternally with God and one another. While we await the full arrival of the kingdom, we are called to live as Jesus' disciples empowered by Christ's Spirit, to enjoy life with God, one another, and creation, and to do all we can to share God's blessings with all people.

Part 7: The End and Eternity

This is the part of the story that has yet to be written, but regarding which the biblical authors offer a collage of images: the return of Jesus to gather the faithful, the final defeat of all that threatens our relationship with God and one another, vindication of the righteous and judgement of the wicked, eternal life with God and one another. Few state this vision of blessing as eloquently as the writer of Revelation:

> And I heard a loud voice from the throne saying,
>   "See, the home of God is among mortals.
> He will dwell with them as their God;
>   they will be his peoples,
> and God himself will be with them;
>   he will wipe every tear from their eyes.
> Death will be no more;
>   mourning and crying and pain will be no more,
> for the first things have passed away." (21:3–4)

> Then the angel showed me the river of the water of life, bright as crystal, flowing from the throne of God and of the Lamb through the middle of the street of the city. On either side of the river is the tree of life with its twelve kinds of fruit, producing its fruit each month; and the leaves of the tree are for the healing of the nations. Nothing accursed will be found there any more. But the throne of God and of the Lamb will be in it, and his servants will worship him; they will see his face, and his name will be on their foreheads. And there will be no more night; they need no

light of lamp or sun, for the Lord God will be their light, and
they will reign forever and ever. (22:1–5)

Finally, after ages of humanity's toil and struggle to live rightly with God
and one another, the relationships central to the created order are restored.
A new realm of blessing awaits humanity. In its midst stands the tree of life,
no longer beyond the grasp of God's human creatures, and its leaves are for
the healing of the nations.

Bibliography

412Teens.org. "What does the Bible Say about Dating or Courting?" https://412teens. org/qna/what-does-the-Bible-say-about-dating-or-courting.php.

Abebe, Nitsu. "America's New 'Anxiety' Disorder." *The New York Times*, April 18, 2017. https://www.nytimes.com/2017/04/18/magazine/americas-new-anxiety-disorder. html.

Anti-Defamation League. "With Hate in their Hearts: The State of White Supremacy in the United States." https://www.adl.org/education/resources/reports/state-of-white-supremacy.

Anti-Defamation League."Christian Identity." https://www.adl.org/resources/back grounders/christian-identity.

Bartholomew, Craig G., and Michael W. Goheen. *The Drama of Scripture: Finding Our Place in the Biblical Story*. Grand Rapids: Baker Academic, 2014.

Baumeister, Roy F., and David A. Butz. "Roots of Hate, Violence and Evil." In *The Psychology of Hate*, edited by Robert J. Sternberg, 87–102. Washington DC: American Psychological Association, 2005.

Beinart, Peter. "The Right's Islamophobia Has Nothing to do with National Security." *The Atlantic*, November 30, 2017. https://www.theatlantic.com/politics/ archive/2017/11/the-new-islamophobia/547130/.

Bell, Alistair. "Americans Worry that Illegal Immigrants Threaten Way of Life, Economy." *Reuters*, August 7, 2014. https://www.reuters.com/article/us-usa-immigration-worries/americans-worry-that-illegal-migrants-threaten-way-of-life-economy-idUSKBN0G70BE20140807.

Berman-Vaporis, Irene, Lawson Parker, and Rosemary Wardlesy. "Peril, Progress, Prosperity: Women's Well-Being Around the World." *National Geographic*, November 11, 2019, 74–81.

Bible Info. "Dating." https://www.bibleinfo.com/en/topics/dating.

———. "The Three Wise Men: What Were Their Names." https://www.bibleinfo.com/ en/questions/what-were-names-three-wise-men.

Bible Study Tools. "Dating Bible Verses." https://www.biblestudytools.com/topical-verses/dating-bible-verses/.

Block, Daniel. "Is Trump Our Cyrus? The Old Testament Case for Yes and No." *Christianity Today*, October 29, 2018. https://www.christianitytoday.com/ct/2018/october-web-only/donald-trump-cyrus-prophecy-old-testament.html.

Bower, Peter C., ed. *Handbook for the Common Lectionary*. Philadelphia: Geneva, 1987.

Brueggemann, Walter. *Theology of the Old Testament: Testimony, Dispute, Advocacy*. Minneapolis: Fortress, 1997.

Burton, Tara Isabella. "The Bible Says to Welcome Immigrants. So Why Don't Evangelicals?" *Vox*, October 30, 2018. https://www.vox.com/2018/10/30/18035336/white-evangelicals-immigration-nationalism-christianity-refugee-honduras-migrant.

———. "The Biblical Story the Christian Right Uses to Defend Trump." *Vox*, May 5, 2018. https://www.vox.com/identities/2018/3/5/16796892/trump-cyrus-christian-right-bible-cbn-evangelical-propaganda.

CAIR. "Islamophobia and its Impact in the United States." https://www.cair.com/legislating-fear-2013-report.

Carlson, Tucker. "The Intellectual Roots of Nativism." *Wall Street Journal*, October 2, 1997. https://www.wsj.com/articles/SB875739465952259500.

Chapman University Survey of American Fears. "America's Top Fears of 2018." https://blogs.chapman.edu/wilkinson/2018/10/16/americas-top-fears-2018/.

———. "Fear of Muslims in American Society." October 16, 2018. https://blogs.chapman.edu/wilkinson/2018/10/16/fear-of-muslims-in-american-society/.

Cottee, Simon. "What Motivates Terrorists." *The Atlantic*, June 9, 2015. http://www.theatlantic.com/international/archive/2015/06/terrorism-isis-motive/395351/.

Coulter, Ann. "Ann Coulter: How We Became the World's Suckers on Immigration." *The Hill*, July 29, 2019. https://thehill.com/opinion/immigration/455126-ann-coulter-how-we-became-the-worlds-suckers-on-immigration.

Croft, Scott. "Biblical Dating: How It's Different from Modern Dating." https://www.boundless.org/relationships/biblical-dating-how-its-different-from-modern-dating/.

Currid, John. "Why the Destruction of the Canaanites?" Reformed Theological Seminary. https://rts.edu/resources/wisdom-wednesday-in-class-with-dr-john-currid/.

de Ste. Croix, G. E. M. *The Class Struggle in the Ancient Greek World: From the Archaic Age to the Arab Conquests*. Ithaca, NY: Cornell University Press, 1980.

DeAngelis, Tori. "Understanding Terrorism." November, 2009. http://www.apa.org/monitor/2009/11/terrorism.aspx.

Death Penalty Information Center. "Race." https://deathpenaltyinfo.org/policy-issues/race.

Elliot, Neil. *The Arrogance of the Nations: Reading Romans in the Shadow of Empire*. Paul in Critical Contexts Series. Minneapolis: Fortress, 2008.

Enns, Peter. *The Bible Tells Me So: Why Defending Scripture Has Made Us Unable to Read It*. New York: Harper One, 2014.

———. *Inspiration and Incarnation: Evangelicals and the Problem of the New Testament*. Grand Rapids: Baker Academic, 2005.

Erickson, Millard. *Christian Theology*. 2nd ed. Grand Rapids: Baker, 1998.

Evans, Rachel Held. *Inspired: Slaying Giants, Walking on Water, and Loving the Bible Again*. Nashville: Nelson, 2018.

———. "Is Abolition 'Biblical'?" February 28, 2013. https://rachelheldevans.com/blog/is-abolition-biblical.

Fea, John. *Believe Me: The Evangelical Road to Donald Trump.* Grand Rapids: Eerdmans, 2018.

Fiensy, David A. *The Social History of Palestine in the Herodian Period: The Land is Mine.* Studies in the Bible and Early Christianity 20. Lewiston, NY: Edwin Mellen Press, 1991.

Fiske, Susan T. "Look Twice." *Greater Good Magazine*, June 1, 2008. https://greatergood. berkeley.edu/article/item/look_twice.

Fiske, Susan T., and Shelley E. Taylor. *Social Cognition: From Brains to Culture.* 2nd ed. Los Angeles: Sage, 2013.

Fretheim, Terrence. *The Pentateuch.* Nashville: Abingdon, 1996.

Furman, Richard. "Exposition of the Views of the Baptists, Relative to the Coloured Population In the United States." Charleston, SC: A. E. Miller, 1838. http://history. furman.edu/~benson/docs/rcd-fmn1.htm.

Galli, Mark. "Trump Should be Removed from Office." *Christianity Today,* December 19, 2019. https://www.christianitytoday.com/ct/2019/december-web-only/trump -should-be-removed-from-office.html.

Gaussen, Louis. *The Inspiration of the Holy Scriptures.* Chicago: Moody, 1949.

Gerson, Michael. "The Last Temptation." *The Atlantic,* April 2018. https://www. theatlantic.com/magazine/archive/2018/04/the-last-temptation/554066/.

Glassner, Barry. *The Culture of Fear: Why Americans are Afraid of the Wrong Things.* New York: Basic, 1999.

———. "Narrative Techniques of Fear Mongering." *Social Research* 71 (2004) 819–26.

Green, Joel B. *The Gospel of Luke.* NICNT. Grand Rapids: Eerdmans, 1997.

Hamel, Gildas. "Poverty and Charity." In *The Oxford Handbook of Jewish Daily Life in Roman Palestine,* edited by Catherine Hezer, 308–26. Oxford: Oxford University Press, 2010.

Hanson, K. C., and Douglas E. Oakman. *Palestine in the Time of Jesus: Social Structures and Social Conflicts.* 2nd ed. Minneapolis: Fortress, 1998.

Harvard Pluralism Project. "First Encounters: Native Americans and Christians." Accessed January 27, 2020. http://pluralism.org/encounter/historical-perspectives/first-encounters-native-americans-and-christians/.

Horsley, Richard. *Jesus and the Powers: Conflict, Covenant, and the Hope of the Poor.* Minneapolis: Fortress, 2010.

———. *The Liberation of Christmas: The Infancy Narratives in Social Context.* Eugene, OR: Wipf and Stock, 1989.

Iyengar, Shanto, and Sean J. Westwood. "Fear and Loathing across Party Lines: New Evidence on Group Polarization." *American Journal of Political Science* 59 (2015) 690–707.

Johnson, Allan G. *The Gender Knot: Unraveling Our Patriarchal Legacy.* Philadelphia: Temple University Press, 1997.

Jones, Robert P. *The End of White Christian America.* New York: Simon and Schuster, 2016.

Juel, Donald H. *Mark.* Augsburg Commentary on the New Testament. Minneapolis: Augsburg, 1990.

Juergensmyer, Mark. *Terror in the Mind of God: The Global Rise of Religious Violence.* 3rd ed. Berkeley, CA: University of California Press, 2003.

Kantzer, Kenneth S., ed. *Applying The Scriptures.* Grand Rapids: Zondervan, 1987.

Khazan, Olga. "People Voted for Trump Because They Were Anxious, Not Poor." *The Atlantic*, April 23, 2018. https://www.theatlantic.com/science/archive/2018/04/existential-anxiety-not-poverty-motivates-trump-support/558674/.

Kimmel, Michael. *The Gendered Society*. 4th ed. Oxford: Oxford University Press, 2011.

Korte, Gregory, and Alan Gomez. "Trump Ramps Up Rhetoric on Undocumented Immigrants: 'These Aren't People. These are Animals.'" *USA Today*, May 16, 2018. https://www.usatoday.com/story/news/politics/2018/05/16/trump-immigrants-animals-mexico-democrats-sanctuary-cities/617252002/.

Koukl, Greg. "The Canaanites: Genocide or Judgement?' Stand to Reason. January 1, 2013. https://www.str.org/publications/the-canaanites-genocide-or-judgment#.Xi8hQWhKjD5.

Kuhn, Karl Allen. *Having Words with God: The Bible as Conversation*. Minneapolis: Fortress, 2008.

———. *The Heart of Biblical Narrative: Rediscovering Biblical Appeal to the Emotions*. Minneapolis: Fortress, 2009.

———. *Insights from Cultural Anthropology*. Minneapolis: Fortress, 2018.

———. *The Kingdom According to Luke and Acts: A Social, Literary, and Theological Introduction*. Grand Rapids: Baker, 2015.

———. "Natural and Unnatural Relations between Text and Context: A Canonical Reading of Romans 1:26–27." *CurTM* 33 (2006) 313–29.

Labberton, Mark. "Political Dealing: The Crisis of Evangelicalism." April 20, 2018. https://www.fuller.edu/posts/political-dealing-the-crisis-of-evangelicalism/.

Lanier, Greg. "We Three King of Orient Aren't." https://www.thegospelcoalition.org/article/three-kings-orient-arent/.

Lenski, Gerhard E. *Power and Privilege: A Theory of Social Stratification*. 2nd ed. Chapel Hill: University of North Carolina Press, 1984.

Lerner, Gerda. *The Creation of Patriarchy*. Oxford: Oxford University Press, 1986.

Lindsell, Harold. *Battle for the Bible*. 6th ed. Grand Rapids: Zondervan, 1977.

Malina, Bruce. *The New Testament World: Insights from Cultural Anthropology*. 3rd ed. Louisville: Westminster John Knox, 2001

Malkin, Michelle. *Open Borders Inc.: Who's Funding America's Destruction*. Washington, DC: Regnery, 2019.

Mathewes, Charles. "White Christianity is in Big Trouble. And it is its own biggest threat." *Washington Post*, December 19, 2017. https://www.washingtonpost.com/news/posteverything/wp/2017/12/19/white-christianity-is-in-big-trouble-and-its-its-own-biggest-threat/.

Mattson, Stephen. "American 'Christianity' has Failed." *Sojourners*, January, 25, 2017. https://sojo.net/articles/american-christianity-has-failed.

McKibben, Bill. *Hundred Dollar Holiday: The Case for a More Joyful Christmas*. New York: Simon and Schuster, 1998.

McLeroy, Leigh. "What Does the Bible Say About Dating?" https://www.exploregod.com/what-does-the-bible-say-about-dating.

Miesel, Sandra. "Wise Men from the East and the Feast of the Epiphany of our Lord." https://www.catholicworldreport.com/2019/01/06/wise-men-from-the-east-and-the-feast-of-the-epiphany-of-the-lord/.

Mohler, R. Albert, Jr. "Homosexuality and the Bible." https://sbts-wordpress-uploads.s3.amazonaws.com/equip/uploads/2010/09/homosexuality-and-the-bible.pdf.

National Association of Social Workers. "The Role of Female Leadership in Social Work Organizations." http://www.socialworkblog.org/practice-and-professional-development/2015/12/the-role-of-female-leadership-in-social-work-organizations/.

National Coalition Against Domestic Violence. "Statistics." https://ncadv.org/statistics.

National Immigration Forum. "Polling Update: American Attitudes on Immigration Steady, but Showing More Partisan Divides." April 17, 2019. https://immigrationforum.org/article/american-attitudes-on-immigration-steady-but-showing-more-partisan-divides/.

Neyrey, Jerome, and Eric C. Stewart, eds. *The Social World of the New Testament: Insights and Models*. Peabody: Hendrickson, 2008.

Noll, Mark A. *The Civil War as a Theological Crisis*. The Steven and Janice Brose Lectures in the Civil War Era. Chapel Hill, NC: University of North Carolina Press, 2006.

O'Day, Gail R., and Charles Hackett. *Preaching the Revised Common Lectionary: A Guide*. Nashville: Abingdon, 2007.

Open Bible. "Dating." https://www.openbible.info/topics/dating.

PBS. "Zero Tolerance." *Frontline*, October 22, 2019. https://www.pbs.org/wgbh/frontline/film/zero-tolerance/.

Pontifical Biblical Commission. *The Inspiration and Truth of Sacred Scripture*. Translated by Thomas Esposito and Stephen Gregg. Collegeville, MN: Liturgical, 2014.

Powell, Mark Alan. *Chasing the Eastern Star: Adventures in Reader Response Criticism*. Louisville: Westminster John Knox, 2001.

———. "The Forgotten Famine: Personal Responsibility in Luke's Parable of 'Prodigal Son.'" In *Literary Encounters with the Reign of God*, edited by Sharon H. Ringe and H. C. Paul Kim, 265–87. New York: T & T Clark, 2004.

———. "The Timeless Tale of a Prodigal Son: What it Means both Near and Far." Founders' Day Lecture. Lakeland College, Sheboygan, Wisconsin, February 6, 2007.

Price, S. R. F. *Rituals and Power: The Roman Imperial Cult in Asia Minor*. Cambridge: Cambridge University Press, 1984.

Radmacher, Earl D. and Robert D. Preus, eds. *Hermeneutics, Inerrancy, and the Bible*. Grand Rapids: Zondervan, 1984.

Restuccia, Andrew. "The Sanctification of Donald Trump." *Politico*, April 30, 2019. https://www.politico.com/story/2019/04/30/donald-trump-evangelicals-god-1294578.

Rives, James B. *Religion in the Roman Empire*. Blackwell Ancient Religions, 2. Oxford: Blackwell, 2007.

Rohrbaugh, Richard. "The Social Location of the Markan Audience." In *The Social World of the New Testament*, edited by Jerome Neyrey and Eric C. Stewart, 141–62. Grand Rapids: Baker Academic, 2008.

Schwadel, Philip, and Gregory A. Smith. "Evangelical Approval of Trump Remains High, But Other Religious Groups are Less Supportive." Pew Research Center. March 18, 2019, https://www.pewresearch.org/fact-tank/2019/03/18/evangelical-approval-of-trump-remains-high-but-other-religious-groups-are-less-supportive/.

Scott, Donald M. "The Religious Dimensions of Manifest Destiny." http://nationalhumanitiescenter.org/tserve/nineteen/nkeyinfo/mandestiny.htm.

Serani, Deborah. "If it Bleeds it Leads: Understanding Fear-Based Media." *Psychology Today*, June 7, 2011. https://www.psychologytoday.com/us/blog/two-takes-depression/201106/if-it-bleeds-it-leads-understanding-fear-based-media.

Sewer, Adam. "The Nationalist's Delusion." *The Atlantic*, November 20, 2017. https://www.theatlantic.com/politics/archive/2017/11/the-nationalists-delusion/546356/.

Shaw, Barbara L., and Heather Rellihan. *Introduction to Women's, Gender & Sexuality Studies: Interdisciplinary and Intersectional Approaches*. Oxford: Oxford University Press, 2018.

Smith, Christian. *The Bible Made Impossible: Why Biblicism Is Not a Truly Evangelical Reading of Scripture*. Grand Rapids: Brazos, 2012.

Sparks, Kenneth. *Sacred Word, Broken Word: Biblical Authority and the Dark Side of Scripture*. Grand Rapids: Eerdmans, 2012.

Southern Poverty Law Center. "Hate in God's Name." September 25, 2017. https://www.splcenter.org/20170925/hate-god%E2%80%99s-name.

Staub, Ervin. "The Origins and Evolution of Hate, with Notes on Prevention." In *The Psychology of Hate*, edited by Robert J. Sternberg, 51–66. Washington DC: American Psychological Association, 2005.

Stern, Jessica "What Motivates Terrorists?" *Defining Ideas*, January 21, 2011. http://www.hoover.org/research/what-motivates-terrorists.

Stewart, Don. "Why Did God Order the Destruction of the Canaanites?" Blue Letter Bible. https://www.blueletterbible.org/faq/don_stewart/don_stewart_1382.cfm.

Strauss, Neil. "Why We're Living in the Age of Fear." *Rolling Stone*, October 6, 2016. https://www.rollingstone.com/politics/politics-features/why-were-living-in-the-age-of-fear-190818/.

The Sacred Congregation for the Doctrine of the Faith. "The Declaration on the Question of Admission of Women to the Ministerial Priesthood." November 30, 1975. http://www.vatican.va/roman_curia/congregations/cfaith/documents/rc_con_cfaith_doc_19761015_inter-insigniores_en.html.

Tracy, Steven R. "Patriarchy and Domestic Violence: Challenging Common Misconceptions." *Journal for the Evangelical Theology Society* 50 (2007) 573–94. https://www.etsjets.org/files/JETS-PDFs/50/50-3/JETS_50-3_573-594_Tracy.pdf.

Trexler, Richard C. *The Journey of the Magi: Meanings in History of a Christian Story*. Princeton, NJ: Princeton University Press, 1997.

USA Facts. "Hate Crime Data: the Value in Expanding our Sources." August 3 2019. https://usafacts.org/reports/facts-in-focus/hate-crimes-ucr-ncvs.

U.S. Department of Justice. "Hate Crime Statistics." https://www.justice.gov/hatecrimes/hate-crime-statistics.

Van Dyke, Henry J. *The Character and Influence of Abolitionism!: A Sermon Preached in the First Presbyterian Church of Brooklyn on Sunday Evening December 9th 1860*. New York: George F. Nesbitt and Co., 1860.

Warfield, Benjamin Breckenridge. "The Real Problem of Inspiration." In *The Inspiration and Authority of the Bible,* edited by Samuel G. Craig, 223–26. London: Marshall, Morgan & Scott, 1951.

Warner, Judith, Nora Ellmann, and Diana Boesch. "The Women's Leadership Gap: Women's Leadership by the Numbers." American Progress. November 20, 2018. https://www.americanprogress.org/issues/women/reports/2018/11/20/461273/womens-leadership-gap-2/.

WhyChristmas.com. "All About the Wise Men." https://www.whychristmas.com/story/wisemen.shtml.

Wilson, Brittany E. *Unmanly Men: Refigurations of Masculinity in Luke-Acts*. Oxford: Oxford University Press, 2015.

Zald, Mayer N., and John D. McCarthy. *Social Movements in an Organizational Society*. New York: Routledge, 1987.

Zias, Joseph. "Death and Disease in Ancient Israel." *Biblical Archaeologist* 54 (1991) 146–59.